PHILOSOPHY IN CLASSROOM TEACHING
BRIDGING THE GAP

David Andrew Jacobsen
University of North Florida

Merrill
an imprint of PRENTICE HALL
Upper Saddle River, New Jersey   Columbus, Ohio

Library of Congress Cataloging-in-Publication Data

Jacobsen, David (David A.)
    Philosophy in classroom teaching : bridging the gap / David Andrew
Jacobsen.
        p.   cm
    Includes bibliographical references (p. 267) and index.
    ISBN: 0-02-360123-X
    1. Education—Philosophy.   2. Teaching.   I. Title.
LB14.7.J33   1999
370'.1—dc21   98-26488
                                                                                 CIP

Editor: Debra A. Stollenwerk
Production Editor: Mary Harlan
Design Coordinator: Diane C. Lorenzo
Text Design and Production Coordinator: Custom Editorial Productions, Inc.
Cover Designer: Brian Deep
Cover Art: © Super Stock, Inc.
Production Manager: Pamela D. Bennett
Director of Marketing: Kevin Flanagan
Marketing Manager: Suzanne Stanton
Marketing Coordinator: Krista Groshong

This book was set in New Baskerville by Custom Editorial Productions, Inc.,
and was printed and bound by R. R. Donnelley & Sons Company. The cover
was printed by Phoenix Color Corp.

 © 1999 by Prentice-Hall, Inc.
Simon & Schuster/A Viacom Company
Upper Saddle River, New Jersey 07458

Photo credits: American Philosophical Society, p.p. 111, 189; AP/Wide World Photos, p. 249;
Archive Photos, p. 161; Danish Embassy, p. 239; Library of Congress, p.p. 58, 73, 84, 101, 121,
136, 147, 173, 201, 225; National Library of Medicine, p.215.

Printed in the United States of America

10 9 8 7 6 5 4 3 2 1

ISBN: 0-02-360123-X

Prentice-Hall International (UK) Limited, *London*
Prentice-Hall of Australia Pty. Limited, *Sydney*
Prentice-Hall of Canada, Inc., *Toronto*
Prentice-Hall Hispanoamericana, S. A., *Mexico*
Prentice-Hall of India Private Limited, *New Delhi*
Prentice-Hall of Japan, Inc., *Tokyo*
Simon & Schuster Asia Pte. Ltd., *Singapore*
Editora Prentice-Hall do Brasil, Ltda., *Rio de Janeiro*

FOR LEOPOLD NACHAMOWITZ . . . WHO SAID:

WHAT YOU PUT INTO YOUR HEAD,
NO ONE CAN TAKE AWAY.

PREFACE

Throughout our existence, we, as individuals, have often expressed views about the universe, life, knowledge, and values. This is the "stuff" of philosophy, and so all of us have engaged in the time-honored tradition of philosophizing. However, only the thoughts or philosophy of a few have been profound enough to be incorporated into the traditional body of knowledge we continue to study to this day.

Although we often think of our personal ventures into this field as practical and relevant, it is common for teachers to experience difficulty in perceiving the classroom applicability of philosophy because this discipline often stays in the theoretical realm of preservice and inservice educational programs. Many forays into this field are limited to storing knowledge of philosophical "isms" and as such may be useful in expanding one's informational base. However, I assume that you are probably more concerned with pedagogy—that is, "*how* do I *employ* this knowledge in my classroom teaching?"

The purpose of this book is to provide some answers to the preceding question by giving you a comprehensible introduction to philosophers and ideologies and a discussion of how this material can be applied to educational environments. My intention is not to offer an exercise in the mental discipline approach but to enable you to conceptualize and utilize the philosophical precepts presented in this work.

It is important to note, however, that you cannot employ knowledge unless you possess knowledge. In fact, one of the critical characteristics of a profession involves common practice founded on a knowledge base. Many of our teaching strategies and methodologies (for example, Socratic, didactic, dialectic, deductive, inductive, empirical, pragmatic, tutorial, and guided discovery) are directly based on the classic work of the philosophers you are about to study.

The effective implementation of the preceding methods requires an understanding of key philosophical concepts. Therefore, the purpose of the two chapters in Unit 1 is to provide a conceptualization and a practical, working knowledge of metaphysics and epistemology. In these chapters you will become familiar with the major philosophies of idealism, realism, pragmatism, and existentialism and also be introduced to some of the ways contemporary philosophers view the nature of reality and the sources of knowledge. Additionally, you will encounter many clearly defined philosophical terms, which will enable you to see how educational ideologies such as perennialism and progressivism are grounded in major schools of philosophy. Throughout the unit you will engage in practical applications and exercises with feedback panels, which will allow you to check your understanding of the material.

The significantly longer Unit 2, consisting of Chapters 3 through 9, will introduce you to 16 philosophers who in one or more ways have contributed to the content and methods of education. Each chapter includes a brief life and times of the philosopher, their general philosophical contributions, and classroom applications. The chapter then concludes with a classroom scenario, or teaching episode, that reflects a specific aspect of the philosopher's work presented in *real* schools with *real* students and *real* teachers throughout the United States. As in Unit 1, exercises designed to check your comprehension, expand your understanding, and increase your critical awareness are offered throughout these chapters.

A note of caution regarding the philosophers and the classroom scenarios presented in this book. It is common to label or discuss a philosopher in light of a philosophical "camp"—for example, John Locke is classed with pragmatism due to his foundational work in the area of empiricism. However, Locke also embraced the concept of an all-powerful, all-knowing "God" and an unknowable body of "substance," which could place him in the camp of realism. Furthermore, Locke, like many others, defies categorization in that his somewhat narrow views regarding who should be educated were far from his more politically liberal writings, which had a monumental impact on Jefferson and American democracy. In other words, philosophers had much to say about many things and deserve to be studied as individuals apart from their alleged philosophical camps.

Although there are substantial commonalities, variations also exist within a so-called camp or "ism." For example, the works of Kierkegaard and Sartre are common to a discussion of existentialism, yet on closer examination, significant differences appear between the two.

Certainly, any study of philosophy and philosophers can result in an endless series of controversies. Aristotle may have established deductive reasoning and the apparent universality of a first premise, whereas Francis Bacon questioned the concept of universal knowledge acquired through deductive reasoning and introduced us to inductive reasoning as the primary vehicle for obtaining knowledge.

Plato believed in innate knowledge, whereas Locke, 2000 years later, believed all knowledge was gained through sensory experience. In our own time, the noted perennialist Mortimer Adler charges Locke with having made a philosophical mistake. In his book *Ten Philosophical Mistakes,* Adler goes on to extol Aristotle and the Ancients and point out the "little errors" of the Moderns.

There is much food for thought in the work of Adler and other commentators. However, my purpose is not to analyze strengths and weaknesses, inconsistencies, contradictions, or even possible mistakes. The aim of this book is to establish the relevance and applicability to the teaching-learning process of Aristotle's *deductive reasoning* as well as Bacon's *inductive reasoning,* Socrates' method of *"discovering"* *knowledge,* as well as Dewey's *scientific approach,* and the more specific contributions of the philosophers presented.

As with the philosophers, so with the scenarios. They are not meant to reflect or capture the essence or scope of a particular philosopher's views but merely present a singular, yet real and useful, element of that individual's contribution(s) as applied to classroom teaching. The message to you as a teacher should be clear: philosophy has practical value and can positively affect *what* you teach as well as *how* you teach it.

This work is intended to expand your knowledge of philosophy and establish a link between philosophy and classroom teaching. More important, I hope that you will engage in a valuable experience that will encourage you to utilize this information as you involve yourself and your students in the endless search for knowledge, wisdom, and truth.

ACKNOWLEDGMENTS

First and foremost, I would like to express my gratitude to the principals, teachers, and hundreds of students who extended to me the privilege of visiting their schools throughout the nation and whose participation provided much of the practical basis for the book. I also wish to thank Professor James W. Bell, who over the years taught me the relationship between writing and editing, my reviewers Myra J. Baughman, Pacific Lutheran University; Elizabeth A. McAuliffe, Salve Regina University; Albert H. Miller, University of Houston; Harrey Newfeldt, Tennessee Technological University; and Trevor J. Phillips, Bowling Green University, and especially my editor, Debbie Stollenwerk, whose guidance and insight were invaluable throughout the project. Dean Donna Evans was instrumental in securing for me a sabbatical leave of absence and Dean Richard Andrews provided a Visiting Scholar appointment at the University of Wyoming, which allowed me to undertake much of the library and field research needed for the writing of the book. Finally, I am indebted to my wife, Lorrie, for her unending support and encouragement, without which this book would never have come to be.

David Andrew Jacobsen

CONTENTS

PARTICIPATING SCHOOLS

COLORADO

FLORIDA

UNIT 1

Philosophy and Educational Ideologies

CHAPTER 1

PHILOSOPHY AND REALITY

After completing Chapter 1, you will:

1. Become familiar with traditional philosophy by identifying specific philosophies presented in metaphysical statements.
2. Increase your knowledge of philosophy by encountering the differing views of reality found in idealism, realism, pragmatism, existentialism, and postmodernism.
3. Increase your awareness of metaphysical applications in the classroom by determining the educational ideology utilized in an actual teaching presentation.

Let me begin by posing the following question: What is your philosophy? Sit back. Relax. Take your time in answering.

Although this question is extremely broad, after some reflection you probably began your reply with "I believe in . . ." or "I think that . . ." or a similar phrase. The point is that all of us engage in philosophical speculation when we reflect on our feelings and attitudes and beliefs regarding a wide range of subjects. All of us at one time or another have pondered human nature, the meaning of life, the accuracy of knowledge, and what we perceive to be the goods and bads and rights and wrongs of the world in which we live. Often, the only difference between us and the philosophers you are about to encounter is that they went beyond reflecting and pondering by formally engaging in what they believed to be rational and thorough investigations of reality, knowledge, and human behavior. In doing so, they went beyond "deep" questions and thoughts by critically speculating about the universe and our place in it (Popper, 1974). They loved wisdom—the root meaning of the Greek word for philosophy—and went searching for it.

In a more formal sense, philosophy involves the systematic development of theories of knowledge, truth, existence, sameness, cause, and good (Hampshire, 1966). This requires a slow and persistent effort to increase our understanding of the world—an understanding that is necessary if we are to make the world a better place. For the moment, it is irrelevant whether *better* means moving closer to universal truths, more accurately comprehending the physical environment, or actually altering the material world. The constant in all three approaches is change. It follows that we must interpret the world to change it, and a good part of this interpretation requires critical or philosophical thought (Marcuse, 1972).

We are often told we live in a dynamic age. Knowledge is now increasing exponentially. It has been estimated that 90 percent of all the scientists who have ever lived . . . are alive! As the 21st century dawns and we move further into the computer age, the amount of information we can retrieve in an instant is endless. A growing challenge for classroom teachers is not so much in the availability of knowledge but, quite simply, in the need to examine this knowledge and reflect on it. Therefore, philosophical applications in the classroom require you to examine ideas, engage in dialogical inquiry, and respect the humanity of your students (Lipman, 1988). In doing these things, you will be able to facilitate the practical role of philosophy in the classroom and thus address the need to "do something" by:

1. Creating alternative ways of viewing existing information.
2. Sharpening students' ability to process and acquire knowledge.

This practical role of philosophy constitutes the central themes or threads that run throughout the book.

WHAT IS REAL?

Down through time, philosophers have grappled with the inquiry into the nature of existence in a variety of ways. Some have argued that reality is beyond the scope of human experience and can be pursued only through the application of the intellect and reason. Others have theorized that reality is limited to what we can discover and experience firsthand. Although these and other approaches obviously differ, a common thread is that of posing reflective questions about the nature of the world and our knowledge of it. In taking this reflective approach, philosophers examine what is already accepted as real, seeing how various theories fit in with what people may believe about observable phenomena (O'Hear, 1985). The branch of philosophy that attempts to answer the question "What is real?" is *metaphysics*. This field is concerned with the reality or nature of human existence (*ontology*) as well as with issues related to the origin and organization of the universe (*cosmology*). Reality is that which has existed, does exist, can exist, and will exist, whether we think about it or not and regardless of how we think about it (Adler, 1993).

The first link between philosophy in general and philosophy in classroom teaching, as mentioned earlier, involves reality or knowledge. Philosophers concern themselves with what is ultimately knowable, whereas teachers and the classroom curriculum focus on what knowledge is necessary and desirable. By definition, *education* is the acquisition of desirable knowledge or values (Frankena, 1965). The process by which students acquire knowledge in the classroom can be undertaken in a variety of ways, as you will see in later chapters. At this point, however, let's take a look at some ways in which teachers *present* desirable knowledge by reading two actual classroom presentations. As you do so, focus on the nature of what is being taught and on how that teacher is transmitting the knowledge involved.

 ## Scenario 1.1

Mrs. Laura Pilkington, a kindergarten teacher at Centennial Elementary School, sat in front of the board and gathered her students about her. The lesson for the day involved prediction as a prereading strategy, and she began by asking the children what they thought was going to happen when they went home. The children closed their eyes and took a few moments to consider her question.

"I'm going to get something to eat," Sarah said.

"I'm going to take a walk with my mom," added Ruben.

"Me and my brother are going to ride our bikes," Francisco said.

"Good job, kids," said Mrs. Pilkington. "What you just did was predict. You think this is going to happen when you get home, but you don't know for sure because it hasn't happened yet, has it?"

"No," responded a number of children.

"Right . . . and what we are going to do now is to look at this book I am holding and predict what we think is going to happen. As you do this, I am going to write your predictions down on this large sheet of paper on our easel. Now let's look at the book for a moment. What is this book going to be about?"

"It's going to be about a turkey," Francisco said.

"What do you think is going to happen to that turkey?" Mrs. Pilkington asked.

"It's going to get eaten for Thanksgiving," Sydney said.

"Okay, we will write down that the story is about a turkey and that the turkey is going to be eaten. When we finish the story, we are going to find out if your predictions were right."

Mrs. Pilkington then proceeded to turn a few pictured pages of the big book and once again asked for observations.

"There's an old lady coming after the turkey," Sydney said.

"Why do you think she is doing that?"

"Because the turkey is eating her berries," Sydney added.

"I think the old lady wants to catch the turkey and eat it," Janelle said.

"Great. Those are very good predictions," Mrs. Pilkington said as she added them to the written list. "Now we are going to read the story to find out what is going to happen and when we finish, we will look at our list and see if all your predictions were right."

Mrs. Pilkington then proceeded to read the book *Sometimes It's Turkey; Sometimes It's Feathers.* During the course of the story, the children found that:

1. The old lady found and hatched a freckled turkey egg and decided to raise and fatten the bird.

With permission. Centennial Elementary School, Denver, Colorado. Mr. Gerald R. Gilmore, Principal.

2. The bird, over a period of time, ate all her berries, grapes, beans, seeds, thorn apples, and even cat food and became very plump for the upcoming feast.
3. On Thanksgiving, the old lady brought the turkey to the table . . . alive, for the turkey, along with her cat, had become her friend.

"Now," continued Mrs. Pilkington, "let's look at our predictions. Was the story about a turkey?"

"Yes," the children answered.

"Okay, then we'll check that one off because we were right about that prediction. Now, did she eat the turkey?"

"Noooo," the children said.

"Did the old lady really chase the turkey?"

"Noooo," the children said again.

"But did the turkey eat things?"

"Yeees!" the children replied.

"So, we got the first one, we didn't get the next two, but we did find out that the turkey was eating the berries and other things. You were very good at predicting and you were super listeners. Now, when you go home today, I want you to think about what you told me you are going to do and see if you are pretty close to what you predicted."

In this lesson, Mrs. Pilkington facilitated the students' comprehension of the concept of prediction. She began by having them generate personal thoughts regarding what might happen when they got home and then proceeded with the book about the turkey, which allowed all the students to consider the same learning material. The students are learning that predictions may or may not be accurate and therefore do not reflect absolute truth or knowledge. It is also possible that the students might learn to understand "reality" as a construction of probability patterns. Note that in the text that Mrs. Pilkington read to the class, the prediction that the turkey would be eaten did not come to pass—which may not necessarily be true for other turkeys in other books. This understanding will undoubtedly be reinforced on the following day when the children share the accuracy of their predictions. Not only will there be differences in the accuracy of the predictions, but also the students will realize that many of their peers engaged in different experiences after they got home. Finally, Mrs. Pilkington has employed an intellectual activity aimed at providing answers to questions regarding such things as belief through a problem-solving approach.

Now let's take a look at another lesson in terms of the nature of the knowledge presented.

Scenario 1.2

Ms. Marianne Milligan, a communications teacher at Rio Grande High School, began her class by distributing an example of a persuasive essay to each of her students and asking them to retrieve their worksheet with the 'power questions.' She

With permission. Rio Grande High School, Albuquerque, New Mexico. Mrs. Judith K. Martin, Acting Principal.

then instructed the students to take out a piece of paper and place their name, the date, and the period in the upper right-hand corner. She told them to title the paper "Dissect an Essay."

"Okay," Ms. Milligan began, "we are now ready to start. Look at the essay on your desk. Every essay has a title. Whatever it is, write it on your sheet under 'Dissect an Essay.'"

"Is this a title page?" Jon inquired.

"You are not going to do a title page. You are just going to use this sheet to undertake the assignment," Ms. Milligan responded. "Now what we are going to do is work on a five-paragraph essay that has a structure that shows you know how to persuade somebody to believe what you think. We are going to start by dissecting the essay bit by bit. These essays you are dissecting are another class's, and they dissected your essays earlier today to get even with you, so everybody is dissecting everybody."

Ms. Milligan then moved to the overhead projector, upon which she had placed a sample essay. She asked the students to look at the first of the power questions on the handout. "We are looking for the theme, which should appear in the introductory paragraph. The theme of this essay (overhead) is, 'I think students with HIV should not, and the key word here is *not*, be allowed to play basketball in school.' So for the answer to number 1, you would write that down. That statement is the theme of the essay, the main idea. Next, it says, 'What is the first reason the author uses to develop the theme?' This usually comes in the first part of the second paragraph. It says here you can't play in the National Basketball Association, so why should you be allowed to play in high school? Is that correct?"

"Yes," Elizabeth said.

"Okay," Ms. Milligan said, "so for number 2 you would write the NBA doesn't allow HIV so why should schools. That is the reason this person is using to support the theme or main idea. The next question calls for citing an example. What does that mean, Robert?"

"It means note or list," he said.

"Or making us aware of an example," Maria added.

"Great," Ms. Milligan said. "Now what is it in the essay on the overhead?"

"All I see is a description of how the NBA works," Mercedes said.

"That's fine because it supports the first reason," Ms. Milligan responded. Using the overhead, she then continued to work through the structure, which called for a second reason and an example to support the second reason and a third reason followed by a support example.

"Now," she continued, "our last power question asks us to identify a concluding sentence in the last paragraph. What is it in this essay . . . Toby?"

"It says 'I don't think HIV victims should be allowed to play basketball.'"

"Good. We have dissected this essay, we've looked at the bone structure of it. We looked at the introduction, reason one and example, reason two and example, reason three and example, followed by the conclusion. Now, let's do it again with another essay on the overhead which takes the opposite position and says students who are HIV positive should, and the key word here is *should*, be allowed to play basketball."

Ms. Milligan then proceeded to work the students through the second persua-sive essay and its structural components. She then instructed the students to repeat the process with the sample essay on their desk by writing the answers to the power questions on their sheets. Ms. Milligan and her bilingual aide spent the re-mainder of the class facilitating the assignment.

Ms. Milligan used a variety of interactive teaching techniques to assist her students in understanding the components of a persuasive essay. She led them through a sequence of main idea or theme followed by developmental reasons, support through example, and conclusion. What the students are learning is that there is a "correct" way to write a persuasive essay. Whereas in this scenario, there is something *absolute* about the structure of a persuasive essay, the first scenario presents a learning experience involving prediction for which the notion of absolute does not apply. Additionally, Ms. Milligan employed more of a philosophical approach, emphasizing the need for certain knowledge of the tangible world via a persuasive essay. A final point to be made is that both lessons are founded on metaphysical views of the nature of reality as expressed in traditional philosophy, to which we now turn.

To keep a lamp burning we have to keep putting oil in it.

Mother Teresa

Idealism and the Nature of Reality

Idealism, realism, pragmatism, and existentialism are often considered the four traditional philosophies. The first two schools are based on the position that reality—for example, knowledge or what we believe to be so—is eternal and unchanging and is therefore absolute. Although many theorists agree on this key point, there are significant differences between the philosophies of idealism and realism.

Idealism has its origins in ancient Greek philosophy, as expressed in the work of Socrates and Plato. For them, the answer to the question "What is real?" was that truth and absolutes are found in the realm of ideas. Both thinkers were influenced by another early philosopher—Parmenides—who said, "What cannot be thought cannot be real." In addition to maintaining that the world is one of ideas, the philosophy of idealism embraces the belief that ideas exist in a universe that is permanent or absolute. Although the course of history has shown that ideas can change over time, these changes simply rep-resent a movement toward a preexisting, ultimate reality. Through this gradual discovery process, human beings refine imperfect truth and come closer and closer to "what is real." As for the source of ultimate reality, ideas are found in the minds of human beings because people are a part of what is thought of as the Absolute, the Universal Mind, or God. Put another way, knowledge and ideas are eternal because their source is eternal.

The presentation of knowledge in the classroom is something you will address on a daily basis throughout your teaching career. As you read the following scenario, see if you can distinguish between the physical object being taught and the idea the teacher wants the students to conceptualize.

Scenario 1.3

Mrs. Traci Connell, a second-grade teacher at David Cox Road Elementary School, began her lesson by asking the children, "What have we been talking about today and a little last week that ticks? Danielle?"

"Our hearts."

"Yes. Our hearts are in our bodies and they tick. Now today we are going to talk about something else that ticks. I'm going to give you two clues and I want you to look up at the board. This is your first clue: It is a poem. I'll read the first verse and then I want you to read the next verse and then I'll finish up. The poem is called 'Big Gears, Little Gears.' Okay, I'll start."

Mrs. Connell read the first verse and then assisted the children with their reading. After concluding, she said, "We have been talking a lot about gears, and this poem is clue number 1. Remember, we are looking for something that is not our heart but that ticks. Here is clue number 2. Watch very carefully as I turn this handle and see what happens to the pointer."

Mrs. Connell then moved about the room so the children could clearly see the demonstration, which involved a handle turning gears that then moved a pointer.

"This represents something, and I would like for you to raise your hand and tell me if you think you know. (Pause.) What do you think this represents? What is it, Deyman?"

"A clock," Deymon said hesitantly.

"Say it louder," Mrs. Connell urged.

"A clock!"

"You are so smart," Mrs. Connell said enthusiastically. "You said this is a clock. Now, when this handle goes around one time, how many times do you think the pointer is going to go around? Bing Jie?"

"Halfway."

"So you think it will go from the top to the bottom?" Mrs. Connell asked.

"Yes," Bing Jie answered.

"Okay. Let's watch and see what happens." Mrs. Connell then proceeded to turn the handle slowly as the children observed both the handle and the pointer.

"Now think about what you saw. We'll come back to this question, but now I want to ask you about something else. We were talking about gears in science and, with what you have seen, what do you think is inside a clock? Frank?"

"Gears," Frank said.

"Right, and later on this morning I am going to show you what is inside that big clock against the wall. Today we are going to start working on time, and you are

With permission. David Cox Road Elementary School, Charlotte, North Carolina. Dr. John Fries, Principal.

going to be able to tell time and show time to the hour by drawing the minute hand and the second hand. First I need to ask you a question. How is the heart like a clock, Laura?"

"It beats and it ticks."

"What happens if the clock stops ticking? Will it still continue to tell time?"

"No," Laura said.

"Why not?"

"Because the gears inside don't move the pointer."

"Very good. Now, what makes your heart beat or move? (Pause.) What do you need to take into your body to make your heart work?"

"Air," Atiya said.

"And what's in the air your heart needs?"

"Oxygen," Atiya replied.

"Great," Mrs. Connell said, "and we can call that *energy*. Now, what kind of energy does a clock need, Bryan?"

"The gears."

"Yes, but what makes the gears turn?" (Pause.) What if we use the word *power* for energy?"

"Oh, batteries," Bryan replied.

"Sure, batteries, or we could plug it in the wall," Mrs. Connell added. "Good thinking. Now let's hold on to that thought and get into our listening positions. We know that for a clock to run it needs gears and energy, but we need to be able to tell time so that it works for us.

"On a clock, like this big one I am holding, the pointers are called *hands*, and you need to know the hour hand and the minute hand. Does anyone know what the long hand on this clock I'm holding is called?"

"The *minute hand*," Astian replied.

"Good, Astian, and of course the short hand is the *hour hand*. Today we are going to learn how to tell time to the hour, but first we are going to see how the hands move on this clock. Now, let's go back to my question about turning the handle and gears and how that moves the pointer."

Mrs. Connell spent the remainder of the class involving the children in a variety of hands-on activities, which included demonstrating the movement of the hands and various times on a large clock, comparing analog and digital timepieces, listening for specific times in the story "Tuesday," and charting those times on a handout called "Time for Frogs." The handout and other seatwork activities allowed Mrs. Connell to interact individually with the children.

On the face of it, one could argue that Mrs. Connell is teaching something extremely observable and concrete. After all, a clock is an item we can touch and experience firsthand. However, from the idealist point of view, time is a concept and is found in the human mind. The "idea" of time and the keeping or recording of time can be found throughout much of recorded history. As such, it is something that has been, is, and always will be, so that it is absolute. Idealists such as Socrates and Plato would say to us that although a timepiece is real in the sense that it is physical or tangible, its very nature requires a beginning and an end. This means that sooner or later a specific timepiece will cease to exist and, because it is therefore not absolute, it is less real than the idea itself. Aristotle would not agree!

Exercise 1.1

Return to the quotation from Mother Teresa, and write a few sentences on how her words might reflect a characteristic of the philosophy of idealism. Then compare your thoughts with the feedback at the end of the chapter.

Realism and the Nature of Reality

The origins of the philosophy of realism are attributed to Aristotle. Although this philosophical school also emphasizes absolute truth or knowledge, it departs 180° from idealism in suggesting that the answer to the question "What is real?" is found in the concrete world, not in the minds of human beings. Whereas the idealist believes that the material world blurs our ability to grasp reality (as expressed in Plato's Allegory of the Cave, discussed later), a realist believes that a study of the physical world best answers the preceding question. The world is physical, not mental, and the universe exists regardless of whether it is conceptualized in the minds of human beings. The realist prioritizes a world of "things" as opposed to a world of "ideas." The way we move toward universal or absolute knowledge is through our interactions with the physical world. We come to know what is real through our experiences and observations of a scientific and orderly world (empiricism).

Pragmatism and the Nature of Reality

As you have seen, two of the major philosophical schools champion the notion of absolute and eternal knowledge or reality. However, the remaining two traditional philosophies, pragmatism and existentialism, reflect a much different point of view.

Pragmatists do not agree with Parmenides' association between thought and reality. They argue that *experience,* not *thought,* is real. Employing Parmenides' assumptions, a pragmatist would say that what cannot be experienced cannot be real. Experience is defined as everything we do in life in a sensory way in addition to everything we believe or think. This implies an interaction not only in a world of things but also in a world of people. The consequences of such interactions may involve changing people, changing the material world, or both. If the notion of permanence (absolutism) is fundamental to the philosophies of idealism and realism, the notion of change (relativism) is the bedrock of pragmatism. A pragmatist believes that reality involves something that has withstood the test of time that experience has confirmed or has not contradicted. However, knowledge is relative in that through a constant, dynamic, and action-oriented process, what we believe to be true today might not hold tomorrow. The Greek philosopher Heraclitus suggested that all things flow and that nothing remains the same; therefore, reality is in a constant state of flux and in a process of becoming, which in no way suggests movement toward preexisting, absolute knowledge. In fact, pragmatists reject the belief that people can acquire absolute knowledge or can perceive ultimate reality.

The premise on which pragmatists rely is expressed in the following syllogism (Lodge, 1970):

> Whatever is transcendental, is out of date:
> Idealism is transcendental
> Therefore, idealism is out of date.

The processing of reality or knowledge serves as a focal point for pragmatists; in fact, pragmatism is often thought of as being a process in and of itself that depends on experimentation and the application of human intelligence. To determine the meaning or usefulness of something, it is implied that the end result of the process is to put information or ideas into practice. The consequences are thought to refine or advance knowledge or that which we believe to be real.

Existentialism and the Nature of Reality

Up to this point, you have seen a focus on interacting with the world of ideas and the world of material things. This interaction allows us to acquire and process knowledge, presumably leading to more general or universal and more accurate views of reality. Existentialism takes issue with the assumption that reality is an expression of the beliefs of the world community. For an existentialist, reality is located in an individual human being and is therefore unique and personal. It follows that the question "What is real?" is not answered through reason. Furthermore, reality or knowledge is not predetermined and is not a priori, the latter being defined as truth that precedes factual information and experience and so is independent of them. Existentialism holds that existence precedes essence, which means that each of us comes into the world in a totally blank way. We have no preexisting or innate knowledge; we have no meaning, purpose, or mission; nothing is imprinted on us in terms of who we are and what we will become. Our "essence"—in other words, that which we will become and that which we will believe—is an ongoing result of the freedom to make choices throughout our life and the responsibilities and consequences of those choices.

Because human beings are shaped by their own individuality, the answer to the question "What is real?" is found in the essence of each person. Thus, reality is not only relative but is also subjective—a pair of ideas that represent the first of many philosophical dualisms you will encounter in this book.

Postmodernism and the Nature of Reality

As you have seen, each of the four traditional philosophies (1) rejects the basic premises of the others and (2) advances particular views on the nature of reality. However, there are significant commonalities, possibly the most prominent being that of a more-or-less cohesive worldview, whether it be absolute or relative. This relatively unified worldview, among other things, separates the traditional philosophies from postmodernism, which reflects a diverse group of commentators and philosophers.

As with the traditional philosophers who preceded them, postmodernists begin with a rejection of previous theories—specifically, those that involve universalizing worldviews. These thinkers describe the modern ideals of science, justice, and art as merely modern ideals carrying with them specific political agendas with no legitimate claim to the status of universals. Postmodernists urge us to recognize the highest ideals of modernity in the West as imminent in a specific historical time and geographic region and to recognize that such ideals bring with them certain political baggage. Such baggage includes the notion of Western supremacy, of the legitimacy of science to tell us how to use and view our bodies, and of the distinction between art and mass culture (Nicholson, 1990). This rejection of universals is a thread that runs though and that, to a large extent, binds the postmodernists. This thread begins with disillusionment with the European Enlightenment and that period's belief that rational thought produced truth and objective knowledge, which in turn were supposed to produce a "better" world for individuals as well as for the collective society. The focal points for achieving this better world were found both in the sciences, which would have an impact on the natural or physical world, and in the arts, which would address the moral progress of human beings. But gradually each domain became institutionalized, and dominant powers "claimed" the truth, which then became a coercive force. Therefore, postmodernists tend to be deeply suspicious toward any form of universal philosophy whose function is to compel consensus. Furthermore, they believe that one cannot grasp society as a whole. What is needed is to fragment what might be viewed by some as a universal society and focus on the fragments themselves. Postmodernists believe that in this way the nature of reality becomes flexible and can more readily become an integrated part of an individual's reality, which in turn can be more easily related to one's experiences (Sarup, 1989).

In addition to arguing that the Enlightenment concept of reality is little more than the outlook of a dominant group, postmodernists are concerned that we actually have an absence of reality! They fear that for many people, reality becomes whatever is shown on television, whatever is promoted in the world of advertising, and whatever is put forth in bookstores and supermarkets by the mass media. For postmodernists, the very distinctions have broken down between reality and a simulation of it, between truth and fiction, and between objectivity and rhetorical manipulation (Farrell, 1994). Although these views could be interpreted as an indictment of the philosophies that preceded them, many postmodernists are not ready to abandon the European and modern search for truth and objectivity—that is, for what is real. They continue to engage in the search but believe that reality is found in the specific cultures and locales of the present, not through the continued revalidation of the absolutes and universals of the past. This theme can be found throughout the works of the postmodernists, including those of Jacques Derrida, Jean-François Lyotard, and Richard Rorty.

Derrida, born in Algiers in 1930, is considered the originator and major exponent of deconstructionism, which attacks the concept of universalism by suggesting that reality is unstable and indeterminant and cannot be grasped in its entirety. He argues that the function of the Enlightenment was to identify and state systematically the rules, principles, or beliefs that underlie epistemological, moral, and social practices . . . a function that he feels can never be complete but always generates further complexity and complications. The unthought (universals) can be real but do not have to be captured in a specific theory; in fact, there is no single way of thinking (Madison, 1993).

Because of a preoccupation with universals, some postmodernists believe that philosophy has run its course and no longer serves a useful purpose. Derrida holds out against the move to dissolve philosophy as a discipline, however, although he does not think that meaning or reality can always be grasped in the form of some proper, straightforward concept (Norris, 1987). For Derrida, philosophy begins in wonder. It is the undertaking that sets reason in motion. Philosophy gives weight and force to reason. Its very energy and enthusiasm are what take it beyond mere accepted knowledge (Sallis, 1987). In his work *Différance*, Derrida develops a major tenet in postmodern literature by arguing that reality is not composed of universals expressed in unambiguous words and concepts but is indeterminant, so that the nature of meaning is constantly shifting (Wood and Bernasconi, 1988).

In his book *The Postmodern Condition: A Report on Knowledge* (1979), Lyotard also dismisses the idea of universal theories. He contends that alleged universals, expressed as scientific knowledge, do not accurately represent reality. For him, scientific knowledge is only a part of total knowledge, the other part being what he refers to as *narrative knowledge,* composed of legends and myths. When these narratives are embraced by the world community, Lyotard labels them *grand narratives.* He suggests that the "myth" of universal knowledge is a fine example of a grand narrative. Because of the absolute character of such narratives, Lyotard rejects them in favor of what he refers to as *little narratives,* which address what people have the right to say and do in a specific culture. There is no attempt to identify the whole and the one; there is a rejection of totality because it is impossible to know what is real without knowing something about a specific society in which the little narratives are situated and applied. These narratives define the norms of the culture in question, and since they themselves are a part of that culture, they are legitimated by the fact that they do what they do (Lyotard, 1979).

Lyotard is especially concerned with reality as being founded on controlled knowledge in a computerized world. In schools today, as well as in the rest of society, information is increasingly acquired through or influenced by what is available through computers. The reference section of libraries is being replaced by computerized programs and databases; knowledge is found not in books but in machines. Lyotard raises the issue of who controls the machines and who has access to them. Once again, as in much of postmodern literature, control suggests power, which in turn suggests the coercive force of conformity to the dominant norms.

Rorty, born in New York in 1931, also expresses concerns about conformity and about the often-mentioned drive toward a global village. He suggests that it is not desirable for humanity to become one and the same. Such a move implies "correctness," which he believes is undesirable and unattainable. A global way of life cannot be built on alleged truths of the human condition because truth or reality is not timeless or universal. However, trying to improve the human condition through debate and discussion that generate new ideas or perspectives justifies the existence of philosophy. Thus, like Derrida, Rorty does not call for the demise of philosophy. However, much of Rorty's work is directed toward a criticism of traditional philosophy. In his book *Philosophy and the Mirror of Nature* (1979), by describing some of the ways philosophy's traditional concerns are embedded in historical contexts and by challenging the practical value of these concerns, he challenges the idea that the academic discipline of philosophy can serve as the ultimate court of appeal in which claims of other disciplines are adjudicated. For him, the task of the philosopher is to find interesting and useful things to say about human beings and their situation (Malachowski, 1990). In *Philosophy and the Mirror of Nature*, Rorty goes on to suggest that the notion of contemplation, of knowledge of universal concepts or truths, makes the Eye of the Mind (the uniquely human abilities of thought, intellect, and insight) the inescapable model for the better sort of knowledge. But to know is to represent accurately what is outside the mind, so to understand the possibility and nature of knowledge is to understand the way the mind is able to construct such representations. The way to increase these representations is by inspecting, repairing, and polishing the mind (or great mirror), which contains various pictures rather than propositions, metaphors rather than statements and other various representations . . . some accurate, some not (Rorty, 1979).

To this end, Rorty is not interested in continuing what he sees as the Western philosophical tradition of trying to discover the foundations of all knowledge. He perceives this undertaking as fruitless because the emphasis on knowledge is too narrow. For Rorty, knowledge must be melded with action and with hope, which allow human and societal problems to be resolved. He believes the role of philosophers should be to do something different from, and more important than, offering accurate representations of how things are. He believes that we need to detach ourselves from the preexistent and that we should not become mired in accounts of nonhuman and human reality. Whatever has been so far proposed as an account of what is or what we ought to do can be changed, corrected, modified, abandoned, or rejected when it proves to be problematic, bothersome, or a blind alley. Rorty sees things (reality) as gray, and in that gray area of our knowledge and understanding, we can expect a good deal of blind groping, guessing, experimenting, trying, and erring (Kolenda, 1990).

In addition to Derrida, Lyotard, and Rorty, feminist writers have made significant contributions to postmodern literature. These writers include Linda Nicholson, cited earlier. Nicholson shares the concern that Western culture has been marked by the philosophical effort to establish universal principles superseding the ideas or concepts of individuals or groups and that these principles were supposedly determined in an "objective" fashion. For her and other feminist scholars, what had most frequently been presented as objective truth, objective good, and objective beauty (supposedly value-free concepts) had actually reflected various cultural assumptions. Moreover, Nicholson suggests that such biases are inevitable; all scholarship reflects the perspectives and ideals of its creators, and in fact, to avoid narrowness, a multitude of points of view need to be included (Nicholson, 1990). Even though Nicholson attacks the concept of unification, she accepts the utility of putting forth theories if they are not global in nature but are used within specific cultural, historical, and political contexts. In doing so, she brings together the need for the objectivity of the Enlightenment and the cultural concerns of postmodern feminism, resulting in inquiry within a social context.

With these schools' respective emphasis on conceptual absolutes, material absolutes, and the objectivity of science, it is not difficult to understand the postmodern feminists' rejection of idealism, realism, and pragmatism. However, with its focus on the individual's role in determining reality, we would think existentialism would be more acceptable to postmodernists. Jennifer Allen addresses this point by suggesting that the fundamental failure of existentialism is hinted at in Simone de Beauvoir's statement that "man represents both the positive and the neutral, as is indicated by the common use of *man* to designate human beings in general" (Allen, 1989, p. 71). The problem is that this description equates the masculine with the human, giving a reductive and misleading account of experience—more specifically, of women's experience. Therefore, there needs to be a break from existential patriarchy. The challenging of partiarchal norms requires consciousness raising, which is defined as the decision to emphasize women's feelings and experiences and to test all generalizations and reading . . . by personal experiences . . . to put all theories to the test of living practice and action. It is important to note that the focus on experience is central to existentialist thought, so Allen is not throwing out the baby with the bathwater. The paramount importance of change and the claim that philosophy is a sustained reflection on lived experience should also be noted (Allen and Young, 1989).

In her work *Throwing Like a Girl and Other Essays in Feminist Philosophy and Social Theory* (1990), Iris Marion Young continues the postmodern attack on the absolute concept of reality by arguing that we need to step back from totalizing theory that risks universalizing particular social perspectives. We should be more concerned with constructing "local" theories, since totalizing theory is suspect, resulting in reified categories and metaphysical ghosts rather than insights about social life and strategies for change (Young, 1990).

Nancy Fraser also addresses the role of social theory by championing what she refers to as *critical scrutiny*, which means cultivating some skeptical distance from the fashionable "postsocialist" distrust of normative, programmatic, totalizing thinking. Her interest is in a perspective that seeks to grasp and transform the social whole—a critical perspective that defends the possibility and desirability of integrating the social and the cultural, the economic and the discursive (Fraser, 1997). Her opposition to totalized thinking and arguments in favor of incorporating forces and influences other than traditional knowledge into the makeup of "reality" are themes that echo through postmodern literature and raise the red flag of wariness toward absolutes, universals, and generalizations transcending the boundaries of local cultures.

Exercise 1.2

Examine the following statements and identify each as being consistent with idealism (I), realism (R), pragmatism (P), existentialism (E), and postmodernism (Pm). Then compare your responses to the feedback at the end of the chapter.

_____ 1. The absolute nature of reality is determined through the observation and classification of existing concrete objects.

_____ 2. Reality is subjective and is found in the eye of the beholder.

_____ 3. Ideas are more real than physical things.

_____ 4. Reality is experience based and is "discovered" through experimentation.

_____ 5. Local regions and specific cultures reflect reality.

Exercise 1.3

So far, Chapter 1 has focused on the nature of reality as being either absolute or relative. What is the position of each of the four traditional philosophies—idealism, realism, pragmatism, and existentialism—regarding this fundamental assumption? Check your comments with the feedback provided at the end of the chapter.

PHILOSOPHY AND EDUCATIONAL IDEOLOGY

Educational ideologies, as expressed in philosophical terms, address a wide range of issues. At the system level, accreditation reports often include the Philosophy of the School, which frequently states the need to assist all students in achieving their maximum potential. Additionally, schools may affirm their commitment to a uniform and equal educational experience and the desired outcomes of that experience. These and other philosophical issues of a more global nature are of critical concern to all involved with educational institutions. However, since the focus of this book is the practical application of philosophy in the classroom, we will look at educational ideology specifically in terms of its impact on what we teach and how we teach it.

Education involves the fostering and transmitting of knowledge through the use of certain types of methods. Although this "philosophical" role of education or the school is easily agreed on, consensus is more complicated regarding the following questions (Frankena, 1965):

1. What knowledge is desirable?
2. Why is knowledge to be cultivated?
3. How or by what methods or processes is knowledge to be cultivated?

We will consider the third question in Chapter 2, but we have addressed the first two questions in this chapter in terms of the nature of knowledge. Educational ideologies are founded on traditional philosophy and embrace differing views regarding the desirability of knowledge and the need to cultivate it. When considering these two questions in light of the role of the school, the educational ideology of perennialism emphasizes the conservative role of transmitting the existing culture (knowledge). The progressivist ideology focuses on the role of evaluating the existing culture, whereas the reconstructionist ideology is concerned with transforming the existing culture. Keep these three roles in mind and think in terms of how philosophy influences the following fable (Reavis, 1956, p. 27).

> Once upon a time the animals decided to do something heroic to meet the problems of the "new world." So they organized a school.
>
> They adopted an activity curriculum consisting of running, climbing, swimming, and flying. To make it easier to administer the curriculum, *all* the animals took *all* the subjects.
>
> The duck was excellent in swimming, in fact, better than his instructor; but he made only passing grades in flying and was very poor in running. Since he was slow in running, he had to stay after school and also drop swimming in order to practice running. This was kept up until his web feet were badly worn and he was only average in swimming. But average was acceptable in school, so nobody worried about that except the duck.
>
> The rabbit started at the top of the class in running, but had a nervous breakdown because of so much make-up work in swimming.
>
> The squirrel was excellent in climbing until he developed frustration in the flying class when his teacher made him start from the ground up instead of from the treetop down. He also developed a charley horse from overexertion and got a C in climbing and a D in running.
>
> The eagle was a problem child and was disciplined severely. In the climbing class he beat all the others to the top of the tree, but insisted on using his own way to get there.
>
> At the end of the year, an abnormal eel that could swim exceedingly well, and also run, climb, and fly a little, had the highest average and was valedictorian.
>
> The prairie dogs stayed out of school and fought the tax levy because the administration would not add digging and burrowing to the curriculum. They apprenticed their child to a badger and later joined the groundhogs and gophers to start a successful private school.

The key to the application of philosophy in this fable is clearly established in the phrase "*all* the animals took *all* the subjects." What is implied here is that the needs of all the animals are the same and therefore absolute. The same can be said of the knowledge itself, for if animals (that is, people) are all the same, it follows that they should all be taught the same subject matter. This position points to the foundation on which the educational ideology of perennialism is based.

Perennialism and the Nature of Reality

The position just described is associated with Robert Maynard Hutchins, considered the founder of perennialism. Using logic in the form of a classical deduction, it is apparent that Hutchins believes that

1. Education implies teaching.
2. Teaching implies knowledge.

3. Knowledge is truth.
4. Truth is the same everywhere.
5. Hence, education should everywhere be the same.

It is apparent that Hutchins's statements are absolute; therefore, it becomes equally apparent that the educational ideology of perennialism is founded on the philosophies of idealism and realism. However, when combining the views of Hutchins and the neo-Aristotelian Mortimer Adler, we find realism, with its focus on matter being the ultimate reality, to be more of a bedrock for perennialism.

In looking at reality and knowledge and therefore at what we teach in the classroom, perennialism offers the following:

1. The curriculum, specifically the subject matter we teach, should encompass the classical body of knowledge that represents universal truth.
2. The role of the teacher is to transmit the classical body of knowledge, for it is unchanging in terms of both content and things of lasting value.
3. The curriculum should be academically oriented because permanent knowledge—as opposed to temporary vocational knowledge or a fleeting encounter with contemporary social problems—is critical for the learner.

In trying to grasp and synthesize organized and universal bodies of knowledge, perennialism utilizes the philosophy of idealism by emphasizing the development of reason and character. This approach leads to the actualization of educated and knowledgeable persons, persons who recognize and carry out their duty and who seek truth and wisdom and live according to these precepts. From realism, in addition to a focus on the concrete, physical world, perennialism champions the development of the student's intellect, which makes it possible to search for the things that are real or eternal in nature. This allegiance to the absolute nature of knowledge and, in fact, the nature of human beings themselves distinguishes perennialism as an educational ideology. This unwavering belief in the uniformity of all things enabled Hutchins to state that "the best education for the best is the best education for all."

Exercise 1.4

Read the following scenario and identify components that represent perennialist applications in the classroom. Then check your responses with those at the end of the chapter.

Mr. Dave Harguth, a chemistry teacher at John F. Kennedy High School, asked the students to move into the lecture/discussion area of the large classroom, which also included a well-equipped laboratory. He began by asking the students to take out their notes and worksheets in order to continue the work on writing formulae and counting atoms in order to determine molecular weight.

With permission. John F. Kennedy High School, Denver, Colorado. Mr. Rick Reynolds, Assistant Principal.

"The first thing we have to do is to learn the system, the language, or what we call the *nomenclature* involved. For this exercise, I have put two rules on the board. The first is that the charges in a compound must be equal but opposite. Remember, equal but opposite, and also remember that when we don't write a subscript in this class, it is understood to be 1. Okay, let's all get started with an easy one. Let's do sodium iodide. Okay, class, sodium is what?"

"Na plus 1," Steve said.

"Okay, Na plus 1 . . . and iodide is?"

"I minus 1," said Vanessa Smith.

"Right, Ms. Smith," Mr. Harguth said. "They are equal but opposite with a plus 1 and minus 1. So, what do we have to do? Do we have to criss-cross?"

"No," Vanessa responded.

"That's correct. All you do then is write the correct formula, which in this case is NaI. Sodium iodide." Mr. Harguth then retrieved an Erlenmeyer flask, told the students he was going to pass it around, and pleasantly implored them not to drop it. "What color is the substance in the flask?" he asked.

"It's violet," Levi said.

"I think it's purple," added Heather.

"Anybody else?"

"Purple," a few more students responded.

"Okay, then," Mr. Harguth said. "Let's call it purple. Even the solid on the bottom looks purple. Now, this element is iodine. We are getting a little bit ahead and we haven't covered this yet, but there's a physical reaction that's occurring in this bottle. That's why I have it sealed; there's a rubber stopper in there and plastic around it with string. That is because iodine vapor is not the greatest stuff in the world to breathe.

"Now iodine has an unusual property in that it goes directly from a solid that you can see here on the bottom of the flask to a vapor, and the term for that is *sublimation*." Mr. Harguth then proceeded to write the term and definition on the board and asked the students to add the information to their notes.

"It never goes to a liquid?" Franco asked.

"No. Not naturally like ice would from a solid to a liquid to a vapor. It goes directly from a solid to a vapor. Dry ice, which is solid carbon dioxide, does the same thing. Okay, now we wrote down (on the board) what we did here as a chemical reaction. We took sodium and combined it with iodine, which formed the compound sodium iodide, the formula for which, again, we have written on the board.

"Now for the really neat part. I'm going to pass around a bottle containing a white powder, and this is what sodium iodide looks like. We started with a purple element and a silvery soft metal, chemically combined them, changed their properties, and we now have a white powder and a new compound.

"Okay, good job. Now let's go back to our worksheet and do number 35, which is copper II sulfide. Let's get some class participation, so I'll have you go to the board if you know how to do it in order to show the class. Now everybody at your seat try it also. If you weren't here yesterday you can look on with someone or if you need extra help, raise your hand and I'll get around to you. And, just as a reminder, some of you write a formula as if the atoms are having one big fight. No. Atoms don't fight like humans; they always snuggle together, so get them close together and again, don't do the criss-cross if the charges are already equal. Okay, let's go."

Using this format, Mr. Harguth and his chemistry students continued to work through a number of formulae for the remainder of the class period.

All things are possible until they are proved impossible—
and even the impossible may only be so as of now.

Pearl S. Buck

Progressivism and the Nature of Reality

If you return to the conclusion of the fable discussed earlier, you will note that a group of ground-dwelling small mammals began their own school. For them, the traditional curriculum of the Animal School was insufficient; they believed the subject matter needed to be expanded to include the practical needs of their offspring. This utilitarian and more contemporary approach reflects the educational ideology of progressivism, which is founded primarily on the philosophy of pragmatism.

Having become familiar with the pragmatist's answer to the question "What is real?" it should come as no surprise that progressivism in the classroom focuses on experience and change, change being viewed as the nature of existence. Nothing is fixed. Nothing is set in stone. Knowledge springs from personal experience, the nature of which is not absolute or eternal. Furthermore, human experience primarily involves problem solving, whether it be the individual's need for food and shelter or the more societal need for things such as solutions to the national debt problem or epidemic drug use. When and if solutions solve problems, they take on the characteristic of being true or real and remain so as long as they continue to function successfully. Once again, however, since the world is dynamic and everything is relative, there is no guarantee that a given solution for a given problem will last for all time.

Returning to the role a school can play, problem solving involves identifying a problem, forming a hypothesis, gathering data, and analyzing data to arrive at a conclusion. Such an approach, along with other problem-solving strategies, requires an evaluation process. Therefore, as opposed to the perennialist's primary role of transmitting existing knowledge, the progressivist prioritizes the role of evaluating the existing body of knowledge. By doing so, as discussed in the work of John Dewey whose positions are fundamental to the progressivist school, experience leads people to growth in the continued direction of progress, and growth leads to even more growth. It is assumed that the end result of this continuous cycle is that of consensus building between individuals and in society itself.

The focus on individuals in progressivist ideology is founded on existentialism, in that an evaluation process requires increased individual awareness and an improved sense of choice and understanding. Choice implies freedom, and it is this concept, along with its inherent responsibilities, that is embraced and promoted in existentialist philosophy.

Exercise 1.5

Reread the thoughts of Pearl S. Buck and then write a few lines on why her expression would complement progressivist ideology. When you finish, compare what you wrote with the feedback at the end of the chapter.

Exercise 1.6

The following scenario presents three mini-lessons offered in one class period. After reading the presentation, identify components that represent both progressivist and perennialist applications in the classroom. Then check your responses with those at the end of the chapter.

Mrs. Ann D. Brown, a sixth-grade teacher at Blanton Elementary School, wrote the followng heading on the board: *Journal Entries for January 19th.* Underneath and to the left she wrote the following passage:

If you could share a peanut butter sandwich with George Washingon Carver, the scientist who developed by-products of peanuts and died in January 1943, what would you talk about?

In the middle of the board, Mrs. Brown wrote the following two sentences:

1. mt rainer is more high that mt shasta
2. we thought youre dog had drown in the mississippi river last night

On the board, below and to the right of the heading, Mrs. Brown asked in writing:

1. What is the only ocean through which the equator does not pass?
2. Is Saudi Arabia in Asia or Africa?

Mrs. Brown then told the students she would give them 10 to 15 minutes to respond to all the areas on the board and added that they could use their atlas and social studies book as references when answering the geography question. She also reminded them that the purpose of having them write about George Washington Carver in their journals was to develop their writing skills and avail themselves of the opportunity to take a risk and to verbally share their thoughts with their classmates if they so desired. Finally, Mrs. Brown directed them to put down their pencils when they were finished and were ready to discuss the assignments.

After an appropriate amount of time and, seeing all the students' pencils down, Mrs. Brown reread the Carver assignment on the board and asked the class who would be willing to go first with a creative journal entry. Brandon raised his hand.

"Okay, Brandon," Mrs. Brown began. "What would you talk about? What would you ask George Washington Carver?"

With permission. Blanton Elementary School, Arlington, Texas. Mr. John DeMore, Principal.

"Dear Diary," Brandon replied. "George Washington Carver invented the peanut butter sandwich. If I could share a PBJ with George, I would talk about how he made it from peanuts before he died."

"Okay . . . you would talk about how he discovered that. Good! Anybody else?" Mrs. Brown inquired. (Pause.) "Right. Traci wants to read hers."

"George Washington Carver was the scientist who developed by-products of peanuts and died in January 1943. If I could share a PBJ sandwich with 'GWC,' we would talk about how he invented by-products of peanuts and we would also talk about how and why he became a scientist."

"Oh . . . that's good!" Mrs. Brown said. "How and why somebody became a scientist. Very good thought. Okay, how about you, Angie?"

"Dear Man in the Moon! I would ask him what it was like to be a scientist, why he liked it, what other ideas he had, and what made him think of by-products of peanuts . . . like peanut butter!"

"Okay. Good job, Angie, and why did you name your journal 'Man in the Moon?'"

"Because he's mysterious," Angie replied.

"Mysterious?" Mrs. Brown inquired.

"Yes . . . and he can't share my secrets."

"Oh, good. I like that. I see your hand, Micheal. Go ahead."

"If I was talking to George Washington Carver, I would ask him why did he develop by-products of peanuts and how come he thought that was a good idea."

"Great," Mrs. Brown said. "Anybody else what to share?" (Pause . . . no takers.) "Well then," she concluded, "you all did a very good job. I'll be collecting the journals and, as usual, will be reading your creative entries and providing some feedback in the areas of organization and writing mechanics.

"Now let's turn our attention to the sentences on the board and see what needs to be corrected. Sarah . . . would you lead us please."

Sarah then went to the board and called on her fellow students to spot problems, which she in turn corrected on the board. When the exercise was finished, Mrs. Brown moved on to the geography questions and had the students "prove" them using the resources she had mentioned at the beginning of the class.

Reconstructionism and the Nature of Reality

Although reconstructionism finds some of its roots in the philosophy of existentialism, it is primarily grounded in the work of pragmatists. The commonalities are found in the beliefs that everything in this world is relative and that human beings process that world in order to change it. As you know, the ideology of progressivism also adheres to these pragmatic positions, but reconstructionists and progressivists go their separate ways in the area of educational roles. Unlike the perennialists, who emphasize the transmitting of the knowledge of the existing culture, and the progressivists, who emphasize evaluating the existing culture, the reconstructionists want to transform the existing culture . . . and they want to do it now! They are critical of contemporary society and are viewed as social activists who address international as well as national concerns.

Progressivists assume that evaluation leads to change but view the process as one that is often adaptive and lengthy. It is a gradual and peaceful unfolding. Reconstructionists see the progressivist ideology as the least doctrinaire because of its empirical and nonteleological assumptions, which lend themselves to a relative or nonuniversal view of social problems and their potential solutions. However, despite its radiant optimism and liberal hopes, it can logically offer no guarantee of the final emergence of the kind of culture and the kind of schools it values most highly (Brameld, 1955). Reconstructionists view the need for change as immediate and are not so concerned with potential social conflict and upheaval. If human beings are to become players or change agents regarding such efforts, they must be equipped to do so, and reconstructionists believe it is the responsibility of the school to provide them with the tools that will enable them to transform the contemporary world.

Most of the reconstructionist literature is found in the works of George Counts (1952, 1962), Theodore Brameld (1950), Ivan Illich (1970), and Paulo Freire (1995). The work of Counts provided the key issue for reconstructivists when he posed the question, "Dare the school build a new social order?" His concern that America's schools did not serve the needs of most of the children arose from the impact of the Great Depression in the 1930s and his belief that only a small, favored group was being prepared for the challenges of a technological and global future. One could argue that Counts was well ahead of his time when, in 1952, he wrote:

> The supreme task of the present and the coming generation in all countries, surpassing any domestic issue, is the development of the institutions, the outlook, the morality and the defenses of a world community. All geographical barriers, including distance, have been surmounted. Retreat into the past is impossible; perpetuation of the present means chaos and disaster?" (Counts, 1952, p. 283).

He further believed that teachers play a critical role in shaping culture, for if they are interested in the lives of children—the central responsibility with which they are charged by the state—they must work boldly and without ceasing for a better social order (Counts, 1962).

Brameld championed the educational role of transforming the existing culture and the need for students to be able to establish useful goals. In his work *Education for the Emerging Age*, Brameld suggested that "we give (goals or objectives) not for the sake of credits or even knowledge as such; we give them so that people of all races, creeds, classes, and cultures may realize a more satisfying life for themselves and their fellows. Knowledge, training, skill—all these are means to the end of such social self-realization" (Brameld, 1950, p. 94).

Illich's contribution is found in his classic work *Deschooling Society* (1970). Illich was a worldly man who had been educated in Europe and had worked in Puerto Rico, the United States, and Mexico. His experiences led him to question whether the world could afford schools that, in his opinion, excluded most of its children, made dropouts of the lower classes, and served as strait-jackets for thinking about education (Smith and Smith, 1994). In *Deschooling Society*, he answered this question by showing that the institutionalization of values leads inevitably to physical pollution, social polarization, and psychological impotence: three dimensions in a process of global degradation and modernized misery. Therefore, Illich's contribution to the reconstructionist movement is not an attempt to abolish schools but is an effort to deinstitutionalize the educational experience.

Finally, in the work of Freire, we find a method that provides the tools with which common people can transform the existing culture. Freire saw a connection between language and power and believed if people had a command of language and a high degree of literacy, they could become agents of change. Working mostly in Brazil and Chile, Freire developed a central argument, expressed in his *Pedagogy of the Oppressed* (1995), which stated that the important thing, from the point of view of libertarian education, is for the people to come to feel like masters of their thinking by discussing the views of the world explicit or implicit in their own suggestions and those of their comrades. This view of education starts with the conviction that education cannot present its own program but must search for this program dialogically with the people (Freire, 1995).

Clearly, the transforming role of education is expressed in the action-oriented literature of reconstructionism, which emphasizes the need for institutional change. Concepts such as change and freedom can produce discomfort regarding what is and what might be, and their complexities and implications are evident in the following passage.

From *The Dialectic of Freedom*, Maxine Greene

Celebrations of the Constitution and the Bill of Rights continue, but day after day their complex affirmations dwindle into slogans. Very often such slogans are used to justify alien undertakings: they are referred to in connection with so many mean-spirited and violent causes that their normative power seems to have drained away. Stunned by hollow formulas, media-fabricated sentiments, and cost-benefit terminologies, young and old alike find it hard to shape authentic expressions of hopes and ideals. Lacking embeddedness in memories and histories they have made their own, people feel as if they are rootless subjectivities—dandelion pods tossed by the wind. What does it mean to be a citizen of the free world? What does it mean to think forward into a future? To dream? To reach beyond? Few even dare to ponder what is to come.

And yet, those of us committed to education are committed not only to effecting continuities but to preparing the ground for what is to

(continued)

come. With this in mind, I want to explore some other ways of seeing, alternative modes of being in the world; and I want to explore implications for educating at this moment of "reform." My focal interest is in human freedom, in the capacity to surpass the given and look at things as if they could be otherwise. John Dewey sought freedom "in something which comes to be, in a certain kind of growth, in consequences rather than antecedents" (1960, p. 280). We are free, he said, "not because of what we statically are, but in so far as we are becoming different from what we have been." To become different, of course, is not simply to will onself to change. There is the question of being *able* to accomplish what one chooses to do. It is not only a matter of the capacity to choose; it is a matter of the power to act to attain one's purposes. We shall be concerned with the kinds of conditions necessary for empowering persons to act on what they choose. It is clear enough that choice and action both occur within and by means of ongoing transactions with objective conditions and with other human beings. They occur as well within the matrix of a culture, its prejudgments, and its symbol systems. Whatever is chosen and acted upon must be grounded, at least to a degree, in an awareness of a world lived in common with others, a world that can be to some extent transformed.

Reprinted by permission of the publisher from Greene, M. (©1988). *The Dialectic of Freedom.* New York: Teachers College Press, by Teacher's College, Columbia University. All Rights Reserved. pp. 3–4.

SUMMARY

It is obvious that if we are going to bridge a gap, we have to build a bridge. That construction process began in Chapter 1 with the introduction of the philosophies of idealism, realism, pragmatism, existentialism, and postmodernism and their respective views of the nature of reality—or their responses to the question "what is real?" Philosophical speculation regarding this question is called *metaphysics*, and the answers significantly influence the educational ideologies of perennialism, pragmatism, and reconstructionism. These ideologies serve as critical pieces of the bridge that directly connects philosophy to classroom practice. With specific regard to metaphysics, by trying to define the nature of reality or knowledge, philosophy provides direction for classrooms in terms of *what* knowledge should be presented. For example, Robert Hutchins and Mortimer Adler did more than simply establish the tenets of perennialism, which are founded on the philosophies of idealism and realism; they attempted to operationalize perennialism by collecting what they considered to be the body of knowledge that would constitute the curriculum of a school.

Their efforts culminated in the publication of the 54-volume Great Books of the Western World, which included the classic works of literature, philosophy, and science. The notion that an academic curriculum delivers an absolute body of knowledge is consistent with the perennialist view that the role of education is to transmit the existing culture. Progressivism, which is founded on pragmatism, stresses the need to evaluate the existing culture—which can be a lengthy process—whereas reconstructionism, founded on pragmatism and existentialism, focuses on the *immediate* need to transform the existing culture.

Chapter 1 introduced the first of the two threads than run throughout this book: creating alternative ways to view existing information. In Chapter 2, we turn to the question "How do we know?" as we take up the second thread: sharpening students' ability to process and acquire knowledge.

Questions for Discussion

1. How do the philosophies of idealism, realism, pragmatism, existentialism, and postmodernism differ from one another in terms of how they answer questions about the nature of reality? After comparing and contrasting the five philosophies, with which one are you most comfortable? Explain.
2. In your own words, how would you define *metaphysics*?
3. What is considered a significant difference between a philosophy and an educational ideology?
4. Why is perennialism thought to be founded on idealism? Why is progressivism grounded in pragmatism?
5. Although progressivism and reconstructivism are both founded on the philosophy of pragmatism, they differ significantly. What is the most important difference?
6. What are some of the potential reconstructivist elements discussed in the thoughts of Maxine Greene?
7. It has often been said that schools tend to transmit cultural knowledge rather than evaluate or transform the culture. Why do you think this might be so?
8. What are your thoughts on the question "What is real?" and how might your perspective affect your behavior as a classroom teacher?

Suggested Field Laboratory Activities

1. Review a number of lessons or curriculum guides in terms of their content and try to determine whether the knowledge is being presented as absolute truth or relative knowledge.
2. Given the opportunity to observe a number of classroom presentations, see if you can identify elements of the traditional philosophies of idealism, realism, pragmatism, and existentialism.

3. Try to locate a copy of the philosophy statement of your school or system. Then try to determine whether that statement is primarily based on the educational ideology of perennialism, progressivism, or reconstructionism.
4. If possible, observe a number of lessons and determine the degree to which they are transmitting knowledge, evaluating knowledge, or transforming knowledge.
5. If possible, plan and implement a brief lesson pesenting a classical or absolute piece of knowledge.
6. Given the opportunity, plan and implement a small-group discussion that allows students to evaluate the knowledge or position presented at the onset of the exercise.

Exercise Feedback

Exercise 1.1

The passage from Mother Teresa states that to keep a lamp burning, we must provide it with fuel. We might say that the function of a lamp is to provide light. If, like an idealist, we think of light as absolute truth, it would follow that the fuel or oil that moves us toward absolute truth is the acquisition of information bringing us closer to certainty. This information is called *knowledge* that moves us in the direction of eternal and universal ideas.

Exercise 1.2

1. (R)   Realism is founded on the belief that what is real is materialistic and eternal.
2. (E)   Existentialism emphasizes the individual and subjective nature of reality.
3. (I)   Idealism focuses on the nonmaterial world.
4. (P)   Pragmatism states that knowledge or truth is relative and is acquired through human reason and exploration.
5. (Pm) Postmodernism states that knowledge is found in specifics, not universals. Reality is reflected in local societies, not the universal or global community.

Exercise 1.3

Both the philosophies of idealism and realism adhere to the position that reality, or knowledge, is absolute or eternal. For the former, reality is found in the human mind in the form of ideas, whereas the latter takes the position that reality is manifested in the physical or material world. Pragmatists point to the relative nature of knowledge, which is in a constant state of flux and is not eternal in nature. Existentialists view reality as subjective and individually determined by our specific and personal experiences in life—experiences that formulate a human being's essence.

Exercise 1.4

Many perennialist influences appear in Mr. Harguth's classroom. Among them are the emphasis on a classically accepted body of knowledge, such as chemical formulae; a focus on the teacher's presentation of rules, the set knowledge of specific examples; the demonstration of a specific reaction, sublimation; and the computation of a number of specific chemical formulae, which provides opportunities for practicing the nomenclature presented.

Exercise 1.5

Progressivism is founded on the principles of pragmatism, one of which stresses the relative nature of knowledge. Therefore, in the classroom, progressive educators are more concerned with processing information as opposed to disseminating "truth." Pearl S. Buck's statement could be interpreted as supporting this position by suggesting the relative nature of the concept *impossible*. Impossible is not absolute even if it may be so only as of now.

Exercise 1.6

If you focus on the three different assignments Mrs. Brown wrote on the board, the question regarding George Washington Carver is progressively based in that it is extremely divergent and does not have a "right" answer. Mrs. Brown is after creativity and is encouraging self-expression prior to the journal writing assignment.

The two sentences in the middle involve a grammar lesson and are more perennialist in that specific rules or information are being applied to the incorrectly written statements on the board.

The final statements on the right side of the board have elements of both educational ideologies. The location of Saudi Arabia could be considered memorized, absolute information, whereas the first question involving the ocean and the equator could entail the application of information in a problem-solving process for the purpose of producing something that had *not* been memorized. Such an emphasis on problem solving would be progressivist, whereas memorizing the location of Saudi Arabia would be more in line with perennialist ideology.

CHAPTER 2

PHILOSOPHY AND KNOWLEDGE

After completing Chapter 2, you will:

1. Enhance you comprehension of the concept of knowledge by distinguishing between the terms *knowledge* and *belief.*

2. Increase your knowledge of epistemology by matching sources of knowledge and descriptions of "how we know."

3. Increase your awareness of epistemological applications in the classroom by determining the educational ideology presented in actual teaching scenarios.

In Chapter 1 you became familiar with the first theme addressed by the philosophers you will encounter in Unit 2. In the chapter you are about to read, we will explore the foundations of the second theme, which is the sharpening of students' ability to process and acquire knowledge. First, however, we must establish a distinction between this second theme and educational learning theory addressing overall behavior including information acquisition.

To begin, educational learning theory is teacher centered in that instructors can theoretically select one of the three most commonly used learning theories (behaviorism, information processing, and constructivism) and implement that theory in their learning environment. These theories discuss in detail the various factors that influence a student's behavior. For instance, behaviorism is based on the assumption that teachers can adequately describe what people do in terms of observable behaviors and that these behaviors are acquired through experience via simple conditioning or learning. The key feature is the focus on observing both student behavior and the environment, which in turn allows for predicting and controlling behavior—the essence of behaviorist learning theory. The degree of this conviction is shown in the following statement (Hunkins, 1989):

> Give me a dozen healthy infants, well-formed, and my own specified world to bring them up in, and I'll guarantee to take any one of them at random and train him to become any type of specialist I might select . . . a doctor, a lawyer, artist, merchant-chief, and yes, even into a beggar-man and thief, regardless of his talents, penchants, tendencies, abilities, vocations, and race of his ancestors.

Cognitive psychologists, who concern themselves with information processing, believe that a student's behavior is always based on cognition—the process of knowing or thinking about the situation in which the behavior occurs. As a result, they are concerned with the organization of knowledge, information processing, and decision-making behavioral aspects of the cognitive realm. The types of questions that cognitive psychologists ask include:

1. What are the students thinking about during problem solving?
2. What cognitive processes do these students engage in?
3. How might effective learning strategies be taught?

Constructivism consists of at least two schools of thought. These are sometimes called *empirically oriented constructivism* and *radically oriented constructivism.* The former holds that knowledge is anchored in the external environment and exists independently of the learner's cognitive activities. This approach focuses on helping learners construct accurate conceptions. The latter maintains that knowledge resides only in the constructions of the learners and that we cannot teach precise representations of "truth." We can only negotiate shared meanings with students and provide them with opportunities to construct useful understanding by overcoming obstacles or contradictions that arise as they engage in purposeful activity.

It should be obvious that educational learning theory is concerned with such things as human reason and empiricism and is therefore grounded, to some degree, in philosophy. The distinction to be made here is that our second theme or thread is solely concerned with the methodologies philosophers have used to answer the question "How do we know?" and the ways those methods can and should be applied in the classroom. These methods, or conditions of knowledge, or processes we use in attempting to attain knowledge, are called *epistemology*.

WHAT DO WE KNOW?

As with many things of a philosophical nature, the question to be answered is not the first question to be asked. Because "knowing" implies a "knowledge" of something, the first question to be addressed is, "What is knowledge?" In Chapter 1 you saw that the primary concern of metaphysics is knowing what can be known. Now we will see that epistemology entails (1) the knowledge we have, and (2) knowing about knowing (Adler, 1993).

If we view knowledge as matters of fact that we have ascertained through reason, feeling, and action, much of what we consider to be knowledge may not be knowledge at all, though there are elements of knowing as presented in the following examples:

1. I know how to find my classroom.
2. I know how to solve a classroom management problem.
3. I know how to track a student's progress.
4. I know my students.

5. I know that Cheyenne is the capital of Wyoming.
6. I know what my principal says is true.

If we are to think in philosophical terms, we must view the purpose of ac-quiring knowledge as moving closer to certainty or truth. With regard to the above statements, competence is not truth; recollection is not truth; and being familiar with someone is not truth. Truth is information that we recognize to be genuine that yields the characteristically human sort of knowledge that distin-guishes us as adult cognizers from machines, other animals, and even our child-hood selves (Lehrer, 1990). Much of the knowledge we think we have, there-fore, falls more into the realm of belief. Whereas belief is fallible, knowledge is infallible; belief is uncertain, but knowledge is certain because knowing re-quires three things:

1. Something must be sure.
2. Something must produce evidence justifying assurance.
3. What is sure must be true.

Much of our knowledge pretends to nothing more than probability. We guess, have hunches, and believe on whatever evidence is available and for the time being take what we believe to be true. If we are wise, we go on testing our beliefs and searching for further evidence that will confirm or refute them (Aaron, 1971).

Our students come to us with a lot of beliefs with varying levels of commit-ment. On some ideas or issues, they will be pretty sure they "know," whereas on others they will be absolutely confident that they "have the answer." The value of bringing epistemological theories into the classroom is found in the practical application of using their beliefs, as well as others, as a point of departure and by addressing skeptical questions regarding human knowledge (McGrew, 1995). This should not be viewed as an exercise in contradiction or the nega-tion of existing beliefs but should be seen as a justification process. For ex-ample, Plato introduced a notion of knowledge as justified true belief, or as true belief "tied down" or supported by reason or explanation as opposed to sensory knowledge. Aristotle believed knowledge is not itself sensory but is al-ways occasioned by sensory experience. For him, the "active mind" synthesizes, analyzes, and judges information collected through the senses. Descartes used clarity and distinctness as general criteria for absolute certainty or knowledge. Locke believed the mind is blank and that we conceptualize through the ab-straction of sensory experience. Kant's justification involved combining a priori knowledge with experience, whereas William James focused on assimilating, validating, corroborating, and verifying (Moser and vander Nat, 1995).

For many philosophers down through the centuries, justification has found its roots in doubt or skepticism or simply questioning that which was held to be true. Some ideas have withstood such scrutiny; others have not. As you know from Chapter 1, some philosophies would state that altering knowledge is a fine-tuning process that brings an idea or object closer to absolute truth, whereas others would suggest that the conceptualization of eternal knowledge is not the end result of the quest. Regardless, the commonality is found in the pursuit of knowledge and the clear understanding that knowledge is characterized not by what we believe to be so but by a process of inquiry that increases our level of certainty. Let's take a look at how this can be applied in the classroom.

We are now at a point where we must educate our children in what no one knew yesterday, and prepare our schools for what no one knows yet.

Margaret Mead

 # Scenario 2.1

Mr. Shaun Wallace, an eighth-grade American history teacher at Alexander Middle School, began his class with an overhead projector and transparency showing the unit, slavery and abolition, and the following objective: the students will understand the struggle between slave owners and slaves and will create a list of ways slave owners tried to control the slaves.

Mr. Wallace also distributed a unit organizer that would allow each student to provide or respond to the following: unit title, unit objective, description, key vocabulary, lesson content, activities, homework assignments, and due dates. He then distributed a two-page handout from *A Narrative of the Life of Fredrick Douglass*. He informed the students this was also going to be a pacing exercise and that throughout the reading they would spot-check 15 terms.

"What kind of a book does this handout come from?" Mr. Wallace asked.

"An autobiography," Barry replied.

"And how was it he knew so much about slavery?"

"He was a slave," Kelly said.

"What were some of the things he did that were important?" Mr. Wallace continued.

"He freed himself," Alicia said.

"And how did he do that, Jamie? What is one of the first things he did?"

"He taught himself how to read," Kelly added.

"Okay. Now in the first paragraph of the handout, what does Fredrick Douglass tell us that he didn't know?"

"He didn't know how old he was," Tina said.

"Yes, and how was that a way of controlling somebody, Tina?"

"I don't know."

"How old are you?" Mr. Wallace inquired.

"Thirteen," Tina said.

"And if you didn't know that you were thirteen, would that affect you?"

"Yes."

"How?"

"I might not know how I should act or how people should act toward me."

With permission. John McKnitt Alexander Middle School, Huntersville, North Carolina. Mr. Jimmy Poole, Principal.

"Fine, so not knowing something is the same as being ignorant, and Douglass tells us that being ignorant, or lacking knowledge, was one way of controlling slaves. Okay, let's continue with the reading. He talks about being separated from his mother at a very early age and believes his father was white and possibly the master of the plantation located in Maryland. So, he didn't know his age and knew little about his parentage. Should we add this last one to the list?"

"Yes," said Greg, "because that was another example of ignorance."

"What else was important about that?"

"He didn't have his parents around to help him," Nicole added.

"Okay. Now, why do you think the slave owners wanted to destroy family bonds?"

"If you didn't know who they were you could never go looking for them and you would be alone and wouldn't have anybody to turn to, " Kim answered.

"Right, " said Mr. Wallace, "and if a slave was sold and didn't have any family members there would be no reason or desire to return to where he or she had been raised."

"He did get to stay with his mom at night," Markiss said.

"True, but as you can see in the passage he said, 'I do not recollect of ever seeing my mother by the light of day,' and when he was about seven years of age 'I was not allowed to be present during her illness, at her death, or burial.'

Douglass also tells us about whipping, particularly the whipping of his aunt Hester. What does he say about that?"

"He says he was terrified," Karen replied.

"And horror-stricken at the sight," Amber added.

"So what do you think that tells us?" Mr. Wallace asked.

"It was another form of control," Ron said.

"Okay, so we will add whipping to our list. What were some of the other ways the owners controlled slaves?"

"They didn't give them much in the way of clothes," Scott said.

"How does that serve to control people?" Mr. Wallace asked.

"They had to rely on the master or they might freeze to death," Scott said.

"You mean they were dependent?"

"Yes," Scott replied.

"What else did they need."

"Food," Scott added.

"Anything else?"

"Shelter," David said.

"So being dependent is a form of control, and we'll put that on our list also. Good job. How about another one?"

"Well, you can't run away or cause trouble if you are tired," Cedric said.

"And how do you keep people tired?"

"Lots of work and not much sleep," Cedric responded.

"Yes, so we will add both of those to our list, and you can double-check to see if you have all these forms of control written down on your unit organizer. Tomorrow we are going to see how slaves tried to end the control by the slave owners."

One of the goals of Mr. Wallace's lesson centers on helping his students increase their awareness of some of the ways people attempt to control other people. However, in keeping with one of the goals of Black History Month, the time during which Mr. Wallace presented this lesson, he is dealing with beliefs his students hold regarding the nature of slavery—beliefs that may well be founded on what statisticians refer to as a "narrow database." By exposing his students to the autobiography of Fredrick Douglass and additional works of a historical nature, Mr. Wallace is expanding that database and may be facilitating a movement from recollecting to knowing. This kind of movement allows us to elevate a student's level of certainty and is the key to answering the question "What is knowing?"

Exercise 2.1

After rereading the quotation from Margaret Mead, do you think her view of knowledge would be more compatible with that of a perennialist educator or a progressivist educator? Check your response with the feedback found at the end of the chapter.

Exercise 2.2

Write a brief paragraph in your own words describing the difference between believing and knowing. Then check your thoughts with the ones provided in the feedback section at the end of the chapter.

HOW DO WE KNOW?

So far, we have addressed the first function of epistemology. We now turn to the second function—what Adler calls knowing about knowing. There are a lot of things we may properly claim to know: what we like and dislike, behavior that is right and wrong, what is virtuous or sinful, mathematical truths, what is beautiful and what is ugly. Although some of these examples involve ethics and aesthetics, we need to be concerned with perceptions, observations, empirical generalizations, scientific theories, and the like, including knowledge of matters of fact and matters of logic (Kyburg, 1983).

These concerns take the form of theories of knowledge describing the process by which we come to know, undertaken with a view to discovering how far or under what conditions this process is successful. Hopefully we can discover a process in which we will be safe from error, or at least can determine within what limits we can carry out such a process (Prichard, 1950). The end result of this process is that of enabling us to possess information, providing a more solid foundation on which our knowledge is based. We might also think of this result as a rationale or a more objective defense of what we may have merely believed to be true. Therefore, the basic question in modern philosophy has been how certain knowledge is attained and verified (Papanoutsos, 1968).

Although the methodologies that philosophers have created as well as employed are quite varied, it is generally agreed that there are three ways of answering the question "how do we know?" or "finding out": through reason, through feeling, and through action. Take a few minutes to read the following scenario and consider which of the three approaches is being employed.

Scenario 2.2

After completing the Pledge of Allegiance in both English and Spanish, Mrs. Sue Doyle began her first-grade class at Centennial Elementary School by showing the children a piece of chalk, a map of the United States, and a map of Europe.

"When we look at the map, which direction is north?" Mrs. Doyle asked.

"Up," said a few of the children.

"At the top of the map," another replied.

"And the bottom is . . . " Mrs. Doyle asked.

"South."

"And we also have . . . ?"

"West and east," responded the class.

"You guys are beautiful. That was a fine review. Yesterday we worked on the map of the United States and found the Pacific Ocean, the Atlantic Ocean, Colorado, and Florida. We said Florida was a peninsula. Who remembers what a peninsula is?"

"It's a place that has water on three sides," Brittany said.

"Perfect! You're fantastic. Now, today you are each going to get a brand-new piece of chalk and a magnifying glass. We are going to make a scientific discovery, and you will be able to share this knowledge with your families!"

"What is knowledge?" Jennifer asked.

"Knowledge is all the wonderful things we learn, and since it's always fun when we get things to look at, please find your map of Europe. Now we reviewed north, south, east, and west, so put your finger to the north of Europe. Now slide your finger down, or south, until you come to a country. (Pause.) This country is Ireland. Good. Now go east until you touch another country and write the letter *E* right in the middle. That whole land is England and is sometimes called the United Kingdom. It is surrounded by water so it is an . . . ?"

"Island," Nick and the children said together.

"Super. Now, there is something in England called the white cliffs of Dover, so if you will take your chalk, color in that whole bottom section of England because that is approximatly where the cliffs are found. They are very tall and very white, and we are using our chalk because the cliffs are chalk too." Mrs. Doyle then moved about the room to monitor the children's progress.

"Now, please take out your map of the United States. Would you please find the Pacific Ocean by the middle of California. Move your finger east to our home state of Colorado. (Pause.) Then I want you to move your finger north, please, to Wyoming. Use your chalk and put and *X* in Wyoming. (Pause.) You're awesome! Remembering the cliffs in England, what do you think the white *X* stands for?"

With permission. Centennial Elementary School, Denver, Colorado. Mr. Gerald R. Gilmore, Principal.

"Chalk," said Chike.

"Chike, this is your best day. You are great. There is lots of chalk in Wyoming and they are digging this natural substance out of the ground there just like they do in England. Do you know what started chalk? It is something similar to oil coming from the dinosaurs."

"Does chalk come from animals?" Kristina asked.

"Great! You've got it. The animals were little marine animals and were all pressed together for thousands of years, and they had shells that were white so that is how they gave chalk to us. Now, look carefully at your piece of chalk. What can you discover?"

"It's soft on my nose," Mark said.

"And it smells funny," Jill added.

"Anything else?" Mrs. Doyle asked.

"It's cold to me," suggested Megan.

"It feels like it's going on you," added Julia.

"Can you scrape a little off?" Mrs. Doyle inquired.

"Yes," the class responded and then did so.

"Now what does it feel like?"

"Powder," said the class.

"Hooray for all of you. Now let's get our magnifying glass and look at the powder to see what we can see."

Mrs. Doyle spent the remainder of the class working with the children as they observed the characteristics of chalk.

Although many things are going on in Mrs. Doyle's class—including map skills, geographic locations, and land forms—the focal point of her lesson involves chalk. As you could see, she has put a piece of it in each student's hands and they are physically exploring the object through sensory perception and are enumerating the characteristics of chalk. The children undoubtedly have an idea of what chalk is and have now learned that it is the "white stuff" in the cliffs of Dover and if they go 100 miles north to Wyoming, they can find it in the ground. At possibly a more significant level to them, the methodology being employed is allowing them to physically conceptualize chalk. Among other things, they have noted that chalk is soft, smells funny, is cold, and feels like powder if they scrape it. Putting this in philosophical terms, they are acquiring knowledge empirically. This process of perceptually experiencing objects or representations of the material world is one method we can use in our classrooms with our students to enhance their ability to answer the question "How do I know?" Now let's look at another method that teachers can apply.

Scenario 2.3

Ms. Gayle Jaggers, a fourth-grade teacher at McCann Elementary School, began her class by reviewing the previous day's work, which focused on figures of speech

With permission. McCann Elementary School, Nashville, Tennesse. Dr. Larry W. Wells, Principal.

used by poets when conveying their messages to their audience. She then said, "Many times they write with a great deal of emotion, or they write because they feel strongly about something or some issue. Often they are simply inspired because they see something beautiful in nature they just want to write about. It makes them feel so good they just have to tell somebody about it. They have to share it.

"Today we are going to work in our groups on some poems, and we will be talking and learning about some of the unique ways poets have of expressing their feelings. Each group will have a different poem, and we are going to examine them. One group has a poem about the Olympics because that's coming up pretty soon. Another group is going to read about a blacksmith who was an important member of the community during the pioneer days. I also picked one called "The Friendly Book" just because you know how much I enjoy books, and I think it has an important message. Then we will read a poem about an airplane and a pilot in the city.

"These poems have in them the figures of speech we have learned such as similes and metaphors. Your assignment may include finding examples of alliteration or onomatopoeia. Now on your sheet you will have assigned tasks to do regarding your poem. You might be asked to find a metaphor, and there's a definition on the sheet explaining and reminding you of what that is in case you have forgotten. I will walk around to help you. You may not find a metaphor in your poem. If you don't, just write that your poem does not have an example of a metaphor and go on to the next task.

"Remember when we work in our groups that you will work on a task by yourself and then read your answer to the members of your team to see if you agree so that you can come to a consensus. Also, remember that the purpose of working in teams is to get a job done more efficiently and be more productive than an individual. So when we work together and pool our minds and our brains, we get the job done much more quickly. Why do you think four people could do some tasks more quickly than one individual? (Pause.) Brad?"

"They could help some of the other people," Brad said.

"Help how?" Ms. Jaggers asked.

"Having an answer."

"That's right. Sometimes if you don't have an answer one of your teammates will know it. Now let's take just a few minutes to review how teams work.

"First of all, I need to assign leaders for today who will keep the action moving and monitor the activity. Remember when you work in your teams to use good rules of conversation. What are some of those rules?"

"Don't talk while someone else is talking," Kontessa said.

"That's right. If two or three people are talking at the same time it prevents others from knowing what is going on or from hearing or even concentrating. What are some other things?" Ms. Jaggers asked. "For instance, what do you do if you disagree? Do you say it is dumb idea? Thomas?"

"Nope."

"What could you say? If Valene thinks something is a simile and it isn't , what could you say that wouldn't hurt her feelings, Brian?"

"I could say I wasn't sure because the definition on our paper seems to say something else," Brian responded.

"Good. You can disagree gracefully or even in a positive manner so the other person's feelings are intact. Then you can get others' opinions so that everyone in the group has a chance to carry their share of the load. Now make sure you read your directions, which tell you what to do, and when you finish you will hand your work to your leader. If you are having any trouble with any of the tasks, your leaders can raise their hands and I will come around to work with you. Tomorrow you will share what you learned about your poem with the whole class."

Ms. Jaggers spent the remainder of the class facilitating the cooperative learning activity.

Although the bulk of the scenario involves Ms. Jaggers' discussion of the organization, rules, and rationale for the oncoming cooperative learning experience—an experience that is becoming increasingly common and effective in today's classrooms—the methodology she is using to assist students in "knowing" involves reason. You will recall that each group was given a different poem about such things as the Olympics and blacksmiths. The students have been directed to look for examples of such things as similes and metaphors and, in addition to being given the poems, have been provided with the definitions and explanations of these literary concepts. Therefore, Ms. Jaggers has given them the general or the rules and their task is to determine the specific or the examples. In other words, she has them engage in an exercise that requires utilizing deductive reasoning—one of the many forms of reasoning you will be encountering throughout this book.

The third way of finding out involves action and is often referred to as the *progressivist methodology of learning by doing*. The following scenario shows how that methodology can be applied in the classroom.

 ## Scenario 2.4

Mr. Ernest Boyd, a sixth-, seventh-, and eighth-grade art teacher at Eggers Elementary/Middle School, arranged his classroom into six workstations and made sure that each station had primary color trays and mixing trays. Three to four students were seated at each of the stations.

Mr. Boyd moved into the middle of the room. "As you know," he began, "we have gone through two different steps of introducing color mixing. We started out by explaining what the primary and secondary colors are, and then we individually developed a unique color wheel where you showed six identical shapes and objects and the six primary/secondary colors going in a circle. Today, you are going to use your color trays and your mixing trays, and you are going to do an original background and foreground painting.

"Now," Mr. Boyd continued," background is things that are farther away and past the horizon line on the paper, and foreground involves things that are below the horizon line and in front." Mr. Boyd proceeded to show the students examples of paintings and pointed out the use of background and foreground.

With permission. Eggers Elementary/Middle School, Hammond, Indiana. Mr. Walter J. Watkins, Principal.

He then said, "When you do your painting, I want you to mix and use secondary colors, and you can also use black and white to outline your work. Okay, you can start now and I will be coming around and you can raise your hand if you need some assistance. Let's get going."

For the next few minutes, Mr. Boyd circulated throughout the workstations to make sure that all the students had begun the task of mixing their secondary colors and that they had all the materials they needed to undertake the painting. He then began working individually with the students, beginning with Bobby, who had raised his hand.

"Mr. Boyd, I want to get a lighter shade of green and I don't know how to do that," he said.

"What were the primary colors you mixed in the first place?" Mr. Boyd asked.

"Blue and yellow."

"And which of the two is lighter?"

"Yellow."

"So, how do you think you can get your green to be lighter?"

"Add more yellow," Bobby concluded.

"Good job," Mr. Boyd said. "Go ahead and do it."

"Mr. Boyd," Carlos said. "My colors are all kind of muddy."

"So what do you think you have too much of?" Mr. Boyd asked.

"Water?"

"Right. Water in your paints?"

"No," Carlos replied. "They look okay."

"So?"

"My brush is too wet?"

"Right, Carlos. Get some paper towels and dry out your brush."

Demetria raised her hand, and Mr. Boyd moved to her workstation. "Mr. Boyd, I am having trouble with my background. It doesn't seem to look right."

"Okay. You've got a white sun here, so why is the sky so dark?"

"It's behind the clouds?" Demetria responded.

"Well, it looks pretty bright to me, don't you think?" Mr. Boyd asked.

"Yes," Demetria said.

"Well then, what you need to do is show that the sun gives off rays and therefore the sky should show some of those rays or colors radiating from the sun. What do you think?"

"The sky would have to be a lot lighter," Demetria said.

"Great. Go ahead and tone it down."

Fred, who was sitting at the same station with Demetria, was also having trouble with background and asked Mr. Boyd for some help. "Well," he began, "one thing you want to do is to show distance. What could you do with that tree you have there?"

"I could make it smaller and that way it would look like it was a lot farther away."

"Excellent idea, Fred. Go with it!" Mr. Boyd then crossed the room to help Gregory, who had raised his hand.

"I'm really not sure where to start," Gregory said.

"Well, start with your background and outline everything first before you actually start filling in with your secondary colors," Mr. Boyd said.

"I think when I do the foreground I want to put flowers there. How should I do that?" Gregory asked.

"In the foreground, should your objects be large or small?" Mr. Boyd asked.

"Large."

"Good, and just like with the background, make sure you outline them first. Also, what do objects in the foreground need more of than they do in the background?"

"I'm not sure," Gregory answered.

"They need a lot more detail," Mr. Boyd said, "because they are closer to you and should be more in focus. Let me show you." Mr. Boyd proceeded to demonstrate the use of detail in the foreground, then continued to assist other students as they increased their ability to apply color theory to paintings involving foreground and background.

It should not be surprising that Mr. Boyd's class is extremely student centered. He begins by reviewing the steps in mixing secondary colors, discusses how they will be used in a background/foreground painting, makes sure the students have all they need and understand the task, and then cuts them loose and begins to engage in individualized instruction. This is obviously a hands-on activity where the students are putting theoretical information into practical action. They are reinforcing what they have comprehended in a "learning-by-doing" experience. Put another way, the students are "living it," which further supports the progressivist point of view that education "is" life. Finally, you will note that Mr. Boyd is facilitating the experience and is frequently responding to student inquiries with questions of his own. When all is said and done, the students will have taken what they have learned and furthered their knowledge through the direct application of that information.

If the "what" is the nature of knowledge, the "how" is the pursuit of it—a pursuit that can be founded on a variety of approaches. You have seen how two of them, reason and empiricism, are employed in the classroom. Additional sources or areas of knowledge include (Pollock, 1986):

1. *Intuition:* most commonly thought of as a moment of internal knowing, or something that suddenly moves from the unconscious to the conscious.
2. *A priori:* what is known independently of experience. It seems to be a certain class of important knowledge characterized by stereotypes and intuition.
3. *Memory:* involves the connection of memory and belief and can also be concerned with factual memory plus the purely logical notion of existential quantification.

Reason and empiricism have traditionally dominated the search for knowledge in classrooms, as shown in the continued focus on the academic achievement of scientifically educated students. But it is not surprising that the postmodern distrust of the search for and establishment of universal truth has led to a reexamination of a much different source of knowledge: intuition. One of the most prominent exponents of intuition as a valuable tool in the classroom is the postmodern philosopher Nell Noddings. Noddings believes the educational system has become dehumanized and that the main aim of education should be a moral one—that of nurturing the growth of competent, caring, loving, and lovable persons (Noddings, 1992).

Born in Irvington, New Jersey, in 1929 and influenced by the pragmatism of John Dewey and William James and the existentialism of Martin Buber, Noddings argues that today's overriding emphasis on academic subjects and courses (as shown by their disproportionate share of the credit hours needed to graduate from America's high schools) is unhealthy. She believes that students are being exposed to a homogeneous curriculum that may not promote or enhance their intellectual and moral needs as individuals, all of whom bring a wealth of personal experience to their learning environments. Additionally, the drive toward a standardized curriculum implies a uniformity of knowledge that concerns Noddings, for she believes the goal of a school is not that of a search for absolute truth or the promotion of the ability to employ reasoning to be right or to "win." It is in this arena that she champions intuition. Rather than emphasizing aggressive, argumentative styles, she focuses on the caring and flexibility of interpersonal reasoning that involves listening, connecting, and taking responsibility (Witherell and Noddings, 1991).

Employing intuition makes it possible to move away from absolute principles. Wherever there is a principle, there is implied its exception and, too often, principles function to separate individuals from each other and promote self-righteousness when one holds a principle someone else does not hold. Intuition provides coherence and enlightenment without "proving" anything and, indeed, without claiming to present or to seek moral knowledge or moral truth. The hand that steadied us as we learned to ride our first bicycle did not provide propositional knowledge, but it guided and supported us all the same, and we finished up "knowing how" (Noddings, 1984).

One of the controversies that has surrounded intuition from the time of Plato to the present involves a lack of agreement on its definition. Across the philosophical spectrum, intuition has been referred to as:

- Imprecise thinking
- Knowledge that exists but cannot be proven
- A way of knowing
- The interpretation of omens
- Uncontrolled imagination
- Visions
- Insights
- Nonrational sources of knowledge
- Hunches
- Immediate, unexplained knowledge
- Nonlinear thinking

Noddings is primarily concerned with how intuition is intended for use in education and how it contributes to learning, creating, expressing, and solving problems. She is not so concerned with intuition as grounds for knowing but is more focused on intuition as a "way" of knowing. In the absense of intuition, experiences would consist of a simple series of occurrences without direction or meaning. Experience would be something merely had, not something anticipated, organized, chosen, and evaluated. Intuition seems to have the special function of allowing us, after we have decided in a reflective, conscious mode, to submit ourselves to the world and to be, nonreflectively or directly, spoken to, grasped, and moved by it (Noddings and Shore, 1984).

Revealed knowledge, or revelation, is an additional source of knowledge, although it is often thought of as an external source of a priori knowledge. Revealed knowledge is that which God discloses or, as postulated in Plato's doctrine of the transmigration of the soul, is something implanted in human beings.

Returning to memory as a source of knowledge, much of the factual information we store, particularly with regard to the sciences, involves an accepted body of classical knowledge formulated by authorities. For example, most of us "know" Newton's third law of gravity because he and others have presented it through books and other sources. Few of us sat under an apple tree, got hit on the head by a piece of fruit, pondered the event, and verbalized the principle or law. Obviously, much of what is taught in today's classrooms is founded on authoritative knowledge.

Finally, returning to reasoning, Ms. Jaggers's presentation involved deduction, which is only one of many forms of reasoning. In Unit 2, you will encounter additional classroom presentations that show the application of such forms as the Socratic method, guided discovery, induction, experimentalism, and dialectic. In addition to classroom experiences involving feelings and actions, these methods provide the tools that allow our students to "find out." One of the three methods is discussed in the following passage.

From *Spontaneous Activity in Education,* Maria Montessori

Now it would be exceedingly difficult to limit perceptions strictly to two, especially when dealing with persons placed in an environment abounding in stimuli, who have already stored up a whole chaos of images. But such being the object in view, (referring to a case study lesson) it is necessary to eliminate as far as possible all other perceptions, to arrest those two, and so to polarize attention on them that all other images shall be obscured in the field of consciousness. This would be the scientific method tending to isolate perceptions; and it is in fact the practical method adopted by us in our education of the senses. In the case of cold and heat, the child is "prepared" by the isolation of the particular sense in question; he is placed blindfolded in a silent place, to the end

(continued)

that thermic stimuli alone may reach him. In front of the child are placed two objects perfectly identical in all characteristics perceptible to the muscular tactile sense: of the same dimensions, the same shape, the same degree of smoothness, the same resistance to pressure; for instance, two india-rubber bags filled with the same quantity of water, and perfectly dry on the outside. The sole difference is the temperature of the water in the two bags; in the hot one, the water would be at a temperature of sixty degrees centigrade; in the cold, at ten degrees centigrade. After directing the child's attention to the object, his hand is drawn over the hot bag, and then over the cold one; while his hand is on the hot bag the teacher says: It is hot! While he feels the cold one he is told: It is cold. And the lesson is finished. It has consisted merely of two words, and of a long preparation designed to ensure that as far as possible, the two sensations corresponding to the two words shall be the only ones that reach the child. The other senses, sight and hearing, were protected against stimuli and there was no perceptible difference in the objects offered to the touch save that of temperature. Thus it becomes approximately probable that the child will achieve the perception of two sensations exclusively.

And what about the liberty of the child, we shall be asked?

Well, we admit that every lesson infringes on the liberty of the child, and for this reason we allow it to last only a few seconds: just the time to pronounce the two words: hot, cold; but this is effected under the influence of the preparation, which by first isolating the sense makes, as it were, a darkness in the consciousness, and then projects only two images into it. As if from the screen before a magic lantern, the child receives his psychical acquisitions, or rather they are like seeds falling on a fertile soil; and it is in the subsequent free choice, and the repetition of the exercise, as in a subsequent activity, spontaneous, associative, and reproductive, that the child will be left "free." He receives, rather than a lesson, a determinate impression of contact with the external world; it is the clear, scientific, predetermined character of this content which distinguishes it from the mass of indeterminate contacts which the child is continually receiving from his surroundings. The multiplicity of such indeterminate contacts will create chaos within the mind of the child; predetermined contacts will, on the other hand, initiate order therein, because with the help of the technique of isolation, they will begin to make him distinguish one thing from another.

Montessori, M. (1965). *Spontaneous Activity in Education* (F. Simmonds, Trans.). New York: Schocken Books, pp. 42–44. Reprinted with the permission of Random House.

Exercise 2.3

Read the sources of knowledge and the descriptions given, then match them by placing the letter of the most appropriate description in the space provided. When you are finished, check your answers with those found in the feedback section at the end of the chapter.

_____ 1. revealed knowledge
_____ 2. intuitive knowledge
_____ 3. empirical knowledge
_____ 4. rational knowledge
_____ 5. authoritative knowledge

a. Inductively determining a rule.
b. Espousing a god-given belief.
c. Knowing something in your heart.
d. Embracing Albert Einstein's theory of relativity.
e. Observing the effect of water on earth forms.

EDUCATIONAL IDEOLOGY AND HOW WE KNOW

You have learned in Chapter 1 that a critical consideration of educational ideologies involves the role the school plays in the transmission of knowledge, the evaluation of knowledge, and the transformation of knowledge. Therefore, rather than looking at the specific ideologies discussed earlier, we will focus on the roles and how they tend to influence the strategies as well as methodologies teachers employ in their classrooms.

Transmitting the existing body of knowledge or culture is generally undertaken by organizing common subjects, which results in what we call a *discipline* of study. These disciplines are then presented as courses that in primary and elementary school can be quite broad—for example, reading, science, or social studies. At the high school level, the commonalities in the courses become more specific, so that science may be offered as a semester of botany or zoology, and reading, among other things, becomes American literature. It is assumed that each subject contains an accepted body of information, and it is the teacher's responsibility to transmit that body of information. Techniques like lecture and expository teaching are often employed in the delivery of the curriculum, much of which consists of authoritative knowledge representing the world's "permanencies." Those who consider themselves perennialists certainly emphasize this role, but it should be noted that they recognize reason, as a source of knowledge, to also be important, because both the needs of the learner and the needs of society depend on an ability to engage in critical thinking and be proficient in problem solving.

When is comes to evaluating knowledge, a course structure is still maintained for the purpose of presenting knowledge, but not necessarily in an authoritarian way. As mentioned in the preface, you cannot employ knowledge unless you possess knowledge or, put differently, if you are going to engage in an evaluative process, you have to have something to evaluate. The processes utilized in the evaluation role of the school primarily involve empirical and rational sources of knowledge. Often, the goal in and of itself is to facilitate the student's ability to apply critical thinking skills to a variety of problems. Examples of such skills employed by progressivists who prioritize the evaluative role include the Socratic method, guided discovery, inductive reasoning, structured observation, and dialectic. These classrooms more often than not are student centered, but they are still structured and somewhat uniform in terms of the curriculum and the learning activities. Although the learning environment is directly related to the interests of the students, it is absolutely critical to note that the students themselves are *not* the final arbiters of what they will learn and how they will learn it.

The methodologies applied to the transformational role of the school are similar to those of the evaluational role of the school, in that both emphasize the need to problem solve and engage in a variety of inquiry-type activities. The differences are found more in the areas of the learning environment and the desired outcomes. The learning environment can be more existentialist in nature by focusing specifically on what the students view as problematic and determining how they as individuals intend to solve those problems. This is often undertaken by focusing on themes or units of instruction as opposed to the more common course structure discussed earlier. Modular scheduling is often employed, which allows for a less rigid school day and increased opportunities for tutorial instruction. Again, the teacher's role is to assist and facilitate the learning experiences, which are often more divergent than those found in classrooms emphasizing the evaluative role.

The big difference when prioritizing the transforming role of the school is in the desired outcomes of a given learning experience. As championed by reconstructionists, these classrooms are action oriented, and the intent is to employ empirical and rational sources of knowledge in an effort to change the world in which the students live. Therefore, little in the curriculum is viewed as theoretical, and a sense of urgency dominates the learning environment.

Although the methodologies of reason and empiricism are commonly employed by progressivists and reconstructionists, and to a lesser extent by perennialists, in an effort to answer the question "How do we know?", the reconstructionist desire to produce agents of change and use the schools as institutions for social reform clearly sets it apart from other educational ideologies.

Exercise 2.4

Read the following teaching scenarios and then, in terms of "How do we know?", determine the primary educational ideology reflected. Then compare your responses to the feedback at the end of the chapter.

Scenario 2.5

Ms. Joann DeSantis, a sixth-grade teacher at Eastwood Elementary School, wrote the following sentences on the chalkboard:

With permission. Eastwood Elementary School, Salt Lake City, Utah. Ms. Marcie McDonald, Principal.

1. did you read a copy of science fiction digest my favorite magazine.
2. karens bike is the newer of the five bikes parked hear

She then asked the class, arranged in a traditional, large-group environment, to read the sentences silently to determine whether there were any errors. After providing an appropriate amount of wait-time, Ms. DeSantis walked to the middle of the classroom among the students.

"Is everything okay?" The students responded with a "group" no!

"Why? What is wrong with the first one . . . Lisa?"

"A sentence has to start with a capital, so the first *d* in *did* has to be a capital."

"That's great, Lisa. Go to the board and make the change. Okay, do you have something, Dave?"

"Well, the same goes for *science fiction digest*," answered Dave.

"Why?"

"Because it's the name of a magazine."

"Which makes it . . . ?"

"A proper noun."

"Good job," Ms. DeSantis said as Dave got up from his seat and started for the board to make the changes in the three words."

"Are we through with the magazine?" she continued.

"No," responded Mathis.

"How come?"

"Titles need to be underlined, and *Science Fiction Digest* is a title."

"Excellent, Mathis." Up to the board. "Are we through?" (Pause.) Charley?"

"We need a comma after *Digest*."

"Okay. You can join Mathis. Now are we through?" (Pause.) Kathy?"

"There is a comma after *Digest*, but you're still asking a question, so we need a question mark at the end."

"Yesss! Good job, everybody," Ms. DeSantis said enthusiastically. "Now, let's go on to the next sentence. Is everything okay in this one?" (The group responds with "nays.")

"Great! Who wants to go to the board and spot a problem?" Ms. DeSantis continued this procedure for the remainder of the lesson.

Scenario 2.6

Ms. Ruth Creel, an economics teacher at Rio Grande High School, wanted to teach her students how to fill out a retail order form. She began her class by distributing a sample order form and ads she had removed from a Ward's catalog. She then told the students the areas they would be looking at would be men's wear, women's wear, toys, and "other." She proceeded to write these categories on the board, then placed an order form transparency on the overhead projector.

With permission. Rio Grande High School, Albuquerque, New Mexico. Mrs. Judith K. Martin, Acting Principal.

"This order form you see is identical to the one I have handed you," Mrs. Creel began. "Now, what you are going to do is work through this form as if you were ordering gifts for the upcoming holidays." She then demonstrated on the overhead the appropriate place on the form for them to write in their names and addresses and instructed them to do so.

"Now look on your form," Mrs. Creel continued. "It says item number, which is to the left, then description, page, and monogram. Does anybody know what a monogram is?"

"The number," Casey said.

"Close. It's letters, so if you were ordering clothing, you would put *CM* for your first and last name. The next one is size, and then we have pattern or color and quantity. What is quantity?"

"How many you want to buy," Esteban said.

"Right, and how about the price, each? What does that mean?"

"How much one of them costs," Kristina said.

"Great, and if we have more than one item, what do we do in that last column, which is the total?"

"We multiply the quantity times the price of each," Erika said.

"Excellent, Erika," Mrs. Creel said. "Now look down below and see method of payment. Somewhere along the line you are going to want to establish some credit so that someday you will be able to buy a car or a house."

"My Dad says you have to watch out for credit because they will let you charge more than you can afford and it will take a long time to pay off and you have to pay extra," Miguel said.

"That's a good point, Miguel, and what do we call that 'extra'?"

"Interest."

"Right, so be sure if they give you a $1000 credit line you don't run out and make a thousand dollars worth of purchases. And at Christmas time, that is a very easy thing to do. Now then, there is a little box to check that says 'defer my payments until April.' Do you know what *defer* means?"

"Do not put it on my credit card, " Amy said.

"I don't have to make any payments," Elfriede added.

"You're both right. I can buy something today and it won't show up on my bill until April. Now up here [Mrs. Creel uses the overhead] it says 'satisfaction guaranteed.' What does that mean?"

"It means if you don't like it you can take it back," Margaret said.

"Or exchange it," Trudy added.

"Great!" Mrs. Creel then discussed, with the use of the overhead, the completion of the form by calling the students' attention to the computation of merchandise total, sales tax, and shipping and handling.

"What I would like you to do now is to go through your toy ads and find one item you would really like to buy for your favorite person and circle it. Then I want you to fill in all the necessary information on your order sheet. After that, buy something for your mom from your women's wear ads. Also, purchase two additional items, one each from men's wear and others."

Mrs. Creel used the remainder of the class period to monitor and assist the students' work.

SUMMARY

In Chapter 2 you have seen that knowledge, whether ultimately considered absolute or relative, implies a pursuit. The degree to which we know something depends on our level of certainty. Classroom teachers can enhance their students' ability to pursue knowledge by exposing them to a variety of methodologies that facilitate commonly agreed on sources of knowledge. Those sources (which address the ways we find out through reason, feeling, and action) include revelation, intuition, empiricism, rational thinking, and authoritarian knowledge.

Learning environments that ideologically focus on the absolute nature of knowledge tend to assist students in answering the question "How do we know?" by emphasizing methodologies that are deductive, intuitive, or authoritarian and that promote the transmission and preservation of traditional knowledge. Learning environments that ideologically focus on the relative nature of knowledge more commonly employ inductive methodologies in an attempt to enhance self-discovery and promote critical thinking skills. These environments are centered more around "how" a student thinks than around "what" a student knows or believes.

Although belief contains varying levels of certainty and knowledge, our most cherished scientific achievements and our most worthy practical attainments depend on a more significant kind of knowledge. This kind of knowledge rests on our capacity to distinguish truth from error, and (for all learning environments) this requires an analysis of knowledge (Lehrer, 1990). The bottom line for teachers is that epistemological applications in the classroom will help students move in the desirable direction of establishing objective as opposed to subjective positions when answering the question "How do I know?"

Questions For Discussion

1. In the attempt to answer the question "How do we know?", what methodologies would be most commonly employed by idealists, realists, pragmatists, and existentialists?
2. Why would perennialist educators be more inclined than progressivist educators to rely on authoritative knowledge?
3. What are two potential sources of intuitive knowledge?
4. Although all educational ideologies, including perennialism, progressivism, and reconstructionism, utilize human reason as a methodology for answering the question "How do we know?", they differ in the application of this source of knowledge. What are some of those differences?

5. Which educational ideology would be most compatible with the methodology described in the passage from Maria Montessori?
6. Is there anything that is common to all the activities involved in "knowing?"
7. How can we show that knowledge is truth? After analyzing the thoughts of Nell Noddings, do you believe that it is necessary for knowledge to be true?

Suggested Field Laboratory Activities

1. Undertake a half-dozen or so observations of classroom presentations and determine if they are centered around reason, feeling, or action.
2. Review a number of lessons or curriculum guides to determine if or how often specific sources of knowledge (revelation, intuition, empiricism, rational thought, authoritative knowledge) are employed.
3. Discuss with your fellow preservice teachers what you consider to be the most important ways to answer the question "How do we know?"
4. Given the opportunity, prepare and implement a lesson that employs a deductive methodology.
5. If possible, prepare and implement a lesson that employs an inductive methodology.

Exercise Feedback

Exercise 2.1

The words of Margaret Mead suggest the dynamic nature of knowledge in a world that will be different in the future. The progressivist could interpret this knowledge as being relative and would be likely to assume that educational experiences must be flexible to prepare students for the unknown. Perennialists would agree that we can not be sure of what tomorrow holds but could also share Mead's belief that whatever comes to be will be compatible with existing knowledge and reflective of the orderly movement toward eternal truth.

Exercise 2.2

Belief is frequently viewed as something we think is so because of our feelings or attitudes or values, with the level of certainty often based on subjectivity and intuition. Knowing is often thought of as increasing that level of certainty by establishing a more objective foundation through the application of a variety of organized methodologies or theories that focus on how we come to know what we do.

Exercise 2.3

1. revealed knowledge   Espousing a god-given belief.
2. intuitive knowledge   Knowing something in your heart.

3. empirical knowledge   Observing the effect of water on earth forms.
4. rational knowledg.   Inductively determining a rule.
5. authoritative knowledge   Embracing Albert Einstein and his theory of
                                  relativity.

Exercise 2.4

In the lesson presented by Ms. DeSantis, we can assume that the students have learned the appropriate rules of grammar and are now in the process of applying them to the two specific examples she has written on the chalkboard. We can further assume these are examples with which the students are not familiar. The students, therefore, are engaged in analyzing examples in terms of rules. Put differently, they are going from the "general," which they have previously learned, to the "specific," with which they are currently being challenged. This of course represents deductive reasoning, which would be more commonly employed by perennialist educators.

At Rio Grande High School in Albuquerque, New Mexico, Ms. Creel is showing her students a blank order form and through a question-and-answer format is facilitating the students' ability to comprehend that format as well as the terms presented in it. Although she is "leading" the students, they are verbalizing conclusions on their own. The final activity asks the students to take what they have learned and apply it to a specific problem Ms. Creel has presented. The problem requires the students to order something for their mother from the women's wear ads provided. This is a practical exercise intended to teach the pros and cons of credit card use and the ability to correctly fill out order forms—a common task in our society. The practical utility of the lesson coupled with the hands-on nature of the activity promotes the ability to do something. These techniques or methodologies are frequently found in progressivist learning environments.

UNIT 2

Philosophers and Classroom Applications

CHAPTER 3

THE ANCIENTS: SOCRATES, PLATO, AND ARISTOTLE

After completing Chapter 3, you should be able to accomplish the following objectives:

1. You will become familiar with the Socratic view of reality by identifying statements as being consistent or inconsistent with Socrates' philosophy.

2. You will become familiar with the Socratic method by identifying the steps of the method in a teaching scenario.

3. You will acquire proficiency in applying the work of Plato to classroom teaching by identifying statements as being consistent or inconsistent with his philosophy.

4. You will acquire proficiency in applying the work of Plato to classroom teaching by discussing the features of guided discovery presented in an actual classroom lesson.

5. You will increase your knowledge of Aristotle's contributions to classroom teaching by identifying statements as being consistent or inconsistent with his philosophy.

6. You will increase your knowledge of Aristotle's contributions to classroom teaching by attributing a list of statements to either Aristotle or Plato.

7. You will increase your awareness of logic as a source of knowledge by briefly describing the steps in Aristotle's method of deductive logic.

Our search for ways of implementing philosophical axioms in our classrooms begins with Socrates, Plato, and Aristotle, though philosophy, or the love of wisdom, existed long before their time. As early as 600 B.C. the Ionian Greeks, through trade, had been influenced by Eastern cultures and had experienced an intellectual awakening. Thinkers such as Thales and Anaximenes focused on water and air as the primary substances; they believed all else to be founded on these substances, thus giving rise to the idea of eternal laws. For Pythagoras, the law of the universe was mathematics. Xenophanes taught that this universe of eternal laws was ruled over by a supreme being, "all eye, all ear, all intellect" (Scramuzza, 1958, p. 163).

Influenced by Xenophanes, Parmenides also moved in the direction of a supreme being by challenging existing beliefs based on opinion or unquestioned acceptance of earlier values and emphasizing the primacy of human reason in the search for permanence and universalism. Around the same time, Heraclitus argued that change was the only reality, which completed the dualism of permanence versus change—a dualism we examine in our classrooms to this day.

Others followed, including Anaxagoras, who refined the dualism issue; Protagoras, who discussed factors that made it difficult to ascertain the existence of a supreme being; and the Sophists, who focused primarily on contemporary culture and human behavior.

From studying what has come down to us from these early thinkers, we know that metaphysical questions were posed and discussed prior to the time of Socrates, Plato, and Aristotle. However, as we will see, these three philosophers of the ancient world not only explored dualisms such as permanence versus change, the mind versus the material world, and the senses versus reason; they also provided us with methodologies and strategies that can and should be employed in our schools to facilitate the students' pursuit of knowledge.

SOCRATES, 469–399 B.C.

As you know, Socrates was not the first Greek to ask fundamental philosophical questions, nor did he necessarily direct questions toward new or unique problems. What set him apart was his combination of traditionalist metaphysics and progressivist epistemology. Regarding the former, Socrates was convinced of the universality of right and wrong and good and evil and rejected the moral relativism of the Sophists. He further believed the human mind was capable of attaining that knowledge of universals through an endless critical examination of anything and everything.

Having proclaimed himself a "gadfly," Socrates devoted his life to exposing misconceptions, clichés, and conventional dogmas, substituting the belief that there was an essential relationship between knowledge and virtue. He connected knowledge with moral behavior, assuming that a good life depends on a knowledge base. We need to act on knowledge if we are to behave in a right or a good way. Therefore, Socrates' purpose was the development of thought, not the imparting of knowledge (Armstrong, Henson, and Savage, 1993).

The tool he employed in addressing the epistemological question "How do we know," which he believed would bring people closer to that universal body of knowledge (which in turn would promote the good life), became known as the Socratic method.

Life and Times

Of all the philosophers you will be wrestling with in this book, Socrates is unique in that we know nothing of him from his own hand. Because his fellow Greek citizens had focused on conversation as central to Athenian life, all of

Socrates' teachings involved verbal discourse. Therefore, the thoughts we attribute to him have been preserved by others, including Aristophanes, Xenophon, and especially Plato.

As to Socrates' birthplace, we are told he was born in the city of Athens to a mother who was a midwife and a father who was a stonecutter. He apparently served in the army and distinguished himself as a soldier. During his adult life he appeared all but oblivious to the material world. His looks were common, his clothes were common, and he was not known to have worked a day in his life. Certainly, Socrates could have provided more than a modest home for his wife, Xanthippe, and his children. However, his priorities focused on a boundless curiosity, intolerance of sacred cows, and great physical and moral courage, all of which established him as the idol of young Athenian men. His followers could have provided financial security had he allowed them to do so, but he did not view himself as a classical teacher and would not accept fees. By today's standards, we might refer to Socrates as selfish, in that his wife and children more or less fended for themselves while he devoted himself to the "simple joy of living, without pretense or snobbery but with careless gaiety and with an interest in everything that went on" (Davidson, 1957, p 459).

This image, coupled with his occasional projection of an apparent lack of knowledge, enabled him to disarm those who knew everything and to encourage those who knew nothing. Though Socrates was a philosophical giant, he maintained his own sense of modesty for, as the story goes, when Chaerophon asked the Oracle whether there was any living person wiser than Socrates, the Oracle replied that there was not. Socrates interpreted this reply to mean that he was the wisest because he realized and admitted his own ignorance and set out on a quest for abiding truth and wisdom (Stumpf, 1966).

As we now know, Socrates left no stone unturned in his quest for the good life through intellectual inquiry, and he often asked questions that forced people to think a good deal more than they wanted to (Wolff, 1989). Though his focus on inquiry did not take hold during his lifetime, his reliance on this method and his stature among Athenian youth were enough to convince the ruling aristocracy that he was a threat to existing institutions.

As a result, Socrates was executed. But his ingestion of the hemlock was optional, in that the condemned could choose exile as opposed to death. The fact that Socrates surrounded himself with his followers during his last days and remained loyal to his convictions may have validated his philosophy for the generations that followed. Certainly, his words spoke as loudly as his actions when he said, "Wherefore, O judges, be of good cheer about death and know of a certainty, that no evil can happen to a good man, either in life or after death" (Plato, *Apology;* in Jowett and Loomis, 1942, p. 60).

Philosophical Contributions

As stated earlier, what we know of Socrates comes to us primarily from the works of Plato, and over the years a debate has raged over the so-called *Socratic problem.* In essence, where does Socrates stop and Plato start? Put differently, how much

*The unexamined life is not
worthy of a man.*

Socrates

of the "Old Gadfly's" philosophy as presented by Plato can we actually attribute to Socrates?

Most scholars agree that Plato appears to have added to Socrates and put his work in literary form (Ozmon and Craver, 1990). Much has been written as to the specifics of these revisions, but few disagree with the proposition that Socrates was an original philosopher who developed a new method of intellectual inquiry (Stumpf, 1966). A primary source of support for this statement is found in the works of Aristotle, who possessed independent knowledge of Socrates and believed that the foundation of his methodology consisted of two major philosophical contributions: (1) Socrates was the first to make general definition a necessary and important feature in philosophical speculation, and (2) he was the first to make the systematic use of inductive arguments an essential feature of his philosophical method (Gulley, 1968).

This method is the *Socratic method,* which is unsurpassed as a means of correcting errors (Mill, 1924). Socrates' use of this method clearly set him apart from his contemporaries not because of the questions he asked but because of the way he asked them and the goal of the inquiry itself. That goal was *gnothi seauton* or "know thyself." More accurately, this expression means that the mind turns around and examines itself. Socrates was telling us that our progress as human beings depends on an intelligent examination of what we believe to be true, which will enable us to reinforce what we know and reconsider what we do not know. This process depends on four basic principles (Wolff, 1989, p. 7):

1. We must put convictions to the test of self examination . . . and in doing so, achieve genuine happiness.
2. There are valid principles of thought and action that are true for all men and women.
3. True principles of right thinking are within all of us.
4. Some people (Socratic teachers) can ask questions that prod the task of self-examination.

A closer reading of these principles reveals to us the essence of Socratic thought and, possibly for the first time, links knowledge and morality or, put differently, intelligence and virtue. Let's focus on the relationships that Socrates believed would lead us in the direction of happiness.

To begin, we need to direct our thoughts intelligently to acquire knowledge. This requires a critical examination of the world in which we live: our traditions, our customs, our beliefs, and a host of societal and ethical problems. This examination, or questioning, allows for a more accurate conceptualization and application of universal and enduring moral principles.

It is critical to understand at this point that, according to Socrates, the use of reason does not give birth to knowledge. Knowledge already exists, and the more knowledge we are able to uncover, the closer we come to what Socrates believed to be a universal body of truth and morality. Our journey along this path ennobles us, and we taste more of the fruit of the good life.

As mentioned earlier, the intellectual tool Socrates gave us that would continually move us closer toward universal truth and thereby create a more satisfying life was the Socratic method, an inquiry approach that employs the following steps (Bronstein, Krikorian, and Wiener, 1955, p. 2):

1. A focus upon an ill-considered statement.
2. Questions that point out inconsistency in answers which produces an awareness of inadequacies.
3. A redefinition of the original statement, concept, generalization, etc.
4. The new definition or conceptualization that becomes subject to the same critical examination.

In essence, we have an endless cycle of belief, confrontation, and potential revision. For Socrates, nothing is sacred; everything—politics, ethics, art, and so on—is subject to the cycle that continually brings us closer to the universal body of knowledge that he believed to be a gift from God. He further believed that wrongdoing is the product of ignorance. Therefore, the acquisition of knowledge through intelligent inquiry not only brings us closer to universal knowledge but also improves the human condition by bringing us closer to universal moral behavior. This relationship clearly establishes for us the essential aspect of the Socratic method. This method was intended to be more than an exercise in reasoning. The end result was to bring us closer to universal truth, which would in turn promote the good life.

> *Make it thy business to know thyself, which is the*
> *most difficult lesson in the world.*

> Miguel de Cervantes

Exercise 3.1

Take another look at the quotation from Cervantes and write a few sentences on how his view corresponds to the philosophy of Socrates. Then compare your work with the feedback at the end of the chapter.

From *The Meno*, Socrates

Meno   What do you mean, Socrates, by saying that we do not learn, and that what we call learning is only a process of recollection? Can you teach me how this is?

Socrates   I told you, Meno, just now that you were a rogue, and now you ask whether I can teach you, when I am saying that there is no teaching, but only recollection; and thus you imagine that you will involve me in a contradiction.

Meno   Indeed, Socrates, I protest that I had no such intention. I only asked the question from habit; but if you can prove to me that what you say is true, I wish that you would.

Socrates   It will be no easy matter, but I will try to please you to the utmost of my power. Suppose that you call one of your numerous attendants, that I may demonstrate on him.

Meno   Certainly. Come hither, boy.

Socrates   He is Greek, and speaks Greek, does he not?

Meno   Yes, indeed; he was born in the house.

Socrates   Attend now to the questions which I ask him, and observe whether he learns of me or only remembers.

Meno   I will.

Socrates   Tell me, boy, do you know that a figure like this is a square?

Boy   I do.

Socrates   And you know that a square figure has these four lines equal?

Boy   Certainly.

Socrates   *And these lines which I have drawn through the middle of the square are also equal?*

Boy   *Yes.*

Socrates   *A square may be of any size?*

Boy   *Certainly.*

Socrates   *And if one side of the figure be of two feet, and the other side be of two feet, how much will the whole be? Let me explain: if in one direction the space was of two feet, and in the other direction of one foot, the whole would be of two feet taken once?*

Boy   *Yes.*

Socrates   *But since this side is also of two feet, there are twice two feet?*

Boy   *There are.*

Socrates   *Then the square is of twice two feet?*

Boy   *Yes.*

Socrates   *And how many are twice two feet? Count and tell me.*

Boy   *Four, Socrates.*

Socrates   *And might not there by another square twice as large as this, and having like this the lines equal?*

Boy   *Yes.*

Socrates   *And of how many feet will that be?*

Boy   *Of eight feet.*

Socrates   *And now try and tell me the length of the line which forms the side of that double square: this is two feet—what will that be?*

Boy   *Clearly, Socrates, it will be double.*

Socrates   *Do you observe, Meno, that I am not teaching the boy anything, but only asking him questions; and now he fancies that he knows how long a line is necessary in order to produce a figure eight square feet; does he not?*

Meno   *Yes.*

(continued)

Socrates   *And does he really know?*

Meno   *Certainly not.*

Socrates   *He only guesses that because the square is double, the line is double.*

Meno   *True.*

Socrates   *Observe him while he recalls the steps in regular order. (To the boy.) Tell me, boy, do you assert that a double space comes from a double line? Remember that I am not speaking of an oblong, but of a figure equal every way, and twice the size of this—that is to say eight feet; and I want to know whether you still say that a double square comes from a double line.*

Boy   *Yes.*

Socrates   *But does not this line become doubled if we add another such line here?*

Boy   *Certainly.*

Socrates   *And four such lines will make space containing eight feet?*

Boy   *Yes.*

Socrates   *Let us describe such a figure: Would you not say that this is the figure of eight feet?*

Boy   *Yes.*

Socrates   *And are there not these four divisions in the figure, each of which is equal to the figure of four feet?*

Boy   *True.*

Socrates   *And is not that four times four?*

Boy   *Certainly.*

Socrates   *And four times is not double?*

Boy   *No, indeed.*

Socrates   *But how much?*

Boy   *Four times as much.*

Socrates   *Therefore, the double line, boy, has given a space, not twice, but four times as much.*

Boy   *True.*

Socrates   *Four times four are sixteen—are they not?*

Boy   *Yes.*

Socrates   *What line would you give a space of eight feet, as this gives one of sixteen feet;—do you see?*

Boy   *Yes.*

Socrates   *And the space of four feet is made from this half line?*

Boy   *Yes.*

Socrates   *Good; and is not a space of eight feet twice the size of this, and half the size of the other?*

Boy   *Certainly.*

Socrates   *Such a space, then, will be made out of a line greater than this one, and less than that one?*

Boy   *Yes, I think so.*

Socrates   *Very good; I like to hear you say what you think. And now tell me, is not this a line of two feet and that of four?*

Boy   *Yes.*

Socrates   *Then the line which forms the side of eight feet ought to be more than this line of two feet, and less than the other of four feet?*

Boy   *It ought.*

Socrates   *Try and see if you can tell me how much it will be.*

Boy   *Three feet.*

Socrates   *Then if we add a half to this line of two, that will be the line of three. Here are two and there is one; and on the other side, here are two also and there is one: and that makes the figure of which you speak?*

Boy   *Yes.*

Socrates   *But if there are three feet this way and three feet that way, the whole space will be three times three feet?*

Boy   *That is evident.*

(continued)

Socrates   *And how much are three times three feet?*

Boy   *Nine.*

Socrates   *And how much is the double of four?*

Boy   *Eight.*

Socrates   *Then the figure of eight is not made of a line of three?*

Boy   *No.*

Socrates   *But from what line?—tell me exactly; and if you would rather not reckon, try and show me the line.*

Boy   *Indeed, Socrates, I do not know.*

Socrates   *Do you see, Meno, what advances he has made in his power of recollection? He did not know at first, and he does not know now, what is the side of a figure of eight feet: but then he thought that he knew, and answered confidently as if he knew, and had no difficulty; now he has a difficulty, and neither knows nor fancies that he knows.*

Meno   *True.*

Socrates   *Is he not better off in knowing his ignorance?*

Meno   *I think that he is.*

Socrates   *If we have made him doubt, and given him the "torpedo shock," have we done him any harm?*

Meno   *I think not.*

Socrates   *We have certainly, as would seem, assisted him in some degree to the discovery of the truth; and now he will wish to remedy his ignorance, but then he would have been ready to tell all the world again and again that the double space should have a double side.*

Meno   *True.*

Socrates   *But do you suppose that he would ever have inquired into or learned what he fancied that he knew, though he was really ignorant of it, until he had fallen into perplexity under the idea that he did not know, and had desired to know?*

Meno   *I think not, Socrates.*

Socrates   *Then he was the better for the torpedo's touch?*

Meno   *I think so.*

Socrates   *Mark now the farther development. I shall only ask him, and not teach him, and he shall share the inquiry with me: and do you watch and see if you find me telling or explaining anything to him, instead of eliciting his opinion. Tell me, boy, is not this a square of four feet which I have drawn?*

Boy   *Yes.*

Socrates   *And now I add another square equal to the former one?*

Boy   *Yes.*

Socrates   *And a third, which is equal to either of them?*

Boy   *Yes.*

Socrates   *Suppose that we fill up the vacant corner?*

Boy   *Very good.*

Socrates   *Here, then, there are four equal spaces?*

Boy   *Yes.*

Socrates   *And how many times larger is this space than this other?*

Boy   *Four times.*

Socrates   *But it ought to have been twice only, as you will remember.*

Boy   *True.*

Socrates   *And does not this line, reaching from corner to corner, bisect each of these spaces?*

Boy   *Yes.*

Socrates   *And are there not here four equal lines which contain this space?*

Boy   *There are.*

Socrates   *Look and see how much this space is.*

Boy   *I do not understand.*

(continued)

Socrates   *Has not each interior line cut off half of the four spaces?*

Boy   *Yes.*

Socrates   *And how many spaces are there in this section?*

Boy   *Four.*

Socrates   *And how many in this?*

Boy   *Two*

Socrates   *And four is how many times two?*

Boy   *Twice.*

Socrates   *And this space is of how many feet?*

Boy   *Of eight feet.*

Socrates   *And from what line do you get this figure?*

Boy   *From this.*

Socrates   *That is, from the line which extends from corner to corner of the figure of four feet?*

Boy   *Yes.*

Socrates   *And that is the line which the learned call the diagonal. And if this is the proper name, then you, Meno's slave, are prepared to affirm that the double space is the square of the diagonal?*

Boy   *Certainly, Socrates.*

Socrates   *What do you say of him, Meno? Were not all these answers given out of his own head?*

Meno   *Yes, they were all his own.*

Socrates   *And yet, as we were just now saying, he did not know?*

Meno   *True.*

Socrates   *But still he had in him these notions of his—had he not?*

Meno   *Yes.*

Socrates   *Then he who does not know may still have true notions of that which he does not know?*

Meno   *He has.*

Socrates   *And at present these notions have just been stirred up in him, as in a dream; but if he were frequently asked the same questions, in different forms, he would know as well as any one at last?*

Meno   *I dare say.*

Socrates   *Without any one teaching him he will recover his knowledge for himself, if he is only asked questions?*

Meno   *Yes.*

Socrates   *And this spontaneous recovery of knowledge in him is recollection?*

Meno   *True.*

Socrates   *And this knowledge which he now has must he not either have acquired or always possessed?*

Meno   *Yes.*

Hamilton, E., and Cairns, H. (Eds.). *The Collected Dialogues of Plato Including the Letters.* Copyright 1961 by Princeton University Press, renewed 1989. Reprinted with permission of Princeton University Press.

Socrates in the Classroom

As you know from your reading of Chapters 1 and 2, metaphysics focuses on the nature of reality and axiology focuses on the good life and the beautiful life. Socrates believed the "real" world to be one of ideas that were universal or absolute in nature. He further believed the good or moral life was universal, and so his purpose became that of connecting knowledge and morality. By increasing our knowledge, we come closer to God-given truths.

When taking Socrates into the classroom, we need to consider his work in terms of motive as well as method. Simply stated, the method involves asking questions, eliciting information, and revising conclusions. This educational process leads to asking more questions and facilitates Socrates's motive, which is to bring us closer to absolute truth and to the better or good life. In terms of morality, the way to improve people's behavior is to examine their beliefs and point out contradictions (Seeskin, 1987).

Now we can more clearly see what Socrates would have us teach and how he would have us teach it. The *what*, or curriculum, should be subject centered or developed around what is considered the classic body of knowledge that has come down to us and that continues to expand. The *how*, or instruction, should let students make intellectual discoveries; teachers should not merely tell them things or lecture. Putting the two together, Socrates says to us as educators that knowledge is best wrung out of the students rather than poured into them. However, it is primarily approved subject matter that we may wring out, not usually the kind students choose for themselves (Kneller, 1971).

What this means in terms of method is that we do not tell the students; they tell us! We ask the questions; they provide the responses. Mortimer Adler, in his work *Reforming Education* (1988, pp. 168–169), provides us with the following insights for implementing the Socratic method:

- Socratic teacher-talk is always aimed at getting students to understand and think about something.
- A Socratic teacher poses critical and penetrating questions.
- A Socratic teacher raises good questions clearly enough to engage students in trying to understand and think through the material.
- Imparting information is fine if the purpose is that of leading up to critical questions the student must try to answer.
- The Socratic teacher does not settle for right answers but tries to undermine and test them. The questioning process then leads to increased understanding.
- The Socratic teacher always puts questions before answers. A question in search of an answer is an educational dynamo, whereas an answer in search of a question is a dud.
- Genuine learning requires an active learner. Therefore, all learning is either unaided discovery or aided discovery.

You should not assume that you are always asking questions for which you have the answers. Certainly there were times when Socrates' purpose was to show a "know-it-all" that the person did *not* know it all. On other occasions, he employed self-deprecation and irony to bring out a shy respondent. In either event, it is assumed Socrates knew where he was going, but for us that may not always be the case. We should be asking questions in a teaching context, which means we know, but we should also be asking questions in an information-seeking context, which means we do not know (Santas, 1979).

Now, let's take a look at how the Socratic method, outlined just before Exercise 3.1, and the questioning techniques of the method can be applied in the classroom.

 ## Scenario 3.1

Mr. Jeff Hudgins, a social studies teacher at Glencliff Comprehensive High School, began his law-related education class by asking his students to place themselves in the following situation.

"You have just been accused and arrested," he began, "for a crime that you did not commit. What are some of the things that you expect to happen?"

"Go to jail," Gwen said.

The law-related education classes at Glencliff Comprehensive High School are part of a cooperative program supported by the office of Juvenile Justice and Delinquency Prevention of the U.S. Department of Justice.

With permission. Glencliff Comprehensive High School, Nashville, Tennessee. Dr. S. V. Swor, Executive Principal.

"You think they are going to take you down to jail. Okay. According to what you know about the American legal system, what is going to happen to you once you arrive at the Metro jail?"

"I'm going to sit for a long time," Gwen replied.

"Everybody think that's what's what's going to happen?" (All but unanimous agreement from the class.)

"Okay, Gwen. Then what?"

"I'd probably go before a judge, get convicted, and go back to jail. Isn't that what usually happens?" she asked.

"I haven't been in jail recently," Mr. Hudgins laughed as the class good-naturedly joined in, "but it seems to me somebody would be talking to me after they put me in jail. Agreed?" (Class responds in the affirmative.)

"Okay, then what do you think they are going to say or do?" Mr. Hudgins continued.

"I think they read you your rights," Ratsamy said.

"Read you your rights," Mr. Hudgins repeated. "Let's flesh that out. What are the rights you expect to have?"

"The right to an attorney," Ratsamy said, and Mr. Hudgins wrote it on the board.

"So, are you going to sit in jail?"

"No, but they are going to put you in a holding cell," Ratsamy added.

"Okay, but are they going to offer you a way to get out of jail?"

"Is that getting a bond?" Shameka inquired.

"Yes, and the right is that of bail, so I'll write that on the board. Now, are you going to get to contact anybody?"

"You get one phone call," Jihuan said.

"A phone call," Mr. Hudgins said as he wrote it on the board. "How about if you didn't know your rights. Are they going to read you your rights?"

"Yes," Jason said.

"What are some of the rights they are going to tell you about? (Pause.) Okay, do you have to talk to them?"

"No, you have the right to remain silent," Amanda said.

"Good one."

"Attorney," Lonnie added.

"Okay," Mr. Hudgins said. "We talked about that. How about another one? For instance, are you going to be treated as if you are guilty or innocent?"

"Guilty until proven guilty," Lonnie responded with a smile.

"Okay," Mr. Hudgins said pleasantly, "but how is it supposed to be according to your rights?"

"You are supposed to be treated as if you are innocent," Lonnie said.

"Right, even though some people do have negative experiences. Now you have some basic assumptions built in about the American legal system unless you have been mistreated, and then you are going to have some other assumptions. For the moment, let's turn to the section in our text where you will find a list of the guiding principles of American law. We are going to briefly discuss those principles and then we are going to get into a little story or case study where you are going to have to decide whether or not these principles have been followed. Now, what is the very first principle printed out in blue?"

"Equal justice for all," Sabrina said.

"Where in the world do we get the notion of equal justice for all?" Mr. Hudgins asked.

"The Constitution," Sabrina said.

"The Constitution, very definitely. Can anyone think of a historical document before the Constitution that mentioned the equality of man? A very famous American document? (No response.) What happened when the colonies decided they wanted to break away from the King of England? How did they tell this to the world? (No response.) What was the document written by Thomas Jefferson? 1776? July the 4th? Fireworks? Come on!" Mr. Hudgins urged enthusiastically.

"Declaration of Independence!" shouted the class.

"Yes! Jefferson said, 'We hold these truths to be self evident' and that 'all men are created equal' and have 'unalienable rights,' including 'life, liberty and the pursuit of happiness.'" This is one of our founding documents, and we know that Jefferson based some of his thoughts on the writings of the English philosopher John Locke. Of course, the Declaration of Independence is not in our Constitution but may have led to something added to the Constitution which was . . . ?"

"The Bill of Rights," Paris said.

"The Bill of Rights. Absolutely," Mr. Hudgins said. "The first ten amendments to the Constitution. In this Bill of Rights we find our most precious liberties. One of those is found in the Fifth Amendment, which says you can't be deprived of life, liberty, or property without due process of law. As we know, in the past this didn't work for all people, so the Fourteenth Amendment expanded due process with the Equal Protection Clause, which says that all people will be treated equally under the law in all states. That is where we get the legal basis for equal justice for all," Mr. Hudgins concluded. "Now, what is the second guided principle listed?"

"Due process," Kerry said.

"Okay. Now, what does that mean?" Mr. Hudgins proceeded to lead the students through a discussion of due process followed by the remaining principles, including the adversary system and presumption of innocence.

"Okay," Mr. Hudgins continued. "We have gone through these guiding principles, and now we are going to play a little game. I want you to get in a group of four or five people with whom you're comfortable. What I want you to do is to take some notes and listen carefully to this story of an accident and pretend you are a law clerk to justice of the U.S. Supreme Court. You have been handed a case from Nashville, Tennessee, and have been asked to determine whether or not the four guiding principles of American law we discussed have been followed in this case."

Mr. Hudgins proceeded to share with the groups a case study involving two vehicles with locked bumpers that swerved off a busy road and killed a pregnant mother of three who was waiting at a bus stop to go home. He then provided information regarding the two drivers, one of whom was a "well-connected," well-dressed corporate head who smelled of beer and was driving an expensive automobile. The second vehicle, a 1968 junker, was driven by a 19-year-old minority male dressed in an NBA sports jacket with his cap on backward. This driver also smelled of alcohol.

Mr. Hudgins then discussed the events that resulted in the teenager being locked-up in a drunk tank and the businessman being released on his own recognizance. He continued to review the case study, which resulted in the teenager being convicted and sentenced to a lengthy prison term. At the end, Mr. Hudgins reminded the students that they were analyzing the situation in terms of rights and guiding principles and the possible violation of these rights and principles. He spent the remainder of the class time working with the groups.

What Mr. Hudgins did in the first part of his lesson is to allow the students to express their intuitive beliefs or beliefs founded on various experiences. He then engaged them in an analysis of their responses and led them to a better understanding of the judicial process. Finally, he changed gears and allowed the students to apply principles to a case study, which further promoted a conceptualization of this information. Throughout, Mr. Hudgins was employing many of Adler's suggestions as presented earlier.

Asking more than you answer often can be a difficult task, so you need to continually focus on this critical teaching method, which you will find helpful. It is essential that you intellectually challenge your students. The Socratic method, which requires the learner to reject things previously assumed to be true and seek new levels of knowledge, is a powerful tool you can use to promote critical thinking in your classroom.

Exercise 3.2

Examine the following statements to determine if they are consistent (c) or inconsistent (i) with the philosophy of Socrates. Then compare your answers with those at the end of the chapter.

_____ 1. Human beings discover knowledge; they do not create knowledge.
_____ 2. The Socratic method involves telling students that their responses are incorrect.
_____ 3. There is a direct relationship between acquiring knowledge and fostering happiness.
_____ 4. The Socratic method is primarily intellectual as opposed to attitudinal.
_____ 5. The Socratic method concludes with the student discovering the right answer.

Exercise 3.3

Read the passage from Plato's *Meno* and (1) underline the statement(s) that Socrates would view as ill-considered, (2) circle the statement(s) that produce an awareness of inadequacies, and (3) bracket the boy or slave's statement(s) that reflect an expansion or redefinition of the geometrical concept. Then consult the feedback at the end of the chapter.

PLATO, 427–347 B.C.

In Exercise 3.3 you saw how the Socratic method was used to enable the slave to further his knowledge. What is equally important for your consideration is the argument of the *Meno* that Plato stated at the beginning of this dialogue:

"Can you tell me whether (knowledge) can be taught or is acquired by practice, not teaching; or, if neither by practice nore by learning, whether it comes to men by nature or in some other way, such as luck or diving gift?" (in Teloh, 1986, p. 151).

It seemed to Plato that real a priori knowledge could not be transmitted by word of mouth or by sensible images alone and that the most a teacher could do toward enabling students to acquire (or regain) knowledge is to aid their recollection by suitable questioning (Bluck, 1964). As you will see, Plato's focus on knowledge acquired before birth and recollection as a process has had a significant impact on classroom teaching.

Life and Times

Plato was born in Athens around 427 B.C., a time in which Greek society was basking in the glory of the age of Pericles. His given name was *Aristocles,* which means "best" or "most renowned." This name may have been appropriate in that he was born into an old and noble aristocratic family, which, it is said, traced its ancestry back to Poseidon, god of the sea (Smith and Smith, 1994). In his adult life, he grew to be robust and broad shouldered and adopted the nickname *Plato*, which means "the broad."

Plato's childhood socialization and education were appropriate for the elite of his time and were centered around the fine arts and physical activities. The elitism of the Athenian aristocracy not only influenced Plato's behavior (he was viewed as extremely arrogant) but also helped shape his conceptualization of philosopher-kings and their paternalistic role in a class society.

Plato was one of the many wealthy youths who sat at the foot of Socrates and was profoundly affected by the humble philosopher's death as well as by his life and thoughts. After the tragic passing of his mentor, Plato set out to explore the world and traveled to such faraway places as Egypt and Italy. For a time, he settled in Sicily and developed a lasting friendship with the son-in-law of the ruler of Syracuse. During this period, Plato often espoused his political ideals, which were communistic and so incurred the wrath of the tyrant, who sold him into slavery. However, Plato's ten-year odyssey ended happily when he was ransomed by his wealthy Athenian friends, which made possible his return to the city of his birth.

In 387 B.C., Plato established his school in a small park he had bought that had been named in honor of a hero called Academus—hence, Plato's *Academy*. This center of learning was not a university as we know it, since it focused on training future political leaders. The Academy appears to have been quite informal and often involved what we would refer to as a cooperative learning environment. However, as time went on, Plato's program of teaching expanded to include preparatory studies in mathematics, astronomy, music, and logic. He thought that only by strict discipline could a young mind be made keen enough to move beyond the chaos of the present world and perceive the unchangeable principles of truth (Jowett and Loomis, 1942).

As for tuition, there was none; the criteria for admission included coming from a family of wealth (as well as being 16 years old or older). Money may not have been an issue for Plato, since his inherited wealth, property, and slaves allowed him to maintain his comfortable, unmarried lifestyle.

Knowledge is the food of the soul.

Plato

Unlike Socrates, Plato rarely involved himself in public speaking but chose the written word as his method of communication and used a dialogue format, which gave speech to other persons. He was a prolific writer. No one is certain as to the volume of his work, but at least 25 authentic dialogues have come down to us.

With the exception of making two brief trips back to Syracuse, Plato devoted himself to his work and the Academy, which eventually drew students from all over the Greek world. This may have been due, in part, to his skill at mentoring the eager young. His students loved him as he loved them; he was their friend as well as their philosopher and guide (Durant, 1953).

A testament to the Academy's success was its staying power. Even after Plato's death at the age of 80 in 347 B.C., the institution continued to attract students from beyond the boundaries of Greece for some 900 years. The Christian Emperor Justinian finally closed its doors in 529 A.D. (Jowett, 1942).

Philosophical Contributions

As we saw in an earlier section, Socrates believed that truth is eternal and perfect. Plato also believed in the universality of knowledge, which he referred to as *ideas*—a term that has been incorporated into the philosophy of idealism, covered in Chapter 1.

Plato distinguished between a world of material objects in space and time corresponding to our senses, and a world of abstract ideas corresponding to our thoughts. The first is the world of sensible things, which are independent of our senses but which we learn through our senses. The second—the world of abstract ideas—is independent of our thoughts, though we learn it through our thoughts (Feibleman, 1973). Let's take a concrete look at these statements through the use of an example.

A stool is a material thing that can be experienced through our senses in a variety of ways. Certainly we can observe that a given stool may have three legs and we can sit on it. In other words, it is a physical object. Yet that object is also a concept in that it belongs to a group of things that share common characteristics, such as having legs and functioning as a seat for one person. Concepts are a form of abstractions and, for Plato, abstractions are not only ideas but are eternal. The idea, or concept, of chair has been, is, and always will be, whereas the three-legged stool could be broken and only continue to exist as pieces of splintered wood. Metaphysically, what Plato is telling us is that the *real world* is one of ideas, not physical objects. He further believed, like Socrates, that ideas were unchanging and absolute and were obtained through thought and introspective reasoning—that is, through an intellectual as opposed to a sensory process.

In part, Plato made this point with his Allegory of the Cave, which suggests the material or physical world is unreliable, shadowy, and distorted. He is saying that what we see may not necessarily be so. Seeing, of course, is only one way of sensing physical things. On a more contemporary note, the story of the six blind men of Hindustan illustrates the shadowy world of touch, which leads the blind people to believe an elephant might be a tree trunk (leg), a snake (trunk), or a rope (tail). As the story goes, all of them touched the elephant and were partially correct, yet they experienced imperfect representations and, in the end, all were wrong. In other words, as with Plato, perception does not equal reality or accurate knowledge.

For Plato, perfect ideas are unchanging and absolute because they originate with God and so are preexisting. You may have asked yourself how we come to have knowledge prior to experience—that is, a priori. Plato's response is his theory of the transmigration of souls, in which he postulates that when we die, our soul departs to some other world where all things become known to it. When reborn, the new (physical) body blinds the soul; in reality, all knowledge is there and all that is required is a stimulus to bring it into focus (Barrow, 1976). In other words, all there is to know is within us, and our life is an endless process of discovering this knowledge. Plato calls this process *reminiscence*, which provides the foundation for his belief that genuine knowledge is intellectual and not sensory. This theory also explains how knowledge can change, for as with the blind men of Hindustan, something that appears to be real might be at an imperfect stage on the journey toward absolute truth.

As you are about to see, this pursuit requires that we are ready and willing to learn, that we are open-minded, and that we consciously question and examine what we know and what we think we know and do so in a logical and intelligent fashion. Plato founded this pursuit on the *dialectic,* which is the exercise of pure thought or intelligence. Its object is the vision of the Good, the last stage in the ascent from the Cave. Exactly what Plato meant by dialectic has been much disputed, but we may say that for him, as well as for other philosophers you will encounter in later chapters, dialectic is a purely philosophical activity. This activity gives coherence to the whole of human knowledge and leads finally to a vision of ultimate reality (Lee, 1955).

There's a world of difference between truth and facts. Facts can obscure the truth.

Maya Angelou

Exercise 3.4

Revisit the words of Maya Angelou and briefly discuss how they relate to Plato's view of reality. Then check your thoughts against those at the end of the chapter.

From *The Republic,* Book V, Plato
(On Knowledge and Belief)

"Are we satisfied that, whichever way we look at it, the fully existent is fully knowable, and the completely non-existent entirely unknowable?"

"Quite satisfied."

"Good. Then if there were anything whose nature was such that it was both existent and non-existent, would it not lie between the fully existent and completely non-existent?"

"Yes."

"Then since the object of knowledge is existent, and the object of ignorance, necessarily, non-existent, we shall have to see if there is something between knowledge and ignorance to correspond to this intermediate reality."

"Yes."

"Isn't there something we call belief?"

"Of course."

"Is its function the same as that of knowledge or different?"

"Different."

"So belief and knowledge must have different objects corresponding to their different functions."

"They must."

(continued)

"Then the object of knowledge is what exists, whose reality it is its function to know.—But there's a definition I think I should make before I go on."

"What is it?"

"Let us class together as 'faculties' the powers in us and in other things that enable us to perform our various functions. Thus I call sight and hearing faculties—do you understand the class I mean?"

"Yes, I understand."

"Then let me tell you what I think about them. A faculty has neither colour, nor shape, nor any of the similar qualities which enable me to distinguish other things from another; I can only identify a faculty by its object and its function, and say that one faculty has one object and function, and another faculty another. What about you? What do you do?"

"The same as you."

"Let us go back, then," I said. "Tell me, do you think knowledge is a faculty? Could you classify it otherwise?"

"No; it is the most powerful of all faculties."

"And should belief be classified as a faculty?"

"Yes; it is the power which enables us to believe."

"But a little while ago you agreed that knowledge and belief were different."

"Yes," he (Glaucon) replied, "because no reasonable person would identify the infallible with the fallible."

"Splendid," I said: "we are clearly agreed that opinion (belief) and knowledge are different."

"We are."

"Each therefore has a different object and a different function."

"That follows."

"The object of knowledge is what exists and its function is to know about reality."

"Yes."

But the function of belief is to believe, didn't we say?"

"Yes."

"Is its object the same as the object of knowledge? And are the fields of knowledge and belief the same? Or is that impossible?"

"It's impossible on the principles we've agreed. If different faculties have different objects, and belief and knowledge are two separate faculties, as we maintain, then it follows that the fields of knowledge and belief must be different."

"Then if the field of knowledge is what exists, the field of belief must be something other than what exists."

"Yes."

"Is it the non-existent? Or is it impossible even to believe what does not exist? Consider. Belief is surely directed to something. Or is it possible to believe and yet believe in nothing?"

"No, that's impossible."

"So a man who believes, believes something."

"Yes."

"But what does not exist can hardly be called something—it is, properly speaking, nothing."

"True."

"Now, we correlated ignorance with the non-existent, knowledge with the existent."

"Quite right."

"So belief must be correlated with neither."

"Agreed."

"So belief is neither ignorance nor knowledge."

"So it seems."

"Then does it lie beyond them? Is it clearer than knowledge or less clear than ignorance?"

"No."

"Then in that case," I asked, "do you think it is obscurer than knowledge, but clearer than ignorance?"

"Very much so."

"Does it lie between the two?"

"Yes."

"Belief is in fact an intermediate state."

"Certainly."

"Now we said before that if it appeared that there was anything that was both existent and non-existent, this would lie between pure existence and complete non-existence, and would be the object of neither knowledge nor ignorance, but of a faculty to be found between them."

"True."

"And we now see that what we call belief occupies that intermediate position."

"That is so."

Plato, *The Republic.* Translated by J. L. Davies and D. J. Vaughn. (1895). New York: Macmillan, pp. 191–194.

Plato in the Classroom

We have noted that it is often difficult to separate the views of Socrates and Plato. Possibly the most significant difference is that Socrates focused his investigative skills on one question only: How should one live one's life? Thus, the greatest contrast between them lies in the different scope of their intellectual interests (Kraut, 1992). Although Plato was concerned with living the good life, he was also concerned with the practical aim of improving society. Both, he believed, could be achieved through human intelligence when correctly applied to the design of ideal societies and educational systems (Brumbaugh, 1989). This task would be that of his philosopher-kings, whose formal Platonic education of approximately 50 years would enable them to approach a maximum of intellectual capability and thereby lead the less intellectual members of society. Therefore, the aim of Plato's Academy or school was to discover the abilities of the individual, aid the individual in discovering the knowledge of truth that is within each of us, and prepare the individual for his or her role in society (Webb, Metha, and Jordan, 1992). Today's classroom teachers are equally concerned with implementing units and lessons designed to meet the needs of the individual as well as those of society as a whole.

Education "has become increasingly academic (compare today's kindergarten classes to those of twenty-five years ago), and to some degree we can trace this emphasis to Plato, who believed education should be intellectual...and for the most part, a controlled experience" (Lodge, 1970, p. 11).

Let's recall that, according to Plato, universal truth is already within us and reminiscence reveals to us that absolute body of knowledge. This being the case, the role of the teacher is to bring out what is already in the students' minds. Plato employed a dialectic approach, requiring pupils to arrive at truth through a rigorous examination of questions and ideas, which allowed for the generating of logical explanations. His view of the dialectic, which appears in Book VII of the *Republic* (Plato, 1955, pp. 419–420), was as follows:

1. "It is an intellectual process, but is paralleled in the visible world by the process of sight from shadows to real creatures, and then to the stars, and finally to the sun itself. So when one tries to reach ultimate realities by the exercise of pure reason, without any aid from the senses, and refuses to give up until the mind has grasped what the Good is, one is at the end of an intellectual progress and this progress is called 'dialectic.'"
2. "[The dialectic is] the only activity which systematically sets about the definition of the essential nature of things."
3. "Dialectic, in fact, is the only activity whose method is to challenge its own assumptions so that it may rest firmly on first principles. When the eye of the mind gets really bogged down in a morass of ignorance, dialectic gently pulls it out and leads it up."
4. "Dialectic is the ability to give an account of the essential nature of each particular thing."
5. "[Students'] powers of argument must be developed by an appropriate education and we can regard dialectic as the coping stone of our educational system."

Through the *Meno* and other dialogues, Plato's dialectic provided the foundation for the guided discovery that we commonly use in our classrooms today.

When using guided discovery, the teacher presents a variety of materials designed to move students toward a desired or specific end, then guides or facilitates the *trip*. The bottom line is that the teacher does not tell the student; the student tells the teacher. However, the experience is *guided* in that the teacher *controls* the learning environment by providing specific questions as well as specific materials. In this way, students discover things that have been predetermined and considered educationally valuable, and they do it through problem solving and the application of intellectual processes. Now let's take a look at how Plato's dialectic, employed in guided discovery, works in the classroom.

Scenario 3.2

Ms. Jami Jacobson, a second-grade teacher at Valle Vista Elementary School, wanted her students to increase their knowledge of light and shadow as related to day and night. Her lesson this particular day concentrated on how shadows are formed, how they change, and where they can be found. The materials to be used included an overhead projector, flashlights, a variety of objects with differing sizes and shapes, pencils, markers, and white butcher paper. She began by showing the children two pages in the book *Earth and Sky,* which depicted the earth as it appears in the daytime as well as nighttime.

"If you were out in space," Ms. Jacobson began, "this is what the earth would look like. The sun can only shine on half of the earth at a time because the earth is very large." Ms. Jacobson showed the illustrations in the book depicting day and night as seen from space.

"I didn't have to look at a map or anything or have someone tell me," Manuel said softly. "I just listened to my brother say that if it is daytime here it is dark on the other side of the earth."

"So one side of the earth is daylight and the other side of the earth is . . . ?"

"Night," responded Manuel.

"Night. That's right."

"Yes, and it is like two earths and it only glows on one side," Manuel added.

"That's right," Ms. Jacobson said. "We can't have daylight all the way around the earth. Is that what you are saying? Am I understanding you correctly? Is the earth so big it can only have daylight on one side at one time?"

"Yes," Manuel responded.

"That's great, Manuel! Now what I am going to do is turn on the overhead projector, and I want all of you to move a little to make sure that you can all see that light on the wall. (Pause.)

"It seems as if many of you know a lot about day and night because people like Manuel's brother told him how the differences happen on the earth. I guess one of the things I would like to know is what kinds of things happen when there is light and darkness. Let me show you what I mean."

Ms. Jacobson then asked Eric to stand between the overhead projector and the wall. "What do you notice is happening over here on the wall?"

"Shadow," a number of children replied.

"Right, you see his shadow. Is it a very good shadow?"

"No."

"What would make it better?" she asked. "Raise your hand if you have an idea." (Pause.) "Gabriel?"

"If you moved Eric."

"If I moved Eric. Good! Where should I move him? Further away or closer?"

"A little further back," Gabriel said.

"And we could turn off the lights," Cristal added.

"Okay," Ms. Jacobson said. "Let's try. (Pause.) Did that help?"

"Yes!" the children replied.

"It sure did. Now, if I turn off the overhead light am I going to have much of a shadow?"

"No."

"Right. So what is one of the things I need to make a shadow?"

"A light on," the children said together.

"Okay, I have to have a light." Ms. Jacobson proceeded to the chalkboard and wrote the word *shadow* underneath which she worte the word *light*. "Do we have to use an overhead projector to make a shadow, or can we use other kinds of light?"

"Other kinds."

"What other kinds?" she asked.

"The sun," Morrisa said.

"A flashlight," Martin added.

"Those are good ones. So we have to have a light. Now if I take Eric out of the path of this light, do I have a shadow on that wall?"

"No," said the children.

"I sure don't. What else do I need to do to make a shadow?"

"A person," Pablo said.

"Yes, a person. Could I make a shadow with something else?" The children rapidly responded.

"Your glasses."

"A piece of paper."

"A Christmas tree."

"A car."

"A can."

"Yes," Ms. Jacobson said with a smile. "There's a word for all of those. What is a word we can use?"

"Names or things," Christian said.

"Great. Names or things. Let's use the word *things,* which is a way of saying *objects.*" Ms. Jacobson added the word *things* to her list on the board. She then directed Eric to stand between the window and the overhead projector.

"Now what has happened, Roberta?"

"The shadow is hard to see."

"Right. We have to have a place to show the shadow. I am going to add the word *place* to our list on the board. To make a shadow, what are the three things we need?" (Pause.) "LeSean, what is one?"

"You need a light," LeSean said.

"Good. Will any kind of light work?"

"Yes, probably."

"Right. Light is one thing we need to make a shadow, and any kind of light will do. What is a second thing we need?"

"Paper," Jolene said.

"Does it have to be paper?"

"No, it could be lots of things."

"Things! Great! And finally we need . . . ?"

"A wall," the children said.

"Yes. A wall or a place to show the shadow. That was wonderful. Now we are going to get into groups and we're going to make different kinds of shadows. I'm going to give each group paper, markers, objects or things, and a flashlight, and you are going to try to create as many shadows as you can. You will use your light, your object, and your paper to make shadows and you will outline the shadows with markers. When you finish outlining your shadows on paper, we will place them around the room and talk about what we did. Any questions about how to get started?"

Ms. Jacobson then facilitated and monitored the group activity.

The first thing to note is that throughout the lesson, Ms. Jacobson is asking questions and the students are providing answers based on their observations—that is, the students are telling her, she is not telling them. Second, by using a variety of materials the students *discover* that an object, a light source, and a place are needed to produce a shadow.

Guided discovery is just one method that can be used to acquire knowledge through a problem-solving approach. However, when employing this powerful tool Plato has given us, you will be providing your students with an exciting hands-on, interactive learning environment and will be facilitating their critical thinking capabilities.

Exercise 3.5

Examine the following statements to determine if they are consistent (c) or inconsistent (i) with the philosophy of Plato. Then compare your answers with those at the end of the chapter.

_____ 1. Plato was solely concerned with how an individual could profit from an intellectual life.

_____ 2. One of the goals of Plato's Academy was to improve society.

_____ 3. An absolute and eternal body of knowledge exists.

_____ 4. Thoughts in the mind are more real than physical objects in the material world.

_____ 5. Students determine what is to be learned in a guided discovery approach.

Exercise 3.6

Read the following scenario and list three techniques the teacher employed to promote guided discovery. Check your answers against those at the end of the chapter.

Mrs. Leah Nemeth, a third-grade music teacher at Centennial Elementary School, began the lesson by having the children sing "Scotland's Burning." After one verse, she asked them to listen to the sounds and have their hand movements match the ones she was demonstrating. After repeating the verse she said, "Now, here is the pentatonic scale we have been working with (she then played eight notes on a bell tower), and I have a question for you. Do I have enough notes here to play the song we just sang?" (Mixed yeas and nays from the children.)

"Listen to what we've got. (She plays the notes again.) This is the note where we start, and now listen to what we sang."

The children then sang the verse again and Mrs. Nemeth asked, "What do you think? Do we have enough notes?" (Yeas from the children.)

"Okay, let's see!" She then played the notes of the tune and the children chimed in, "Noooooo!"

"Right. I'm just missing one note, aren't I. And that note is . . . ?"

"The bottom one," most of the children said together.

"Yes, and we've already got 'doe,' so we've got to figure out what we need down here. Well, I just happen to have some notes here, so let's try a few and see if one works. Now don't guess. I just want you to listen until we find the sound we want." Mrs. Nemeth then played two notes.

"Nooo," said the children after listening.

"No? Okay, let's try this." She then played two more notes.

"Nooo!"

"Okay. How about this?"

"Yesssssssss!"

"Great! Now let's try to figure out what it is. Count down with me from 'doe.'" The children followed along with Mrs. Nemeth as she counted from one to four. She then asked them to look at the scale she had drawn on the chalkboard and, once again, count down from "doe."

"It's a 'so,'" the children said.

"Yes. The missing note is a 'so,'" Mrs. Nemeth said, "but it's the 'so' below 'doe,' and so we are going to call it 'low so.' The hand sign is the same so let's try it. Ready?"

After singing the notes, Mrs. Nemeth asked, "Now let's see if we have all the notes." She repeated "Scotland's Burning" on the bell tower while the children, who were seated in the three-tiered music room, listened. "Is that it?"

"Yes," responded the children. Mrs. Nemeth went to the board and showed them how the notes looked on the staff. She then said, "Children, get out your books, turn to page 111, and try to find a pattern that looks like the one on the board. Then raise your hand to let me know." She proceeded to work individually with the children.

With permission. Centennial Elementary School, Denver, Colorado. Mr. Gerald R. Gilmore, Principal.

ARISTOTLE, 384–322 B.C.

Socrates and Plato had much in common and, as we noted in discussing the Socratic problem, it can be difficult to distinguish between their philosophical contributions. This of course is because we only know Socrates through Plato and because their metaphysical and epistemological points of view were very similar. As you are about to see, this will not be a problem with Aristotle, the third of our ancient philosophers, in that his views regarding what is real and how we know are markedly different from those of Socrates/Plato.

One of the most striking differences begins with Aristotle's love of collecting, classifying, and categorizing material things, which was his method of organizing knowledge of the physical world. Fortunately for us, he loved to lecture and write, and his library and collected works that have come down to us have been referred to as the equivalent of the *Encyclopaedia Britannica* of Greece (Durant, 1953, p. 46). Never before had one person so thoroughly mastered the whole body of existing knowledge; never again was it possible for a single individual to do so (Davidson, 1957, p. 342).

Although Aristotle focused on the study of the physical world, knowledge of abstract ideas—which he called *universals*—was his goal just as it was with Plato. The disagreement, as you will see, is in *how* to obtain this knowledge or ultimate truth.

Life and Times

Unlike Socrates and Plato, Aristotle was not a citizen of Athens but was born in the town of Stagira, located approximately 200 miles north of Athens in the city-state of Macedonia. By today's standards, this region would have been considered the frontier, relative to the cosmopolitan world of Athens. Eventually, Aristotle did benefit from living in the capital of Macedonia, where his father, Nichomachus, was a prominent physician who included the grandfather of Alexander the Great among his patients. This profession may have had an impact on Aristotle, because it was customary at that time for fathers to educate sons, and these early experiences undoubtedly focused on empirical observations in the biological sciences. This in turn may have led to Aristotle's preoccupation with collecting and organizing physical things.

Aristotle was orphaned at an early age but inherited money from his mother and property in the town of Chalcis, also located in Macedonia. Because of his family and financial background, at age 17 he was sent to study with Plato; he remained at the Academy for the next 20 years. Like other Athenian youth of that time, Aristotle was well dressed with fashionably short hair. It is said he was quite thin with an extremely sharp wit and was at times arrogant. In addition, he apparently often displayed an air of intellectual superiority, which may have been due to the fact that he was not an Athenian citizen and was viewed as someone from the hinterlands.

Eventually, Aristotle left the Academy, possibly because Plato was in his later years and was focusing on science and mathematics—areas Aristotle had already

The roots of education are bitter, but the fruit is sweet.

Aristotle

concentrated on in his early years with his father. In 347 B.C., he left Athens and settled across the Aegean Sea in Asia Minor, where he spent three years classifying what for him was the knowledge of a new world. During this period, he married and also traveled to the island of Lesbos, which enabled him to initiate his studies in marine life.

Aristotle returned to his native land of Macedonia in 342 B.C. for the purpose of tutoring a 13-year-old prince named Alexander. When Alexander became king and went to Athens, Aristotle accompanied him and continued to provide education in the areas of politics, rhetoric, and the natural sciences. This relationship would benefit Aristotle in two significant ways. The first was that Alexander provided the funds (with a contemporary value probably in excess of $1 million) that enabled Aristotle to open his school. The second was that during the time Alexander conquered much of the ancient world and came to be known as *Alexander the Great,* he literally sent tons of plants and animals and artifacts back to Greece, which made it possible for Aristotle to synthesize the knowledge of his day.

Unlike Plato's Academy, Aristotle's school, or Lyceum, was composed of a series of walkways in an orchard and had no buildings. As mentioned, Aristotle was not an Athenian but was considered a foreigner who could not own property but was allowed to rent the space for his school, which he maintained for 12 or 13 years. The Lyceum continued to flourish for half a century after his departure but eventually declined.

With the death of Alexander the Great in 323 B.C., a wave of anti-Macedonian feeling swept through the country and Aristotle feared the Athenians who returned to power. He was eventually indicted on a charge of impiety, probably provoked by his belief that prayer and sacrifice were of little use. Being acutely aware of the fate of Socrates and knowing that exile was, at that time, an honorable alternative to death, Aristotle returned to his mother's estate in Macedonia and died shortly afterward. Regarding his flight, he is believed to have said, "I do not want to give the Athenians a second chance of sinning against philosophy."

Philosophical Contributions

Most of what we have from Aristotle comes from writings that appear to have been put down on paper for his own use. The work consists of approximately 47 books, which the Islamic scholar Avicenna translated around the year 1000 A.D. Aristotle's work was in turn translated by European scholars into a body of information that was so all-encompassing and persuasive that it was unquestioned until the middle of the second millennium.

Until that time, the major philosophical questions had been metaphysically focused, with specific regard to the nature of reality. For Plato, pure thought in the form of Ideas was the answer, whereas Aristotle viewed reality as a uniting of actuality (form) and potentiality (matter), which established a dualism: both must be united in order for something to be real or to truly exist. Aristotle defined form as an object's essence and attributed form to intellectual knowledge. Matter involves the physical or material world and is experienced through the senses. Let's see how essence and matter are united.

The illustration of Aristotle in this chapter is partly based on a marble bust of the philosopher. The marble is matter; the bust is actuality and is an extension of what was in the sculptor's mind. The latter is specific and is an individualistic shape or form—one of many things the sculptor did with marble. Aristotle believed that human development involved this matter-form process, which would bring us closer to universals because it was cyclical. What does this mean?

Professional educators constantly engage in the three-phase model of teaching, which calls for planning, implementing, and assessing units of instruction. Based on an analysis of those assessments, they revise lessons in an effort to increase the effectiveness of the unit. Therefore, teaching is cyclical, with the intent being that of striving to produce a more perfect or "pure" unit of instruction. Returning to Aristotle and his matter-form relationship, if we consider shape or form to be thought, the cyclical approach moves us closer to pure thought—that is, God. Because God is perfect and is a thinking God, thought is also perfect.

The reason the cyclical approach is critical is because Aristotle believed matter to be in a constant state of motion caused by four things. Let's return to our example of his marble bust. The first cause is the *material cause,* which is some kind of "stuff." In this example, the "stuff" is marble. To have motion, something or someone must move the "stuff." This something or someone is referred to as the *efficient cause,* which, in this case, is the sculptor. The third or *formal cause* involves something matter moves toward—here the likeness of Aristotle. The *final cause* is something it is for, which is the finished statue of Aristotle representing the intention or idea of the sculptor.

Plato recognized the material world of matter as well as the intelligible world of ideas but believed the latter to be more real. Because of this he was *idealistically* focused in terms of what ought to be. Aristotle was more of an empiricist because he thought knowledge, which is within our grasp of reality, is ultimately grounded on perceptual observations (Barnes, 1991). Although perception is a source of knowledge, it is not knowledge itself, for ideas and thoughts spring from or are grounded in material things. What we have here is a marriage of sensing and understanding. Sensing is an individual thing; understanding goes to the general and is an act of our intellect. Sensing and perceiving are one mode of knowing; understanding is a different mode of knowing (Adler, 1985). With this "marriage" concept, Aristotle was more focused on how things are, as opposed to Plato, who was concerned with what ought to be. Aristotle is therefore considered a *realist.*

Aristotle's emphasis on the physical world begins with the position that if we perceived nothing, we would know nothing (Modrak, 1987). However, perception is in and of itself not enough, for to exercise knowledge or even acquire it, we must *think.* Therefore, Aristotle delved into the world of logic, which he defined as truth or reality determined by analysis of thought. His work in this area—which deals with deductive logic, is known as the *Organon.* This work was extremely influential for centuries and is often considered his most important contribution.

Deductive reasoning involves a first or major premise, a second or minor premise, and a conclusion. Put together, all three are called a *syllogism.* The first or major premise Aristotle considered to be a statement of truth, a universal. For example, the major premise of the most classic syllogism is "All men are mortal." As best we know, this statement is irrefutable. The second or minor premise identifies a more specific relationship and employs a component of the major premise. In this case, the minor premise of the classic statement is "Socrates is a man." The third and final component of the syllogism is the conclusion, which is predetermined and inescapable. Logically, the syllogism concludes, "Therefore, Socrates is mortal."

The validity or truth of this conclusion depends on the truth of the major premise. Truths, here synonymous with universals or first principles, are grasped, some by induction, some by perception, some by a kind of habituation and in some other ways (McKeon, 1941). As you can see from this statement, parts of Aristotle's work are flexible in terms of specific answers, yet the following continuum gives us a solid view of his journey toward absolute truth: knowledge of things through senses (no innate knowledge other than a sensory ability) → memory → frequently repeated memory → experience → knowledge → rudimentary universals → true universals.

Aristotle's search was for truth, and the tools he employed were rigorous, systematic, and logical. We now illustrate how those tools are used in today's classrooms.

To be caught up in the world of thought . . . that is being educated.

Edith Hamilton

Exercise 3.7

Return to Edith Hamilton's definition of being educated. Briefly compare her definition to that of Aristotle's. Then check the feedback at the end of the chapter.

From *Metaphysics*, **Book II, Aristotle**

The investigation of the truth is in one way hard, in another easy. An indication of this is found in the fact that no one is able to attain the truth adequately, while, on the other hand, we do not collectively fail, but every one says something true about the nature of things, and while individually we contribute little or nothing to the truth, by the union of all a considerable amount is amassed. Therefore, since the truth seems to be like the proverbial door, which no one can fail to hit, in this respect it must be easy, but the fact that we can have a whole truth and not the particular part we aim at shows the difficulty of it.

Perhaps, too, as difficulties are of two kinds, the cause of the present difficulty is not in the facts but in us. For as the eyes of bats are to the blaze of day, so is the reason in our soul to the things which are by nature most evident of all.

It is just that we should be grateful, not only to those with whose views we may agree, but also to those who have expressed more superficial views; for these also contribute something, by developing before us the powers of thought. (This) holds good of those who have expressed views about truth; for from some thinkers we have inherited

(continued)

certain opinions, while the others have been responsible for the appearance of the former.

It is right also that philosophy should be called knowledge of truth. For the end of theoretical knowledge is truth, while that of practical knowledge is action (for even if they consider how things are, practical men do not study the eternal, but what is relative and in the present). Now we do not know a truth without its cause; and a thing has a quality in a higher degree than other things if in virtue of it the similar quality belongs to the other things as well (e.g. fire is the hottest of things, for it is the cause of the heat of all other things); so that which causes derivative truths to be true is most true. Hence, the principles of eternal things must be always most true (for they are not merely sometimes true, nor is there any cause of their being, but they themselves are the cause of the being of other things), so that as each thing is in respect of being, so is it in respect of truth.

Barnes, J. (Ed.). *The Complete Works of Aristotle.* Copyright 1984 by Princeton University Press. Reprinted by permission of Princeton University Press.

Aristotle in the Classroom

Like many contemporary educators, Aristotle was concerned with self-realization and believed that the growth and development of a human being involved an endless movement toward universals. He further believed this goal was achievable through human reason. As you have seen, this journey begins with perceiving and experiencing the material world, which in turn leads to the verbalization of abstractions. The abstractions, most commonly found in schools in the form of concepts and generalizations, require the use of reason. Therefore, an educational environment should be designed to facilitate the development of a student's intellect.

Aristotle suggests we do this in a number of ways. The first involves searching for truth or, put differently, determining what an object or idea is or what it is not. This process takes us to other intellectual levels, such as knowing what to do and knowing how to do something. One critical method involves the use of deductive reasoning, which you were introduced to earlier in this chapter. Additionally, Aristotle gave us the processes of sorting and classifying and the basic idea of a concept analysis.

Besides developing these methodologies, Aristotle stressed the need for the repetitive practice of activities and the value of teachers telling and explaining information to students. As you will see, like the American philosopher/educator John Dewey, Aristotle believed in learning by doing and went beyond the overt activities of students to include listening and covert thinking, which often are thought of as passive. With his notion that the educational environment is teacher centered in terms of the dissemination/lecture/expository nature of teaching, it should come as no surprise that his curriculum would be highly academic and subject centered. With this in mind, Aristotle's answer to the *Meno*—which began our section on Plato—is that "intellectual excellence is for the most part both produced and increased by instruction" (Loomis, 1943, p. 592).

One such method of instruction is that of a concept analysis, and, as noted, Aristotle provided the foundation for this tool. He did this by suggesting that the definition of an object is based on two critical questions: (1) To what class does the object belong? (2) How does it differ from other objectives? Let's take a look at the initial stages of such an analysis.

Scenario 3.3

Ms. Lori Outten, a developmental kindergarten teacher, asked her children to sit on the floor in a semicircle. She then moved a chair into the open space in the middle and specifically instructed the children to observe what she had placed before them and describe something about it. She further reminded them of previous descriptive exercises in which they had engaged. After a brief period of time, Ms. Outten pointed to Abby, who had raised her hand, and said, "Okay Abby. Start us off. Tell us one thing you see."

"I see a seat," Abby said.

"And what can people do with it?"

"They sit on it!" Abby said with a smile and was joined by the giggles of a few of the children in the class.

"Okay," Ms. Outten continued, "how about somebody else? (Pause.) Kristine?"

"I see four legs."

"That's fine. And what do you think they are made of?"

"I think maybe wood."

"And I think you are right. Britt, thank you for raising your hand. What do you see?"

"I see a back."

"And what color is it?" Ms. Outten asked.

"It is blue," Britt answered.

"So is the seat," Zachary added excitedly.

"Yeah, and the legs are brown," Joshua said with gusto.

"These are excellent observations, children, and thank you very much for just telling us about this . . . "

"Chair!" the children yelled together.

"Yes. A chair," Ms. Outten agreed, thereby labeling the concept which the children undoubtedly knew prior to the activity. "And you have told us that a chair has legs, a back, and a seat. How many of you have chairs in your home?" (All the children raised their hands.)

"Okay," Ms. Outten continued. "Now, how many of you have a love-seat in your home?" (A half dozen or so children raised their hands.)

With permission. Lakeside Elementary School, Orange Park, Florida. Ms. Carol Eberhart, Principal.

"Now, I want you to think very carefully about what I am about to say, especially those of you who have both chairs and love-seats in your home. (Pause.) You all have told me that a chair has four legs, a seat, and a back. Okay, then I guess a chair is a love-seat."

"Noooo!" a number of the children murmured, including Abby.

"Why did you say no, Abby?"

"Cause it's not," she replied.

"Why not?" Ms. Outten urged and was met with no response from Abby or the other children.

"Abby," she continued, "didn't you tell us a chair has a seat and you can sit on it?"

"Yes."

"Just you?"

"Yes."

"So is there a difference?"

"Yes, because me and my sister can sit on the love-seat but I sit on a chair by myself."

"Good job, Abby. So everybody, what do we have to change when we describe a chair? Zachary?"

"It has a seat for just one person to sit on."

"Well done," Ms. Outten said. "Now, I want all of you to close your eyes and I want you to picture your all-time favorite chair, and then we are going to go around the room and share our thoughts."

Not using technical terms, of course, Ms. Outten continued the exercise by having the children talk about their favorite chair, which helped them realize the critical characteristics of the concept. Starting with rocking chair, which Joshua had shared, as a subordinate concept, she then fleshed out the "world" of chair by engaging the children in a discussion of common coordinate concepts such as love-seat and couch and the superordinate concept, furniture. She then had the children return to their desks to use the materials she had provided to draw their favorite chair and facilitated the exercise.

As you can see, Ms. Outten employed the two critical variables given to us by Aristotle. Through the establishment of common characteristics such as legs, back, and single seat, the students were able to isolate the group of things, or concept, called *chair*. By tossing in the love-seat problem and coordinate concepts, she was able to have them further conceptualize the object through the process of differentiation. As a final point, as mentioned in the preface, a particular lesson is not necessarily limited to a single methodology. In Ms. Outten's case, did *she* tell the children or did the *students* tell her? Hopefully, you spotted some aspects of Plato's guided discovery in addition to Aristotle's fundamental concept analysis.

Simple as it may seem, Aristotle also gave us the methods of sorting and classifying information for the purpose, among other things, of making large amounts of knowledge manageable. Let's now look at how this can be undertaken in the classroom.

Scenario 3.4

There were six learning centers in the early childhood classroom at Centennial Elementary School. The morning before Thanksgiving, Mrs. Tammy Brown and her
16 children sat on the floor around an 11′ × 5′ white tablecloth on which had been
drawn a grid composed of 55 one-foot-square cells. The children were very excited because they had brought vegetables and were going to make a "friendship
soup" at the end of the day. However, Mrs. Brown's primary objectives involved
sorting and graphing.

"Lauren brought celery today," she began. Where do you want to put the celery
on our graph?" The child placed the celery on the first row.

"That's fine. Mary, what did you bring today?"

"Tomatoes."

"Are you going to put them on a different row?"

"Yes," she said and placed them above the celery.

"Paul, I see you also brought some celery. Where are you going to put your
celery?" (Pause.) Do you see any other celery on the graph?"

"Next to Lauren's celery."

"Good job! Now, how about Rose's turnip. Does that go next to anything?"

"Noooo," the children replied.

"Great," said Mrs. Brown, so Rose, where are you going to put your turnip?"

"Up above those."

"Right, and you are starting a new row way over there."

After going around the circle, Mrs. Brown checked to make sure that all the children had placed their vegetables on the graph. "Now look at what we have created," she said. "What have we done? (Pause.) Albert?"

"We put them on the paper."

"Is there any special way we did that?"

"The ones that are the same are together."

"Yes, we put the vegetables that were the same together on the graph. Now let's
look closer. How many of you brought green beans today?"

"Two."

"And how many brought peas today?"

"Two. One, two cans of peas. Now you're going to have to help me count all of
these carrots. How many carrots?"

"One, two, three, four, five," the children concluded with a shout.

"Great!" Mrs. Brown then let the children count all the remaining vegetables.
"Okay, here's a tricky queston. Are you ready to think about it? Which vegetable
did more children bring?"

"Carrots."

"Carrots," Mrs. Brown repeated. "How do you know that, Jake? What made you
say that? What did you see about the carrots that told you that there were more carrots for our soup today?"

"I saw five of them."

With permission. Centennial Elementary School, Denver, Colorado. Mr. Gerald R. Gilmore, Principal.

"Yes . . . and they almost went off our graph," she replied with a smile. "Okay. Now let's try something different. Right now we sorted our vegetables by the kind of vegetable, but can you think of another way you might want to sort these vegetables? Anybody?" (Some confusion on the part of the children.)

"Watch, please. I am going to sort them a different way and let's see if you can figure it out." Mrs. Brown then put all the green beans, peas, and celery in one group.

"What do you think? What is there alike about all these vegetables?" (Mixed response from the children.)

"Well, let me give you a hint. I can't put the carrots over here. They don't match this group. Can you figure out why?"

"Because they're orange!" Larry yelled excitedly, "and all of those are green!"

"That's great, Larry. Give me five. Okay. That was my tricky one. Now you figure out your tricky way to sort the vegetables and then we will make our soup."

Although the preceding lesson is quite simple, the process of sorting and classifying is critical to the conceptualization of the material world and involves a methodology employed on a regular basis in today's classrooms. Coupled with the foundational aspects of a concept analysis and the usefulness of deductive reasoning in acquiring knowledge, it goes without saying that Aristotle has had a significant impact on the way educators teach students in today's learning environments.

Exercise 3.8

Examine the following statements to determine if they are consistent (c) or inconsistent (i) with the philosophy of Aristotle. Then compare your responses to those at the end of the chapter.

_____ 1. Reality is limited to the material world of objects.
_____ 2. Perception is important regarding the acquisition of knowledge.
_____ 3. Deductive reasoning is founded on a first premise, which is a statement of truth.
_____ 4. A concept is a group of things that share common characteristics.
_____ 5. Teaching and learning imply an interactive process that is unending.

Exercise 3.9

Read the following statements and place an X in the column of the philosopher who would most agree with that statement. Then check your answers against the ones in the feedback section at the end of the chapter.

STATEMENT	PLATO	ARISTOTLE
1. Reality exists only in the realm of ideas.		
2. Teachers should promote the development of abstractions.		
3. Teachers should implement sensory experiences.		

4. Guided discovery should be used in the classroom to assist students in the learning of preexisting truth.
5. Truth involves the process of remembering.
6. Teachers promote the retention of knowledge by assisting students in the processes of sorting and classifying objects.

Exercise 3.10

Briefly describe the function or nature of each step in Aristotle's deductive method. Then compare your responses to those found in the feedback section at the end of the chapter.

_____ 1. First or major premise
_____ 2. Second or minor premise
_____ 3. Conclusion

SUMMARY

The Ancients—Socrates, Plato, and Aristotle—have given us a storehouse of types of inquiries and methodologies. Socrates and Plato provided the foundations for the philosophy of idealism by suggesting that, metaphysically, reality was to be found in the ideas of humans and that these ideas were absolute truth—that is, God-given. Aristotle emphasized the importance of sensory perception, which he believed to be the initial step in the acquisition of knowledge. He saw knowledge as absolute. He not only stressed the need to acquire knowledge but also believed a key goal of human life was to think and to think intelligently. Finally, his work provided the basis for the philosophy of realism.

In terms of methodology, as shown in the chapter, today's teachers employ a variety of strategies bequeathed to us by the Greek philosophers. These strategies include the Socratic method of Socrates, Plato's guided discovery, and Aristotle's use of deductive reasoning, in addition to the techniques of analyzing concepts and classifying objects.

Finally, today's classrooms emphasize an academic approach to the subject matter. We can, in part, trace this priority to the ancient philosophers, who believed the essence of education to be the acquisition of a universal body of absolute knowledge for the purpose of continually bringing human beings closer to a world of truth and a world of happiness.

Questions for Discussion

1. According to Arnold Stumpf, Socrates developed a new method of intellectual inquiry. What are at least three components of the Socratic method?
2. Do you believe Socrates was as humble as he purported to be? Why? Why not?
3. What alleged threat did Socrates pose to Athenian society and to the Greek rulers of the time?

4. What is one significant difference between the Socratic method and Plato's use of the dialectic?
5. What is a priori knowledge? According to Plato, how do we obtain such knowledge?
6. What is the purpose of Plato's dialectic?
7. How does Plato distinguish between knowledge and belief?
8. Most historians attribute the philosophy of idealism to Socrates/Plato and the foundation of realism to Aristotle. What were the metaphysical differences between these Greek philosophers?
9. What were the components of Aristotle's metaphysical dualism? How were they united?
10. What is a syllogism and how does it work?
11. According to Aristotle, what is the difference between theoretical knowledge and practical knowledge?

Suggested Field Laboratory Activities

1. Review the lessons in a given unit of instruction (see curriculum guides or teacher-prepared units) and study the plans that are Socratic or open-ended, teacher-led discussions.
2. Select an abstraction (concept/generalization) and develop a lesson plan that employs the Socratic method. Given the opportunity, present the lesson to a class.
3. Review prepared lesson plans and curriculum guides and determine how many employ Plato's guided discovery. Also, select one example of a didactic lesson and revise it to reflect a guided discovery approach.
4. Develop a lesson plan that employs Plato's guided discovery. Given the opportunity, implement the lesson.
5. Scenario 3.3 depicts a concept analysis. Select a common concept, such as car, mammal, or house. As Aristotle would have us do, determine what class the concept belongs to and determine how it differs from coordinate concepts, like train, reptile, and hotel. Develop a lesson plan that would allow you to implement this concept and, given the opportunity, do so.
6. Develop a lesson plan in which you determine a first premise and then you assist the students in engaging in deductive reasoning and the production of a syllogism. Given the opportunity, implement the lesson.
7. Organize a learning experience that will allow the students to comprehend the difference between theoretical knowledge and practical knowledge.
8. Organize a lesson plan that provides the students with an opportunity to sort and classify information. Implement the lesson if possible.
9. Observe teacher presentations and write down some examples of the way they present universals in the form of ideas and universals in the form of material things. Determine if one form is being used significantly more than the other.

Exercise Feedback

Exercise 3.1

As you know, Socrates believed in the individual search for truth, which in turn would lead to the good or moral life. Cervantes' classic work *Don Quixote* presents us with the gentleman from La Mancha, who seeks truth in his passions and his deeds. *Know thyself* becomes a chivalric quest of a comical hero whose story is a voyage to eventual self-discovery (Murillo, 1988).

Exercise 3.2

1. (c)   Consistent. Knowledge resides with God.
2. (i)   Inconsistent. The role of the teacher is limited to asking questions.
3. (c)   Consistent. Knowledge leads to truth, which in turn leads to happiness.
4. (c)   Consistent. The process enables the student to analyze preconceived notions, revise the knowledge, and move closer to truth.
5. (i)   Inconsistent. The method brings the student closer to the right answer or absolute truth.

Exercise 3.3

1. The initial ill-considered statement is, "Meno's slave, to whom Socrates has addressed the question, supposes that the sides must double in length of the others."
2. The statements that produce an awareness of inadequacy involves Socrates' drawings in the sand.
3. The statement that reflects the slave's expansion or redefinition of the geometric concept begins with, "Eventually, the slave realizes that . . ."

Exercise 3.4

Plato shows us that things (facts) may not be what they seem in his Allegory of the Cave. Though we may perceive something as factual, a multitude of "shadows" can, as Maya Angelou says, obscure the truth.

Exercise 3.5

1. (i)   Inconsistent. The educated person also had to improve the lot of others.
2. (c)   Consistent. Due to his concern with society, Plato is often considered an early reconstructionist.
3. (c)   Consistent. This is also expressed by Socrates.

4. (c)   Consistent. A cornerstone of the philosophy of idealism.
5. (i)   Inconsistent. That which is to be learned is predetermined by the teacher—hence the term *guided*.

Exercise 3.6

Specifics you might have listed include the following:

1. Mrs. Nemeth had a predetermined objective.
2. The students used hand movements to interpret the music.
3. The students attempted to determine whether sufficient notes were present.
4. The students tried to determine what notes needed to be added.
5. The students attempted to determine the actual musical pattern employed.

The three basic techniques employed show Ms. Nemeth had determined the object, used questions and demonstration to "guide" the students toward the desired conclusion, and allowed the students to "discover" the conclusion.

Exercise 3.7

Edith Hamilton's focus was on thinking as a cornerstone of being educated . . . and so it was with Aristotle. For him, to be educated was a process of growing, developing, and moving ever closer to universal truth through the application of human reason.

Exercise 3.8

1. (i)   Inconsistent. The search for truth includes, but is not limited to, the material world.

2. (c)   Consistent. Learning through the use of one's senses is emphasized throughout Aristotle's work.

3. (c)   Consistent. Aristotle believes there are absolute truths that are used as a starting point when one acquires additional knowledge.

4. (c)   Consistent. This statement is a definition of a concept.

5. (c)   Consistent. For Aristotle, learning is cyclical.

Exercise 3.9

STATEMENTS	PLATO	ARISTOTLE
1.	X	
2.		X
3.		X
4.	X	
5.	X	
6.		X

Exercise 3.10

1. First or major premise: This statement is global in nature and presents a universal truth.
2. Second or minor premise: This statement is more specific and establishes a connection to the universal truth.
3. Conclusion: This third and final statement is a logical outgrowth of the relationship established between the first two statements. It is convergent and inescapable.

CHAPTER 4

CHALLENGING THE ANCIENTS: DESCARTES, BACON, AND LOCKE

After completing Chapter 4, you should be able to accomplish the following objectives:

1. You will gain an understanding of the philosophical contributions of Descartes by identifying statements as being consistent or inconsistent with his philosophy.

2. You will increase your knowledge of Descartes' impact in the area of philosophical inquiry by discussing one major way his quarrel with the Ancients affects classroom teaching.

3. You will expand your knowledge of methods of learning by identifying a number of statements as being consistent or inconsistent with the philosophy of Francis Bacon.

4. You will become familiar with Bacon's methodology by briefly describing how his method of reasoning facilitates his famous quotation, "Knowledge is power."

5. You will increase your awareness of ways to implement inductive reasoning by briefly discussing one Baconian method employed in an actual teaching scenario.

6. You will increase your understanding of the ways the Ancients were challenged by identifying statements as being consistent or inconsistent with the work of John Locke.

7. You will increase your knowledge of how empiricism is utilized in the classroom by describing how Locke's method is employed in an actual teaching scenario.

The time between the era of Socrates, Plato, and Aristotle and the three philosophers you are about to meet was just short of 2000 years. You might be asking yourself how so much time could elapse without a challenge to the ancient philosophers, for there certainly had to be people of great wisdom during that period. And so there were. However, much of that time was dominated by a religious preoccupation with the next world as opposed to the material world and therefore was characterized by societies not overly concerned with a secular search for knowledge and truth.

The focus on the expansion of culture and education during the ancient Greek period pretty much came to a halt with the 1000-year reign of the Roman Empire, which preserved much but added little (Feibleman, 1973). In some instances philosophy came into play, as shown in the rule of Marcus Aurelieus, who exemplified the Platonic concept of the philosopher-king by employing reason throughout his reign. More notably, in terms of impact, the work of Aristotle was coupled with religion by St. Augustine toward the end of the Roman Empire—around 400 A.D. As you know, Aristotle gave us deductive reasoning, which began with the absolute truth of a first premise. St. Augustine married knowledge with religious belief by establishing God as the giver of these truths. Years later, Thomas Aquinas, who was a disciple of Aristotle, clarified this relationship with the notion that truth or knowledge could not deviate from or contradict revelation. This intellectual dominance, expressed in Christian theology, was equally prevalent in the Muslim world, where Arab philosophy throughout the period was dominated by Aristotelianism.

During the thousand or so years prior to the time of Descartes, Bacon, and Locke, the thinkers of the day, often referred to as classicists and Scholastics, promoted Aristotle's deductive style of thinking, which enabled humans to discover God's predetermined truths. The earlier part of this era is often referred to as the *Dark Ages*, for little formal learning took place and abstract philosophical speculation was rarely undertaken. Eventually, however, a rebirth or Renaissance occurred. In addition to ushering in a focus on science, this period was characterized by political and religious upheaval, which led people to question traditional assumptions about the world in which they lived. Philosophically, the time had come to "challenge the Ancients."

RENÉ DESCARTES, 1596–1650

To come to know René Descartes is to wonder how such a person challenged not only the ancient philosophers but his contemporaries as well. He was not physically imposing and had few friends. He was educated by the church and was a firm believer in the Catholic faith throughout his life. He was not necessarily creative or original; some say it is doubtful whether Descartes produced a single important doctrine such as Plato's doctrine of innate ideas (Jolley, 1990). Furthermore, his famous inclination to "doubt all things" was not unusual in his day, when skepticism was common among Europeans.

What did set Descartes apart was his doubt with regard to the absolute certainty of existing knowledge and his desire to not only revisit that knowledge but to challenge the way in which it was obtained. According to him, our main goal in life is to carry out the activity of knowing in the proper way (Grosholz, 1991). During his time there were those who interpreted his work as saying that, epistemologically, the proper way had not been employed for the past 2000 years.

Life and Times

Descartes was born in 1596 in the small town of LaHaye, located in the area of Touraine about 150 miles southwest of Paris. Although his parents were of sufficient wealth and social position, his mother died when he was a baby and he was raised by his maternal grandmother. Descartes' boyhood was one of sickness and poor health and, as with many such children, he focused on intellectual things and was seen as being exceptional.

At the age of eight, as was the custom for children of some wealth, Descartes was enrolled in the Jesuit college of La Fleche, where he studied until the age of sixteen. This educational experience clearly affected him in two significant ways. The first was that, because of his intellectual ability, he had access to a wide range of knowledge and thought. The second was his enduring concern with the approval of the church and the influence of Catholicism, which was to be a fundamental part of his life.

At the end of this educational period, Descartes did not believe he had acquired any certain knowledge, with the possible exception of mathematics. Therefore, he chose to continue his studies in the area of law and was awarded a doctorate in 1616. After he achieved a certain level of scholarship, one might say Descartes took a U-turn and became a soldier of fortune. For the next few years, he served in the army of Maurice of Nassau in Holland and traveled to many places in that part of Europe.

This period in Descartes' life came to an abrupt halt when, on November 10, 1619, he had a dream that revealed to him a new method for seeking knowledge. He believed this dream to be a divine message and that it was his destiny to put this method before the world. Fortunately, an inheritance allowed him to devote himself to this task for the remainder of his life.

For the next ten or so years, Descartes continued to travel and was basically a loner. He never married, and it is said he often referred to solitude as his "beloved." However, he could not escape the limelight when in 1628 in Paris, at the age of about 32, he had a famous confrontation with a notable French chemist. This scientist, Chandoux, voiced the popularly held view that science could only lead to probable conclusions. In a public forum, Descartes stated that he had formulated a method of reasoning that, through absolute certainty, would allow for the acquisition of knowledge. His speech won large numbers of people over to his viewpoint (Sorell, 1987).

Spurred by this public success, Descartes returned to Holland to continue work on his method of rational inquiry, which he believed could be applied not only to science but to any other type of subject matter. He described his system or method in a work titled *Le Monde*, completed in 1634. However, the world in which he lived remained skeptical, as shown in the condemnation of individuals such as Galileo. Therefore, he played down his ideas, reflecting his conciliatory attitude toward the church. Eventually, he presented his unorthodox work in a less-than-straightforward fashion in his celebrated *Discourse on the Method*, completed in 1637.

Cogito ergo sum: I think, there-fore I exist.

Descartes

During another period of ten years, Descartes continued to write while remaining reclusive. However, in 1647, he looked forward to returning to France to live on a pension awarded by the king. Nevertheless, he remained controversial since church officials believed that his work challenged the medieval establishment (Richetti, 1983). His pension, therefore, was not funded and he returned to Holland, where he spent the next two years.

In 1649, Descartes left Holland for the last time and traveled to Sweden, where he taught philosophy to Queen Christina. The 5:00 A.M. sessions may have indicated the value the queen attached to philosophy; in any case, the combination of poor health, possible depression, and the dawn treks through the snows of Stockholm contributed to pneumonia. Within a year of his arrival in Sweden, Descartes died at the age of 54.

Descartes' *Discourse* was written in French—not Latin, the language used by most European scholars down to his time. His choice of French suggested that he wanted to go beyond the academicians to reach a wider audience. As you will see, his method and focus on epistemology were clearly viewed as a challenge to the establishment, past and present. Even after death, he remained controversial; in 1691, a royal decree banned the teaching of his work in any school in France.

Philosophical Contributions

As you now know, skepticism, doubt, and challenge were characteristic of the times in which Descartes lived. Therefore, his inclination to doubt everything was not unusual. What set him apart from his contemporaries was his effort to utilize doubt as a foundation on which he could seek truth as opposed to merely reaffirming the body of knowledge that had held sway since the time of Aristotle. This rejection of authoritarian knowledge not only conflicted with the approach the ancient philosophers took but also challenged the church, as we have seen. What is sad, of course, is that Descartes considered himself to be a religious person who simply wanted to perfect a method of arriving at certainty with the hope of harmonizing reason with biblical revelation. What he ended up doing was to begin to shift the focus of philosophical inquiry from metaphysics to epistemology, due to his preoccupation with the question of how we can be certain (how we can know). Let's look at how Descartes answered this question.

The Cartesian system begins with a method of doubt. Descartes would accept nothing as true unless he clearly knew it to be so. In his own words, he decided "to believe nothing too certainly of which I had only been convinced by examples and customs" (Descartes, 1986, p. 63). His intent was to establish a certainty on which he could build further certainties or truths. To do this, he began by doubting everything to see if anything was left. As the caption to the illustration of Descartes in this section suggests, the first certainty was that of his own existence. If he is to doubt, he must be thinking, and if he is thinking, he must exist. It follows that if people cease to think, they cease to exist, which leads to the conclusion that thinking is a certain and lifelong process.

Beginning with this premise that he determined to be certain and known, Descartes set about the task of employing a rational method that would establish truth. His break with Aristotelian thought comes with directing human reason in the effort to discover truth as opposed to employing a metaphysical or unknown truth as a foundation for further knowledge. Put another way, Descartes was not just alleging that the Scholastic and ancient philosophers had gotten their principles wrong. He maintained that they lacked proper principles entirely because fundamental axioms had not been built on clear, self-evident starting points (Cottingham, 1988).

Finally, although Descartes is often seen as a philosophical skeptic prepared to take doubt to extremes (Sorell, 1987), one could argue that his method of doubt was actually positive and not negative, because his preoccupation with doubts and certainties provided a path toward ascertaining more accurate thought. Let's turn to what Descartes envisioned as that proper way or method.

Like Aristotle, Descartes' method involves the use of deductive reasoning, but he took issue with Aristotle's view of the nature of the beginning, expressed in a foundational statement. For Descartes, the foundational statement has to be a fact known with certainty, absolute certainty. Whereas Descartes deals with facts, Aristotle deals with universal concepts or metaphysical speculation. In other words, Descartes argues for the need to begin with a *known*; Aristotle begins with an *unknown*. Descartes' method for determining factual certainties is founded on his assumption that

> in place of the large numbers of rules that make up logic, I would find the following four to be sufficient, provided that I made a strong and unswerving resolution never to fail to observe them.
>
> The first was never to accept anything as true if I did not have evident knowledge of its truth: that is, carefully to avoid precipitate conclusions and preconceptions, and to include nothing more in my judgments than what presented itself to my mind clearly and so distinctly that I had no occasion to doubt it.
>
> The second, to divide each of the difficulties I examined into as many parts as possible and as may be required in order to resolve them better.
>
> The third, to direct my thoughts in an orderly manner, by beginning with the simplest and most easily known objects in order to ascend little by little, step by step, to knowledge of the most complex, and by supposing some order even among objects that have no natural order of precedence.
>
> And the last, throughout to make enumerations so complete, and reviews so comprehensive, that I could be sure of leaving nothing out. (Descartes, 1988, pp. 3–6).

The key to the rules or method is that only in the actual application of the mind to specific problems can we come to recognize what it is to see something clearly and distinctly (Grosholz, 1991). Therefore, the method is analytical in that, beginning with Descartes' second point, the *whole* is being broken down into its constituent parts, with the intent being the possibility of discovering as opposed to reaffirming existing knowledge. Descartes is out to discover what is true, although his work leads to the notion that he is looking for things that are certain.

We can see that Descartes did not completely sever his ties with the ancient philosophers, for when he states "in order to think, it is necessary to exist," his foundational certainty becomes an eternal truth. This was an indication that Descartes was prepared to admit that at least some a priori truths existed that must be immune to doubt and that he must be able to rely on in order to avoid doubt (Williams, 1978). Although Descartes was deeply influenced by the Scholastic philosophy that had preceded him, the problems he posed, the questions he raised, and the demands he made for absolute, subjective certainty in knowledge undermined the influence of the 2000-year-old tradition of Aristotelian philosophy (Wolff, 1989). The specific form of this "undermining" involved Descartes' unique approach of establishing reality through reason. Often referred to as the father of rationalism, Descartes not only laid the foundation for the Enlightenment but played a key role in shaping the modern mind (Schouls, 1992).

I never notice what has been done. I only see what remains to be done.

Madame Marie Curie

Exercise 4.1

Reread the quotation by Madame Curie and write a short paragraph on how her words might apply to Descartes' philosophical relationship to the ancient philosophers. Then compare your response to the feedback at the end of the chapter.

From Meditations on First Philosophy, Parts I, IV, Descartes

Already some years ago I have noticed how many false things, I, going into my youth, had admitted as true and how dubious were whatever things I have afterwards built upon them, and therefore that once in my life all things are fundamentally to be demolished and that I have to begin again from the first foundations if I were to desire ever to stabilize something firm and lasting in the sciences. But the task seemed to be a huge one, and I waited for that age which would be so mature that none more fit for the disciplines to be pursued would follow. Thus I have delayed so long that I would now be at fault if by deliberating I were to consume that time which remains for what is to be done. Today then I have opportunely rid the mind of all cares and I have procured for myself secure leisure, I am withdrawing alone and I shall at last devote myself seriously and freely to this general demolition of my opinions.

Yet to do this it will not be necessary that I would show that all my opinions are false, which I could perhaps never achieve anyway. Because reason persuades me that assent is to be withheld no less accurately from the opinions that are not fully certain and indubitable than from the ones that are overtly false rather will it suffice to reject all my opinions if I shall have found any reason for doubting in each one. And therefore nor will these opinions have to be gone through individually, which would be an infinite task. But because—the foundations have been undermined—whatever has been built upon them will collapse spontaneously, I will go right for those principles upon which rested all that which I have once believed.

Namely, whatever I have admitted up until now as maximally true I have accepted from the senses or through the senses. Yet I have found that these senses sometimes deceive me, and it is a matter of prudence never to confide completely in those who have deceived us even once.

In these days I have thus accustomed myself to leading the mind away from the senses, and I have so accurately noticed that there are very few things about corporeal things that be perceived truly, and that many more things about the human mind—and still many more things about God—are cognized, that now I shall without any difficulty turn cogitation from imaginable things to intelligible things only, and ones separate from all matter. And I have indeed a much more distinct idea of the human mind, in so far as it is a cogitating thing—not extended in length, breadth or depth, and not having anything else from the body—, that I have a distinct idea of any corporeal thing. And when I pay attention thereto that I doubt, or that I am a thing incomplete and dependent, then there occurs to me the clear and distinct idea of an independent and complete being, that is, of God. And from this one thing—that there would be such an idea in me, or that I would exist as one having this idea—I so manifestly conclude that God also exists, and that my whole existence depends on him at individual moments, that I might be confident that nothing more evident and nothing more certain can be cognized by the human mind. And now I seem to see a way by which one might get from that contemplation of the true God—in whom, namely, all the treasures of the sciences and of wisdom are hidden—to the cognition of other things.

Descartes, Rene (©1990). *Meditationes de prima philosophia/Meditations on First Philosophy: A Bilingual Edition.* (George Heffernan, edited, translated, and indexed.) University of Notre Dame Press, Notre Dame, Indiana.

Descartes in the Classroom

Let's begin with the important fact that Descartes' works were written in French, which shows that he was more concerned with the educated people of his time than with existing Scholastics. In line with this focus, he also believed human beings are prone to errors and that human nature is weak (Heffernan, 1990). Therefore, the significance of his method was to enable individuals to seek the one truth of each thing, and whoever found it knew as much about it as can be known about it (Benjamin, 1993). Restated, all of us have the capacity to employ reason in the search for knowledge and, equally, should do so.

Descartes would have teachers and students undertake this search in a highly structured way. He was very specific in enumerating what he called *Rules for the Direction of our Native Intelligence*, the first 12 of which are as follows (Cottingham, 1988, pp. 32–33):

1. The aim of our studies should be to direct the mind with a view to forming true and sound judgments about whatever comes before it.
2. We should attend only to those objects of which our minds seem capable of having certain and indubitable cognition.

3. Concerning objects proposed for study, we ought to investigate what we can clearly and evidently intuit or deduce with certainty, and not what other people have thought or what we ourselves conjecture. For knowledge can be attained in no other way.

4. We need a method if we are to investigate the truth of things.

5. The whole method consists entirely in the ordering and arranging of the objects on which we must concentrate our mind's eye if we are to discover some truth. We shall be following this method exactly if we first reduce complicated and obscure propositions step by step to simpler ones, and then, starting with the intuition of the simplest ones of all, try to ascend through the same steps to a knowledge of all the rest.

6. In order to distinguish the simplest things from those that are complicated and to set them out in an orderly manner, we should attend to what is most simple in each series of things in which we have directly deduced some truths from others, and should observe how all the rest are more, or less, or equally removed from the simplest.

7. In order to make our knowledge complete, every single thing related to our undertaking must be surveyed in a continuous and wholly uninterrupted sweep of thought, and be included in a sufficient and well-ordered enumeration.

8. If in the series of things to be examined we come across something which our intellect is unable to intuit (immediate intellectual apprehension) sufficiently well, we must stop at that point, and refrain from the superfluous task of examining the remaining items.

9. We must concentrate our mind's eye totally upon the most insignificant and easiest of matters, and dwell on them long enough to acquire the habit of intuiting the truth distinctly and clearly.

10. In order to acquire discernment we should exercise our native intelligence by investigating what others have already discovered, and methodically survey even the most insignificant products of human skill, especially those which display or presuppose order.

11. If, after intuiting a number of simple propositions, we deduce something else from them, it is useful to run through them in a continuous and completely uninterrupted train of thought, to reflect on their relations to one another, and to form a distinct and, as far as possible, simultaneous conception of several of them. For in this way our knowledge becomes much more certain, and our intellectual capacity is enormously increased.

12. Finally, we must make use of all the aids which intellect, imagination, sense-perception, and memory afford in order, firstly, to intuit simple propositions distinctly; secondly, to combine correctly the matters under investigation with what we already know, so that they too may be known; and thirdly, to find out what things should be compared with each other so that we make the most thorough use of all our human powers.

Descartes gave classroom teachers, through rules and discourse, a valuable method that we and our students should use to better understand the material world in which we live. This task, more or less summarized by rule 12 in the preceding list, is undertaken by beginning with certain knowledge and using that information to establish further knowledge through deductive reasoning. It is interesting to note that Descartes considered his doctrine or method one of his greatest philosophical achievements (Gaukroger, 1989). Now let's see how this approach is used in the classroom.

Scenario 4.1

Mrs. Martha Scribner, a social studies teacher at Glencliff Comprehensive High School, began her law-related education class by informing the students the purpose of the class was going to be to trace how the Fourteenth Amendment has been interpreted over time.

"We are basically looking at a period of approximately one hundred years, from 1865 to 1965," she said. "We have already looked very closely at the wording of the Fourteenth Amendment, and when we are through, you will hopefully understand this amendment a little better and you will also be able to interpret how congressional acts and Supreme Court decisions have either advanced or regressed civil rights and human rights during that period. So we will be looking today at legislation and legal cases in trying to determine how those interpretations have affected the intention of the Fourteenth Amendment and rights.

"Now the first thing I am going to do is divide you into four groups and ask you to do some brainstorming as to what your rights are." Mrs. Scribner spent a few minutes organizing the groups and then went to the board at the front of the classroom.

"I'm going to write three categories on the board," she continued. "You can have political rights, economic rights, and social rights. Now, off the top of your head, can anyone give me an example of what you think would be a right in any one of those categories?"

"A political right would be the right to vote," Sara said.

"Good. Good example, Sara." Mrs. Scribner then wrote Sara's example in the political column. "What about an economic right?"

"Own land," Maurice said.

"Sure," said Mrs. Scribner. "That could be an economic right. Can we change *land* to *property?*"

"Okay," Maurice replied.

"I've got one," Lon said. "How about being able to move around or go where you want to go."

The law-related eduction classes at Glencliff Comprehensive High School are part of a cooperative program supported by the Office of Juvenile Justice and Delinquency Prevention of the U.S. Department of Justice.

With permission. Glencliff Comprehensive High School, Nashville, Tennessee. Dr. S. V. Swor, Executive Principal.

"Let's see. How and where can I write that on the board? How about unrestricted movement or travel?" Mrs. Scribner asked.

"Okay," Lon said.

"And where will we put it on the board?"

"Under social rights."

"Yes. We could put it there. Now, in your groups, see if you can think of two or three more example for each category."

The students then spent the next few minutes brainstorming and listing examples of their political, economic, and social rights.

"Okay," Mrs. Scribner continued. "Let's see what you have come up with. Who has another political right?"

"The right to work and a minimum wage," Latisha said.

"Would that be—political, economic, or social?" Mrs. Scribner asked.

"Economic," Latisha replied.

"Good. Is it okay if I put 'fair wages'?"

"Sure," Latisha said.

"How about the right to have a job or choice of work?" Jo added.

"Choice of work," Mrs. Scribner repeated. "Can you actually tell me where you are given that as a constitutional right? (No response.) "Let me put it another way. If having a job was a constitutional right and you were unemployed and could not find work, what could you do?"

"Sue," Jo said

"Sure. So if that was a constitutional right, look how many people would be suing the government. So, does the government guarantee that you will have a job?"

"No," Jo concluded, "but there are supposed to be guarantees that you won't be discriminated against."

"Good thinking," said Mrs. Scribner. "That's another issue, so let's talk about it." She then facilitated discussions regarding discrimination and other examples of rights, including the right to a public education, citizenship, search and seizure, contracts, trial by jury, marriage, and religion.

At the end of the discussions, Mrs. Scribner said, "Now, in our groups, we are going to try to determine how specific legislation and/or court cases had an impact on political, economic, and social equality." An interactive handout included the following:

Thirteenth Amendment
Civil Rights Act of 1866
Fourteenth Amendment
Fifteenth Amendment
Slaughterhouse Cases
Civil Rights Act of 1875
U.S. v. Cruikshank
Civil Rights Cases of 1883
Plessy v. Ferguson
Civil Rights Act of 1964
Heart of Atlanta Motel v. U.S.
Voting Rights Act of 1965

"What you are going to do is determine how far these interpretations went in achieving the rights that you have mentioned and that we have written on the board. For example, starting at the top with the Thirteenth Amendment, think about whether it advanced any of the political, economic, or social rights we have discussed. As you work through the sheet, you can also add rights we did not put on the board. What I will be looking for when we discuss your work tomorrow is how well you support the degree to which specific equalities have been affected. Keep in mind that you are looking for retreats as well as advances."

After providing some additional information, Mrs. Scribner spent the remainder of the class working with the groups on a needs basis.

What we see here is that Mrs. Scribner began with a certainty: the Fourteenth Amendment as it appears as part of the U.S. Constitution. She then initiated an analytic process by establishing categories of rights and asking the students to brainstorm, in a small-group format, examples for each of the categories. Court cases and acts were then offered to further analyze and eventually determine the current interpretation of the Fourteenth Amendment. This interpretation completed the journey from *certain* knowledge to *new* knowledge.

Exercise 4.2

Examine the following statements to determine if they are consistent (c) or inconsistent (i) with the philosophy of Descartes. Then check your responses against those at the end of the chapter.

_____ 1. A primary concern is how we, as human beings, obtain knowledge.
_____ 2. Deductive reasoning should be employed to rediscover truth.
_____ 3. The focus of philosophical inquiry should involve metaphysical questions.
_____ 4. The foundation for new knowledge is certain knowledge.
_____ 5. Deductive reasoning employs more intuition than analysis.

Exercise 4.3

As you have seen, Descartes believed himself to be religious, yet he was hounded throughout his life by the church, and after his death his works were banished in France. Briefly discuss why his work would find disfavor if implemented in a classical educator's classroom. Then compare your response to the feedback at the end of the chapter.

FRANCIS BACON, 1561–1626

Sir Francis Bacon is generally given credit for introducing the systematic study of science. In taking a scientific approach, he differed from every other philosopher prior to his time, since he aimed at practice rather than theory. Although his concerns about the accuracy of existing knowledge paralleled those of Descartes, he rejected the French philosopher's dependency on deductive reasoning, which he felt failed to apply knowledge to the real world. In addressing these concerns, Bacon is considered to have laid the foundation for pragmatism. Here for the first time was the voice and tone of modern science (Durant, 1953).

Life and Times

Bacon was born in London on January 22, 1561. His family was privileged, having both social and political connections. While his mother, Lady Anne Cooke, daughter of the chief tutor of King Edward VI, was considered a religious and conservative person, his father, Sir Nicholas Bacon, was a worldly man who served as Lord High Chancellor during the reign of Queen Elizabeth I.

The young Bacon was thought of as solemn and was physically frail. As was the custom of the time for a boy of his station, Bacon entered Trinity College, Cambridge, at age 12, remaining there from 1573 to 1575. Although his somewhat carefree youth was interrupted by his father's premature death, Bacon was able to support himself through his work in the law and through the generosity of the Earl of Essex, whose gift of property provided a tidy income. In later years, it was this same Essex who attempted to overthrow the government of Elizabeth and was tried and executed. Bacon was a member of the prosecuting team that sent Essex to the gallows, and many of his peers considered his behavior toward a benefactor to be a serious flaw in his character.

Nevertheless, his political abilities could not be denied. Bacon was elected to the House of Commons at the unusually young age of 23 and prospered during the reign of James I by holding the offices of Solicitor General (1607), Attorney General (1613), Lord Keeper of the Seal (1617) and, finally at age 57, Lord Chancellor. Although he had already been knighted and titled as Baron Verulam prior to ascending to the high office once held by his father, this final and most prestigious appointment brought him the title Viscount St. Albans, which placed him among the elite of his country.

During this time, at the somewhat advanced age of 45, Bacon married, but he continued to focus his attention on his political standing and a need to maintain a publicly affluent lifestyle. As with his relationship with Essex, these years were not without controversy. Although his thoughts and essays may have been lofty, his personal behavior was more in keeping with the political times and included the common practice of accepting bribes. Such charges ended his political career, earned him four days in the Tower of London, and resulted in a fine of £40,000. It comes as no surprise that Bacon remarked, "The higher one goeth the fewer true friends he shall have," and, "Sincerity in politics is unprofitable."

Turning to his private life, Bacon now had the luxury of sufficient time to pursue his writing based on his fascinating background of scholarship and statesmanship. Eventually, his dedication to these pursuits contributed to his undoing. On a visit during a snowstorm in the spring of 1626, he was struck with the idea of using cold to retard putrifaction. He stopped at a village, bought, killed, and stuffed a fowl with snow, and proceeded to observe this experiment.

Knowledge is power.

Francis Bacon

Exposure brought on what was probably an upper respiratory infection, and he died shortly thereafter.

Philosophical Contributions

In challenging the ancient philosophers, Bacon took a position similar to that of Descartes, for he too did not believe that humankind already possessed a body of truth that was merely being reworked. He did not think of truth as already known and that people should simply fall back on the intellectual attainments of the past and accept them without critical scrutiny (Davidson, 1957). Taking this position a step further, Bacon believed most of the knowledge of his time to be false because it was based on insufficient examination of the concrete world. Aristotelian "truth" had been in place for quite some time and Bacon was wary of this intellectual choke-hold, for if you start with the assurance of knowing something, you are less likely to reconsider it than if you start with no preconceived point of view.

Bacon's challenge came with focusing his life's work on the sciences and the application of natural philosophy to the social condition. At that time, people had begun to examine the physical world and had produced some great discoveries—particularly in the area of astronomy—that influenced Bacon's thinking. He believed that knowledge could be attained through amassing data, carefully intepreting the data, and conducting experiments founded on organized observations.

Philosophically, this approach radically differed from that of Plato, who, as you know, believed that forms (the essence of an object) were ideas that existed in the metaphysical realm. Bacon believed that forms belonged to the empirical, not metaphysical, universe. Put another way, Bacon's view was that reality or truth is found *in* nature, not *beyond* nature.

In addition, Bacon challenged the deductive methodology of Aristotle by replacing it with inductive reasoning, which focused on the acquisition of knowledge through a process of going from the specific to the general. For Bacon, logic was a matter of the pious observation of facts of experience, and he was primarily concerned with his method as opposed to the nature of reality itself (Butler, 1968).

Although (like Descartes) Bacon challenged the ancient philosophers, he was not considered a skeptic, as was his French contemporary. Bacon believed we could "know" and, through his inductive method, simply wanted to question and examine the body of existing knowledge. He too was concerned about the validity of an idea or an object based on the intuitive truth of a first premise in a syllogism. He believed that "stuff" got in the way, which he defined in the form of the following four Idols:

1. Idols of the Tribe: Perceptions in the mind can get in the way, for people as a group can color a belief—that is, we believe what we want to believe.
2. Idols of the Den: Individuals interpret what they learn in light of their favorite theories and align things with existing experiences.
3. Idols of the Market Place: Errors arise through human interaction, particularly through words that are often vague and inaccurate.
4. Idols of the Theater: Errors that have been accepted based on previous reasoning or authority.

For Bacon, the way to eliminate these barriers was to pursue truth through induction. His method of reasoning stressed the careful observation of facts as opposed to the deductive method of reasoning from abstraction. This new instrument, or Novum Organum as he called it, was founded on the following *Three Tables of Investigation:*

- Table of Affirmation, which requires the assembling of known instances of a phenomenon.
- Table of Negation, which requires the investigation of negative instances.
- Table of Comparison, which involves the study of variations in different phenomena to see if there is any correlation between various changes observed.

Put in a less formal way, the method calls for listing all cases or instances in which something happens, listing all cases or instances in which something does not happen, listing all cases or instances in which something happens in differing degrees, and, finally, processing the preceding information in an attempt to "discover" knowledge. In short, simple observations lead to general information.

Bacon believed that the only trustworthy knowledge came through observing nature. Beyond this, human beings could know nothing. With his new scientific (inductive) system would come power. By observing and obeying nature, human knowledge and power could meet. Bacon thought that scientific knowledge would transform society and possibly human nature itself (Smith, 1994).

With its focus on the physical world, inductive reasoning still serves as the basis of scientific thought and achievement (Griese, 1981).

Commentators have suggested Bacon's work may have fallen short in that he had no grasp of the modern concept of a hypothesis, whereas others have noted that his character and lifestyle were inconsistent with his thoughts as expressed in his writings. Regardless, he certainly went well beyond his self-assessment that he merely "rang the bell that called wits together."

I have walked with people whose eyes are full of light but who see nothing in sea or sky, nothing in city streets, nothing in books. It were far better to sail forever in the night of blindness with sense, and feeling and mind then to be content with the mere act of seeing. The only lightless dark is the night of darkness in ignorance and insensibility.

Helen Keller

Exercise 4.4

Return to the quotation by Helen Keller and briefly discuss how her words and thoughts might reflect Bacon's view of the human perception of knowledge. Then compare your response to the feedback at the end of the chapter.

From *Aphorisms*, Book 1, C–CVI, Bacon

An entirely different method, order, and process for carrying on and advancing experience must be introduced. For experience, when it wanders in its own track, is, as I have already remarked, mere groping in the dark, and confounds men rather than instructs them. But when it shall proceed in accordance with a fixed law, in regular order, and without interruption, then may better things be hoped of knowledge.

Moreover, since there is so great a number and army of particulars, and that army so scattered and dispersed as to distract and confound the understanding, little is to be hoped for from the skirmishings and slight attacks and desultory movements of the intellect, unless all the particulars which pertain to the subject of inquiry shall, by means of Tables of Discovery, apt, well arranged, and, as it were, animated, be

(continued)

drawn up and marshaled; and the mind be set to work upon the helps duly prepared and digested which these tables supply.

But after this store of particulars has been set out duly and in order before our eyes, we are not to pass at once to the investigation and discovery of new particulars or works; or at any rate if we do so we must not stop there. For although I do not deny that when all the experiments of all the arts shall have been collected and digested, and brought within one man's knowledge and judgment, the mere transferring of the experiments of one art to others may lead, by means of that experience which I term literate, to the discovery of many new things of service to the life and state of man, yet it is no great matter that can be hoped for from that; but from the new light of axioms, which having been educed from those particulars by a certain method or rule, shall in their turn point out the way again to new particulars, greater things may be looked for. For our road does not lie on a level, but ascends and descends; first ascending to axioms, then descending to works.

Then, and then only, may we hope well of the sciences when in a just scale of ascent, and by successive steps not interrupted or broken, we rise from particulars to lesser axioms; and then to middle axioms, one above the other; and last of all to the most general.

This understanding must not therefore be supplied with wings, but rather hung with weights, to keep it from leaping and flying. Now this has never yet been done; when it is done, we may entertain better hopes of the sciences..

Montagu, B. (Ed.). (1831). *The Works of Francis Bacon,* vol. XIV. London: William Pickering.

Bacon in the Classroom

The numerous and varied experiments Bacon undertook underscore his value to classroom teachers. What he gave us was a system, a method, which involved the undertaking of painstaking observations and the accumulation of facts that in turn would lead to an all but inescapable conclusion. This system combined with Bacon's "acute sense that science means invasion of the unknown, rather than repetition in logical form of the already known, makes him . . . the father of induction. Endless and persistent uncovering of facts and principles not known . . . such is the true spirit of induction (Dewey, 1921, p. 34).

The application of inductive reasoning in the classroom allows students to go from example to rule or from specific to general. Students are not trying to discover what they already know; they are, one would hope, engaged in the exciting pursuit of *new knowledge*. This hope is best reflected in the following quotation from Bacon:

> "'Prometheus first struck the flints and marvelled at the spark, [rather than]. . . when he first struck the flints he expected the spark'" (in Perez-Ramos, 1988, p. 288).

As you have seen, Bacon was primarily concerned with science and believed that with his new scientific system (inductive reasoning) would come power. By observing and obeying nature, human knowledge and power could meet. Bacon thought that scientific knowledge would transform society and possibly human nature itself (Smith and Smith, 1994). The application of his method in the classroom, however, need not be limited to the sciences, for it can be employed by students moving from isolated facts to conclusions in any subject discipline. To emphasize this point, let's observe Bacon in action in a reading/literature class.

Scenario 4.2

Mrs. Pamela A. Halvorsen, a sixth-grade teacher at Blanton Elementary School, began her lesson by saying, "If you've moved before, you have discovered that there are some advantages and disadvantages to moving. Let's talk about what those might be. Who can share some advantages of moving . . . Brian?"

"You might get a chance to do something you didn't have a chance to do before," Brian said.

"All right, Brian. Experience something you hadn't experienced before. Example please?"

"I might have a bigger house," Brian added.

"Yes, your house might be bigger," Mrs. Halvorsen said. "I can remember having to share a room as a child with my brother, and I was so excited to move because the new house had a room just for me. Okay. Cortney, how about another advantage?"

"I might meet some new kids."

"That's a good one, Cortney. You might make new friends. Do you have one, David?"

"I might get a chance to go to a better school," David said.

"Yes, that could happen," Mrs. Halvorsen said, "and I see you are smiling, Emi, so I guess you had the same idea? (Emi nods in the affirmative.) Good. Who has another advantage to moving?"

"I might move to a nicer neighborhood," Fernando responded.

"So, you are changing neighborhoods and maybe things are improving not only in the neighborhood but with some of the other things you have shared," Mrs. Halvorsen concluded. "Now let's focus on disadvantages or things that might not be so good about moving. Would you like to start us off, Gabby?"

With permission. Blanton Elementary School, Arlington, Texas. Mr. John DeMore, Principal.

"You might have to move away from your best friend," Gabby offered.

"That's a good one. How about you, Javier? You just recently moved?"

"Well, I came to a new school which is okay but when I left I missed some neat field trips."

"That's true, Javier. When you move you are usually going to miss out on some things," Mrs. Halvorsen said.

"Yeah, and the school might also have bad food," Javier added.

"The new school?" Mrs. Halvorsen inquired.

"Any school I guess," Javier said with a laugh and was joined by his classmates.

"Okay, anything else?" Mrs. Halvorsen continued with a smile.

"Well," Jason said thoughtfully, "if you move to a new country the economy might be the pits."

"That could be very true, Jason. You might experience culture shock when you go from an economy like we have in the United States to a country that is more dis- advantaged than we are and, of course, it could work the other way as well. You've all done a great job and I know we could share a lot more about the pros and cons of moving but, for the moment, we have enough to move to our chapter and better understand how Yuki is feeling about leaving her home.

"As we know, she is probably homesick and all of us have had those feelings. She has been through a lot of changes, so let's talk and see if we can catch on to what she is feeling here. Who would like to start reading today? (Pause.) Krystal?" Krystal then read a brief passage from Yoshiko Uchida's book *Journey Home.*

On concluding, Mrs. Halvorsen said, "Let's talk about that one segment that says, 'if she had to say many more farewells, she felt as though there would soon be nothing left of her old self.' What does that mean to you? If you have said goodbye to friends, can you put yourself in Yuki's place? Monuplea?"

"Well, I think she is saying that every time she leaves or departs from somebody, she leaves a part of herself."

"Excellent, Monuplea, so when you are saying goodbye a little part of you stays behind with that person, and Yuki had been saying a lot of goodbyes at this point and the author is trying to get you to feel what Yuki is feeling. Let's continue our reading."

Mrs. Halvorsen called on Nathaniel, who read a long passage that concluded with the following:

> On the first night Yuki went to the restroom, at the rear of the coach (train). Just as she opened the door to go in, a blonde woman with two children pushed past her. She glared angrily at Yuki and muttered, "go back to where you belong, you damn Jap."

"Let's talk for just a few minutes about this passage," Mrs. Halvorsen began. "Did you expect this author to use words like that in this book?"

"No," the students replied in unison.

"Then why do you think the author has used the word *damn,* which is the first cuss word we have seen in a book this year?" Mrs. Halvorsen asked.

"Because it expressed the blonde woman's strong feelings of hatred for the Japanese," Phillip replied.

"How did it make you feel when you read it?" Mrs. Halvorsen said. "Were you shocked?"

"No," Rakahya said. "Maybe that happened to the author."

"So you are saying that perhaps Mr. Uchida, who wrote this book, may have experienced this in his own life and he is retelling it in such a way that it makes you have the real impact of the feelings he felt?" Mrs. Halvorsen inquired.

"Yes," Rakahya responded.

"Fine," Mrs. Halvorsen continued. "Think back for a second to things that have been said to you in your own life that you felt were really hateful. (Pause.) Now, how many think they know how Yuki felt?" (Most of the students raise their hands.)

"Okay. Now you are going to find a partner and you are going to read the rest of this chapter back and forth together and, after you finish, I want you to complete your reader response sheets together. What you will be doing in your summary is drawing conclusions, based on our talks and the readings, with regard to the impact on moving in terms of feelings as well as events." Mrs. Halvorsen spent the remainder of the class time moving from group to group and monitoring the activity.

What is critical for you to note in this scenario is that though most groups would come up with similar conclusions, unlike Plato's guided discovery, the end result or goal or conclusion arrived at by the students was not predetermined by the teacher. As you know, when employing inductive reasoning in classrooms, the teacher is assisting the students in the process of generating or observing specifics and then moving toward general statements or conclusions. In the above scenario, Mrs. Halvorsen both provided the opportunity for the students to express personal examples of the pros and cons of moving and had them focus on additional information as presented in the story. The end result is that the students are going to arrive at a potentially open-ended conclusion(s) through this process.

Exercise 4.5

Examine the following statements to determine if they are consistent (c) or inconsistent (i) with the philosophy of Francis Bacon. Then compare your answers with those at the end of the chapter.

_____ 1. The primary function of knowledge is to improve the human or social condition.
_____ 2. The sole function of inductive reasoning is to validate existing truth.
_____ 3. People should intellectually and critically examine the world in which they live.
_____ 4. Preconceived points of view are frequently reconsidered.
_____ 5. Philosophy should focus on concrete issues.

Exercise 4.6

Read the following scenario and discuss one way the teacher gave the students an opportunity to engage in inductive reasoning. Then compare your response to the one offered at the end of the chapter.

Mrs. Joy Warner, a kindergarten teacher at David Cox Elementary School, had her children working on a unit in dental health. She organized her room into a number of learning centers, including a dentist's office, where the children counted each other's teeth, cavities, and fillings and put the information on a chart; a play dough center, where the children made models of mouths; and art center, where the children painted a tooth with a toothbrush, practicing correct toothbrushing strokes; and a nutrition center, where Mrs. Warner interacted with a few children at a time. Three children sat with her, while one aide and one parent volunteer worked with the children in the other learning centers.

Mrs. Warner showed the children a picture of some food. "What kind of food is this?" she asked.

"It looks like meatloaf," JuRelle said.

"Look a little closer."

"Cake."

"Yes, it does look like cake or a kind of sweetbread. And what is the stuff on the top?"

"Icing," Melina said.

"And maybe nuts," Nirav added.

"Great," Mrs. Warner said. "Now what do we have here?"

"Strawberries."

"Good, Jessica. What about this one?"

"A tomato," Preston said.

"Okay." Mrs. Warner continued to hold up the pictures and have the children identify the food in each. She then turned toward the felt board, on which she had placed cutouts of a happy tooth and a sad tooth.

"What we are going to do now is sort these pictures. Some of these are pictures of food that can make your teeth happy, while others make your teeth not so happy. I'm going to put all the pictures in the middle and choose one, and then you are going to tell us where the picture should go.

"Okay. Now let me model it first to show you. This is cake and I am going to put the cake right up here under the sad tooth. Why do you think the cake would make the tooth unhappy? Melina?"

"Cavities," Melina replied.

"What might cause a cavity?" Mrs. Warner asked.

"Sweet things," Melina said.

"Yes. Cavities can be caused by eating too many sweet things, but what makes them sweet?"

"I know. It's sugar!" Melina exclaimed.

"Very good," Mrs. Warner said. "You put sugar in things to make them sweet. Now let's go back to our pictures to see if they should go under the happy face or sad face. JuRelle, you do one for us."

JuRelle reached out, picked up a picture, and said, "tomatoes."

"A complete sentence, please."

"Tomatoes are healthy for your teeth."

"Very good, JuRelle. I like that word healthy. Okay, Preston?"

"Strawberries are good for your teeth."

"Right. A strawberry is a fruit and is does have some sugar in it, but if you are going to eat the natural sugar in it we know that is better than when you put sugar into foods to make them sweet like candy and cake."

Mrs. Warner continued to have the students classify the pictures and place them on the felt board. "Now," she asked. "How many things do we have that are not good for your teeth?" The children counted aloud, one through seven.

"And how many things do we have that are good for your teeth?" The children counted again, one through eight.

"So, which food do we have the most of?"

"Healthy food," the children replied.

"Good. Now I want everyone to think. When we go over to our mural on the floor you are going to draw either one healthy thing or one unhealthy thing."

"I'm going to draw a strawberry," Preston said.

"And where are you going to draw it? Under healthy things or unhealthy things?"

"Healthy."

"Yes, Preston," Mrs. Warner said. "You are going to draw your strawberry under healthy and after you draw it, write the word of the food right under your drawing."

Mrs. Warner then sat on the floor next the the children and monitored their progress with a focus on an inventive spelling exercise that allowed her to diagnose their progress on writing and their use of phonetics. These observations gave her information for future, individualized instruction. She was also able to review with them their work in this integrated learning experience, which included numbers, sets, language development, health, communication skills, writing, and art.

JOHN LOCKE, 1632–1704

As with his contemporaries, John Locke struggled with the theory of innate ideas. Descartes modified it, Bacon developed inductive reasoning thereby questioning the theory, and John Locke offered the idea of the *tabula rasa* ("blank slate"), which suggested there were no innate ideas in the mind. The concept of the tabula rasa suggests that at birth the mind is a clear slate, a white paper, on which the data of experience are impressed (Gutek, 1988).

This notion of the tabula rasa was the starting point for Locke's work. As mentioned earlier, this era was one in which the material world was being scientifically investigated. Astronomers told us about the heavens and physicists such as Isaac Newton told us about the nature of matter and space. Being a philosopher, Locke was also caught up with these issues, but he told us that matter lacks qualities until human sense perceptions put them there (Feibleman, 1973). As you are about to see, Locke's preoccupation with acquiring knowledge through sensory perception established him as the most influential champion of liberalism in the 18th century (Runes, 1963).

Life and Times

Locke was born at Wrington, Somerset, England in 1632. Because his mother died when he was quite young, the task of educating Locke was left to his father, a puritan who believed in the virtue of hard work. His father's values and his relatively poor health and lack of stamina may have contributed to his focus on learning and knowledge. Thanks to the fact that Locke's father practiced law and owned a little land, the youth, at age 14, was enrolled at the Westminister School, which at that time was considered one of England's great public schools.

During these years, Locke studied classical languages but was not enamored of the "lean" curriculum, which established classical literature as the source of knowledge. In line with this thinking, he also found it difficult to accept Scholastic philosophy and enjoyed the pursuit of various schools of thought. It is believed that Descartes, who was approaching the end of his days at this time, was one of the first philosophers Locke enjoyed because it showed him viable alternatives to the classicists or Schoolmen (Edwards, 1967).

Eventually, Locke earned both a bachelor's and a master's degree at Oxford University and thrived in the academic environment. He remained in Oxford for the next 30 years and, in 1660, became a lecturer in Greek rhetoric and moral philosophy. His interests also included the somewhat embryonic profession of physician, and Locke eventually was invited to be a member of the prestigious British Royal Society—the most respected scientific organization in England.

You are undoubtedly familiar with Locke's influence on the writings and political philosophy of Thomas Jefferson. Although we will focus primarily on Locke's epistemological work, it is important to note that, through his association with Lord Anthony Ashley Cooper (who eventually became Lord Chancellor of England), Locke was taken with the place of philosophy in the world of politics. Additionally, Cooper was considered to be a "liberal," and he and his cronies, including Locke, were in a difficult position with their constant opposition to King Charles II and King James II. Therefore, Locke fled to Holland—a significant event in his life because it finally gave him the time to organize, write, and present his thoughts to the world.

Eventually, Locke returned to England to serve as Commissioner of Appeals during the reign of William and Mary, who themselves had come to England from Holland. He remained in their service until 1700, when he retired and spent his four remaining years quietly. Locke considered himself a "sober" man, and the story is told that when offered an appointment as minister of the court to Berlin, he declined because hard drinking was indispensable to a minister at that court and he was the "soberest man in the kingdom" and could not be of any use there.

Locke did not marry, but for the better part of a dozen or so years he lived at the home of Lady Damaris Masham, who said of him the day he died in 1704, "His death was like his life, truly pious, yet natural, easy and unaffected."

*There is nothing in the mind ex-
cept what was first in the senses.*

John Locke

Philosophical Contributions

The rejection of the theory of innate ideas provided the rationale for Locke's concept of tabula rasa and sets the stage for his views on how we learn. For Locke, all knowledge comes from experience through our senses. The mind is at birth a clean sheet, and sense experience writes on it in a thousand ways, until sensation begets memory and memory begets ideas. All this seems to lead to the startling conclusion that since only material things can effect our senses, we know nothing but matter and must accept a materialistic philosophy. If sensations are the stuff of thought, matter must be the material of the mind (Durant, 1953).

Locke's concern with how we know—which, as we have seen also preoccupied Descartes and Bacon—was a further move away from ancient and medieval thought. He too believed that truth could be determined through reason but also believed that reason was founded on human sensation followed by reflection. This theory was expressed in what many consider to be Locke's most significant philosophical work, *An Essay Concerning Human Understanding.* This essay has been described as a journey out of the ludicrous complications of the history of philosophy to the sweet simplicity of thought as a natural activity (Richetti, 1983).

This essay undoubtedly provided the foundation for empiricism. For the empiricist, sensory experience is the only source of knowledge about which we can be sure. The epistemological question of how we know is answered through our senses. We know because we see things, touch things, hear things, smell things, and taste things.

Locke suggested the most common way we experience things is through our sight, which reinforced his emphasis on *how* we experience something as opposed to *what* we actually experience. His call for an acute awareness of experience and his concentration on how ideas or knowledge are gained by the mind are considered to be major philosophical contributions (Ozmon, 1990).

Locke himself was much more reserved in assessing the value of his work. Early in the chapter you learned that Bacon identified impediments to truth or knowledge that he called *Idols*. Bacon's influence on Locke is shown in his discussions on impediments, which he referred to as rubbish. He saw himself as "cleaning ground alittle and removing some of the rubbish that lies in the way to knowledge" (Richetti, 1983, p. 50).

Locke's method for "removing the rubbish" was to experience (through the senses) the physical world first and then develop ideas. Unlike Plato, he did not believe that innate ideas were already in our minds or that truth and knowledge were preexisting and dormant within our souls. The beginnings of knowledge were to be found by empirically determining the primary qualities of objects in the concrete world. For Locke, primary qualities are those properties or characteristics that are essential to the very existence of the object. They are physical and they are measurable and so are observable. Therefore, the way we gain knowledge is to experience what an object *appears* to be. Because appearance may not necessarily equate to absolute truth or substance, Locke believed it was impossible to obtain absolute knowledge and that we have to settle for what is "probably so."

Nevertheless, Locke believed (empirical) knowledge to be valid for "the notice we have of our senses . . . deserves the name of knowledge; for I think nobody can, in earnest, be skeptical, as to be uncertain of the existence of those things which he sees and feels" (Bronstein, Krikorian, and Wiener, 1955, p. 288).

A drop of water has the tastes of the water of the seven seas: there is no need to experience all the ways of worldly life. The reflections of the moon on one thousand rivers are from the same moon: the mind must be full of light.

Hung Tzu-ch'eng

Exericse 4.7

It is often argued that knowledge through our senses is limited because we cannot experience all the objects of a physical world. After rereading the quotation from Hung Tzu-ch'eng, briefly describe how his words address that concern. Then compare your response to the feedback at the end of the chapter.

From *An Essay Concerning Human Understanding, Vol. 1, Locke*

The way shown how we come by any knowledge, sufficient to prove it not innate.—It is an established opinion amongst some men, that there are in the understanding certain innate principles; some primary notions, characters, as it were stamped upon the mind of man, which the soul receives in its very first being, and brings into the world with it. It would be sufficient to convince unprejudiced readers of the falseness of this supposition, if I should only show (as I hope I shall in the following parts of this discourse) how men, barely by the use of their natural faculties, may attain to all the knowledge they have, without the help of any innate impressions; and may arrive at certainty, without any such original notions or principles. For I imagine anyone will easily grant, that it would be impertinent to suppose the ideas of colours innate in a creature to whom God hath given sight, and a power to receive them by the eyes from external objects: and no less unreasonable would it be to attribute several truths to the impressions of nature and innate characters, when we may observe in ourselves faculties fit to attain as easy and certain knowledge of them as if they were originally imprinted on the mind.

But because a man is not permitted without censure to follow his own thoughts in the search of truth, when they lead him ever so little out of the common road, I shall set down the reasons that made me doubt of the truth of that opinion, as an excuse for my mistake, if I be in one; which I leave to be considered by those who, with me, dispose themselves to embrace truth wherever they find it.

Locke, J. *An essay on human understanding.* Annotated by A. C. Fraser (1959). New York: Dover Publications, Inc., pp. 37–38. Reprinted with permission of Dover Publications, Inc.

Locke in the Classroom

Locke believed that philosophy should be of practical use. As you have seen, his work was based on the importance of physically experiencing the material world in an effort to acquire useful information. In this way, he established a connection between consciousness and knowledge (Ayers, 1991). This practical focus is clearly reflected in Locke's political philosophical writings regarding individuals and society and in his doctrines regarding life, liberty, and property.

Although Locke may have been politically liberal, his views on who should be educated were narrow and in line with the times. Nevertheless, unlike many of his predecessors, he did address specific educational concerns in his work *Some Thoughts Concerning Education,* which consisted of a number of letters he wrote to a friend anxious about his son's education. In these letters, Locke discussed such things as individual aptitude, health, and character and the need for play. More specifically, he emphasized the use of example and practice and the need to organize learning in a slow and cumulative fashion. Many of these thoughts appeared as principles of learning, ten of which are as follows (Yolton, 1971):

1. General methods and rules are more of a concern than subject matter and curriculum.
2. Virtue is a more important aim of education than specific instruction in particular subjects.
3. The learning of a method of study is of greater value than factual knowledge.
4. Large (educational) classes do not allow for constant attention and particular application to every single student.
5. The right way to teach children specific subjects is to give them a liking to what you propose them to learn.
6. Regarding specific learning, give the students one simple idea, and see that they take it right, and perfectly comprehend it before going any farther, and then add some other simple idea that lies next in the way toward the objective.
7. Just as there is an order of idea acquisition, there should be an interconnection of subject matter.
8. What is taught should not be presented as a task or burden. If learning is recreational, it is motivational.
9. The process of learning is helped when teachers teach the students how to gain mastery over themselves.
10. Learning is not to be permissive, but the guides and controls ought to be child centered; they ought to arise from the child's own character and motivational structure, subtly manipulated by the teacher.

As you could well predict at this point, Locke believed in learning by doing and promoting learning through a sensory interaction with the environment. Let's look at how this process works in the classroom.

Scenario 4.3

Ms. Jenny Newhall, a first-grade teacher at Monclair Elementary School, asked her students, who were grouped at tables, to come toward the board and sit on the floor in such a way that everyone would be able to see the displayed materials. After she praised the students for their orderly behavior, she began her lesson.

"Who can tell me what we have been talking about this week. It's just one word. Adam?"

"Gas," Adam replied.

"That's good but not the one I am looking for. How about something bigger than gas?"

"Matter," Adam said.

"Matter! Okay," Ms. Newhall responded. "We're talking about matter. Now, two things tell us something is matter. Do you remember one of them, Annie?"

"Weight."

"Good, Annie. It has to have weight. Does that mean 'wait, don't talk anymore?'" (Nay response from the class.) "What does it mean, Nancy?"

"It means it weighs something," Nancy said.

"Right," Ms. Newhall said. "You could put it on a scale and see if it is heavy or light. What else does matter have to have? It has to have weight or . . .?"

"Take up space," Paul answered.

"Yes, take up space. Do we take up space?" (Class responds yes.)

"So, are we matter?" Ms. Newhall asked. (Class responds yes.)

"Does the chair at your desk take up space?" she continued. (Class responds yes.)

"And does your desk have weight? Does it weigh something?" (Class responds yes.)

"Then is it matter?" (Class responds yes.)

"Ok! Now we said there are three kinds of matter. Who can name me one of those three kinds?"

"A solid," Stephen said.

"Right. A solid is one. Who can name another?" Ms. Newhall asked.

"A liquid," Markail added.

"Good, Markail, and now we have one more? Megan?"

"Gas," Megan responded.

"Right. A gas. You boys and girls are really doing a good job. We have solids, liquids and gases. What did we say those things were made up of? Remember those two big words that we learned? (Pause.) Well, everything is made up of tiny little things. What are those things called, Kelly?"

"Atoms."

"Atoms. That's right, Kelly. And what happens to atoms when they don't like being alone? What do they do or what do they make, Casey?"

"Mickey Mouse heads?" Casey replied.

"Yes, Casey, you remember the shape but what do we call it?"

"A molecule," Casey answered.

"That's a good job, Casey, because molecule is a big word," Ms. Newhall said. She then continued her review by having the children demonstrate a water molecule with plastic balls; identify molecular drawings of a solid, liquid, and gas; and arrange definitions of the three under their labels on the board.

Ms. Newhall concluded by saying, "Okay, we have had a quick review and now it is time to do our experiments. Just turn around while I walk over to one of the tables. Today I am going to do the experiments but tomorrow you will do them yourselves."

Ms. Newhall then sat down at the table and said, "First of all, when we learn to be scientists, what did I say we have to use better than anything else? Sean?"

"Our eyes."

"Right, Sean, and we have been practicing using our eyes, haven't we. Now (pointing to the table next to her, on which she had placed some water cups) I would like you to raise your hand and tell me what you see."

"Water," Myron observed.

"Okay, water. What else do you see, Kara?"

"I see cups."

"You see cups. How about you, Rebecca?"

"They are about the same height."

"Okay, John?"

"One has a top like this." (John spreads his arms open.)

"You mean one has a top that is wide and the other is narrow?" Ms. Newhall inquired.

"Yes," John responded.

"Okay, good for you. Sharon?"

"You can see little white things."

"Yes you can and what do you see, Julie?"

"You can see a reflection in the water and you can see right through it," Julie said.

"Exactly. Good observation, Julie. You can see a reflection from the water. How about you, Jeremy?"

"It takes the same shape the cup has," Jeremy said.

"Good. Good! It takes the same shape as this cup. One more thing, Janine?"

"One looks like one is higher than the other."

"Okay. Now," Ms. Newhall said after retrieving a small box and placing it on the table, "what is in this box I have just placed on the table?"

"Baking soda," Mary said.

"Yes, and what do we do with baking soda, Mary?"

"Brush our teeth and get other things clean."

"Right and what room do we usually see it in?"

"The kitchen."

"Yes because we use it to bake. Now then, what does baking soda look like, Rayron?"

"It's white."

"What else, Bobby?"

"It looks like flour," Bobby added.

"Anything else?" Ms. Newhall asked.

"It looks like salt," Jordan said.

"One more, Patty," Ms. Newhall urged.

"It looks like snow."

"Good job, everybody. Now, what do you think is going to happen if I put a spoonful of this baking soda into the water? (Pause.) Kim?"

"I think the water will turn white."

"You think it will turn white. All right, that is one idea. Toni, do you have another idea?"

"I think it is going to settle."

"Okay. What does settle mean, Toni?"

"It means it will settle in the water."

"So where does it go?" Ms. Newhall prompted.

"It goes to the bottom," Toni answered.

"Good, Toni. Anything else, Jeffrey?"

"Bubbles."

"Bubbles maybe. Anything else?"

"It is going to turn wet," Annie said.

"What is going to turn wet?" Ms. Newhall inquired.

"The white stuff," Annie responded.

"Okay. Now, shall we try it and see what happens? (Yes response from the enthusiastic children.) And what part of your body are you going to use for me?"

"Eyes," the children answered.

"Good. Now I am going to take a teaspoon of the baking soda and drop it into the water. Watch carefully. Okay, here we go. (Pause.) Now, what did we see? Patty?"

"Bubbles."

"Yes, we saw some bubbles just like we said. What else did we see, Stephen?"

"It settled."

"Yes, it settled just like Toni said. What else happened? (Pause and no response from the children.) Well, when I first put the baking soda in the water, do you remember what it looked like?"

"It looked dark white," Adam said.

Ms. Newhall held up the cup and said, "Does it still look that way?"

"No," the class responded.

"Okay. Now, if I put the baking soda in the other cup, what do you think will happen?"

"The same thing," a number of children said.

"You mean there are going to be bubbles and dark white color and then the baking soda will settle?"

"Yes," the children answered. Ms. Newhall dropped a teaspoon of baking soda into the second cup and the children erupted into laughter when, in fact, they observed something totally different. "What happened?" Ms. Newhall asked, raising her voice in order to be heard.

"It exploded!" Adam answered.

"What does *explode* mean, Adam?"

"It overflowed the cup."

"But you all told me the same thing would happen. Now you need to put on your thinking caps. Why do you think this one settled out and the other one overflowed? What was different, Markail?"

"You tricked us! You put a chemical in it."

"You're so clever, Markail. Okay, come up here with your partners from Table A and just smell the two cups." Ms. Newhall then provided an opportunity for all the children in the class to smell the cups.

"Now," she continued, "raise your hand if you know what I did."

"You put vinegar in the one that overflowed," Mark observed.

"Right, it was vinegar and I did that to trick you on purpose. You know that I told you that you have to use your eyes but that is only one thing you should use. We have been learning about liquid, solid and gas but often your eyes cannot see a gas. So, what else do we use other than eyes?"

"Your brain," Markail said.

"Yes, that's true, but what gave you the clue about the vinegar, Markail?"

"My nose."

"Yes, so you had to use your eyes and your nose, and we need to learn that you have to use more than your eyes when you are a scientist. Now let's try two more experiments that involve a liquid, solid or gas."

As you know from your reading, Locke believed the most common use of the senses was sight, and this lesson clearly emphasizes his point. However, and equally important, Ms. Newhall is clearly showing that a reliance on a single "sense" may be insufficient in terms of acquiring knowledge empirically. In any event, the students are actively engaged in the exploration of their environment, and Ms. Newhall's implementation of Locke's methodolgy is providing an opportunity to utilize the senses in answering the question "How do we know?"

Exercise 4.8

Examine the following statements to determine if they are consistent (c) or inconsistent (i) with the philosophy of Locke. Then check your responses against those at the end of the chapter.

_____ 1. Knowledge is acquired through experience.
_____ 2. The concept of tabula rasa is consistent with Plato's theory of innate ideas.
_____ 3. What we know should be more of a concern than how we know it.
_____ 4. Intuition is more reliable than empiricism.
_____ 5. Learning through the senses enables us to acquire absolute knowledge.

Exercise 4.9

Read the following scenario and briefly describe how Locke's empirical methodology was employed in the science lesson. Then compare your response to the one at the end of the chapter.

Ms. Betsy Pechonick, a first-grade intern at Ponte Vedra Palm Valley Elementary School, sat in a chair and asked her students to gather around her on the floor so she could read them *The Tiny Seed* by Eric Carle. On concluding the story she asked, "What do flowers need in order to grow?"

"Sun," John said.

"Water," Ryan said.

"A bunch of dirt," Joshua added

"All good answers," Ms. Pechonick said with a smile. "Anything else?"

"Need some fertilizer," Jan said.

"Gotta have air," Daniel replied.

"And lots of love and care," Keith added.

"That's great, everyone. Now Ryan said water so let's talk about that a little bit. How does the water actually get to the flower? (Pause.) Melissa?"

With permission. Ponte Vedra Palm Valley Elementary School, Ponte Vedra Beach, Florida. In association with Mrs. Julie Clairmont, Directing Teacher. Mr. Michael Parrish, Principal.

"Well, the rain comes down."

"You're right but how does the plant get the rain?"

"Through the soil?" Melissa asked.

"Yes, but how does it get from the soil into the plant?" Ms. Pechonick inquired.

"Oh, through the roots," Melissa answered.

"Great job, Melissa." Ms. Pechonick then instructed the students to return to their tables, on which she had placed a stalk of celery sitting in a glass of red-colored water, a worksheet, and some crayons. Since the children had made prior observations of the celery, she then told them to look at the experiment and discuss among themselves what had happened. She finally informed them that she would know when they were ready when they became quiet.

After a few minutes, Ms. Pechonick said, "I would like one person from the group to stand and tell us what you talked about . . . what happened. Okay, red table no. 2?"

"It's red on the bottom and it is going up," Keith said speaking for table no. 2.

"What's going up?" (No response.)

"Then," Ms. Pechonick directed, "look at the water in the glass and think about the measurements you took yesterday. What do you think?"

"There's less water in the glass," Keith responded.

"Then what happened?" Ms. Pechonick urged.

"It took the water in it."

"Look at the bottom. How did you think that happened? Blue table, please?"

"It went up the holes," John said, "which I think are like tunnels for the water to go up."

"Fine, John." Ms. Pechonick then went to the blue table and cut off the tip of the celery that had been in the water and split it open.

"What do you see?" she asked.

"It's red," the children at the blue table answered.

"What do you think is happening? Red table was very close," Ms. Pechonick added.

"It's sucking up the water," Sarah said.

"All of it?"

"Some of it."

"So what is going to happen?" Ms. Pechonick asked.

"It's going to turn red," Sarah said.

"Specific parts please?"

"The stem and then maybe the leaves," Sarah added.

"Then what do you think will happen?"

"I think all the water will be gone," Sarah replied.

"Could be," Ms. Pechonick said. "What I want you to do now is to take your worksheet and draw an 'after' picture, meaning I want you to draw what you think the celery is going to look like tomorrow. At that time, we will look at your drawings and the celery in the glass and see what actually happened."

Ms. Pechonick spent the remainder of the period moving from table to table and facilitating the observation/coloring exercise.

SUMMARY

As you have read in this chapter, the challenge to the ancient philosophers came in differing ways. Descartes focused on the problem of certain knowledge and was the first to have a problem with the theory of innate ideas. His method involved the need to certify knowledge and then use it as a foundation for new knowledge. But he fell into disfavor with the church, for he focused on human reason rather than religious faith as the only dependable key to knowledge of the universe. Put another way, human reason forces the natural universe to reveal itself (Davidson, 1957). Descartes' emphasis on certainty as opposed to intuition also provided a foundation for the work of Bacon and Locke.

Like Descartes, Bacon did not consider himself irreligious, for he believed that ultimate knowledge resided with God, who he referred to as a "code maker." For Bacon, it was the nature of the best codes (knowledge/truth) to resist all explication and indeed suggested misleading meanings until they were broken (Briggs, 1989). Bacon generated inductive reasoning as the method for "deciphering" the codes and believed that the acquisition of knowledge through this approach would lead to a better world in which to live. In espousing this belief, he helped set the stage for the modern technological conquest of nature as a means of prolonging and improving lives (Lampert, 1993).

Locke also championed scientific knowledge but did not limit himself to that discipline, because he believed that scientific knowledge was general knowledge (Schouls, 1992). Although his primary position—which established sensory experience as the beginning step in the acquisition of knowledge—involved the physical world, Locke addressed the political world as well as the world of human behavior. Certainly his notion that (based on the idea of the tabula rasa) morality is learned behavior did not endear him to his contemporaries.

When looking for commonalities in the contributions of Descartes, Bacon, and Locke, we find two distinctive points that challenged the ancient philosophers. The first was their effort to look for certainty rather than accept received opinion. The second was their primary focus on how we learn, thereby making the method of acquiring knowledge, or certainty, or truth the starting point of philosophy. Now began the great game of epistemology, which in Leibniz, Berkeley, Hume, and Kant waxed into A Three Hundred Years' War that at once stimulated and devastated modern philosophy (Durant, 1953).

Questions for Discussion

1. After thinking of something you believe to be certain, what would be your rationale for its certainty?

2. Analyze the four steps of Descartes' "logic," presented on page 103. What would you identify as strengths or weaknesses of his method as compared to Aristotle's "logic"?

3. In the passage on pages 104–105, how does Descartes go about destroying all his former opinions in light of his position that destroying these opinions is impossible?

4. How did Descartes "challenge" the Ancients?
5. How does Bacon's view of reality differ from Plato's view of reality?
6. What was Bacon's possible agenda or purpose for generating his discussion of the Four Idols?
7. What behaviors of teachers and/or students in the scenarios of this chapter illustrate the reasoning processes of Bacon and Aristotle?
8. Having read the selected aphorisms on pages 113–114, how would you list and describe the sequence of steps in Bacon's method of inductive reasoning?
9. How did Locke's work contribute to the shifting emphasis, during his era, from metaphysics to epistemology?
10. What did Locke contribute that allows many contemporary commentators to refer to him as the founder of empiricism?
11. What was Locke referring to when he used the term *rubbish?*
12. How does the point of view presented in the excerpt on pages 122–123 reflect Locke's epistemology?

Suggested Field Laboratory Activities

1. Select a topic or objective in a text or teachers guide that is founded on an alleged factual statement. Then, generate some ways that you might validate or reject that statement.
2. Design a lesson plan that incorporates Descartes' rules 10, 11, and 12 as presented on page 106.
3. Given the opportunity, implement the preceding lesson plan, audio tape it, and analyze it to determine whether the desired cognitive behaviors of rules 10, 11, and 12 were undertaken by the students.
4. Review a number of teacher lesson plans and curriculum guides and identify examples of inductive reasoning employed as procedures or strategies.
5. Select a concept and develop a lesson plan that employs the steps found in Bacon's method of inductive reasoning.
6. Given the opportunity, have a teacher assist you in planning an appropriate topic to be taught and develop and implement a lesson that employs inductive reasoning.
7. Commentators often have difficulty placing Locke in a philosophical camp such as realism or progressivism. Taking into consideration some of the principles that appear on page 123, identify those employed in your setting and determine the philosophical camp in which they would most appropriately be situated.
8. Review a number of the activities being undertaken in your setting and determine whether you believe them to be tasks, recreational, or a combination of both.
9. Review a number of teacher lesson plans, guides, and so on and identify those that employ aspects of empiricism.
10. Given the opportunity, plan and implement a lesson that utilizes Locke's empirical method.

Exercise Feedback

Exercise 4.1

You could interpret Marie Curie's words to the effect that one should not be shackled by what has transpired in the past but should seek new knowledge or experience. You might add that there is more to be done than simply rework what already exists. A purpose of philosophy is to seek knowledge and not merely replicate it.

Exercise 4.2

1. (c)   Consistent. We establish something that is certain and use it as a base on which to build new knowledge.

2. (i)   Inconsistent. Descartes wants to certify truth; not rework it.

3. (i)   Inconsistent. Descartes' primary concern was with epistemology, not metaphysics.

4. (c)   Consistent.

5. (c)   Philosophically consistent, but Descartes questioned intuition as the basis for "certain" knowledge.

Exercise 4.3

As you know from reading Chapter 1, a classical educator adheres to the idea that a body of absolute and predetermined knowledge exists. When implemented in such a classroom today, Descartes' methodology could reaffirm things that are believed to be true, but his approach could also contradict things held to be true.

Exercise 4.4

Helen Keller's words could lend themselves to Bacon's position that, during the time in which he lived, people took for granted or merely accepted prevailing thoughts or conditions. "Ignorance and insensibility" had no place in Bacon's thoughts, for he believed the constant search for practical knowledge would move humankind away from the darkness and toward a better life. He crusaded against the "blindness" of the mind.

Exercise 4.5

1. (c)   Consistent. This is what Bacon was referring to when he said that "knowledge is power."

2. (i)   Inconsistent. Inductive reasoning may in fact validate existing truth but also has the potential to arrive at new conclusions.

3. (c)   Consistent.

4. (i)   Inconsistent. Bacon believed preconceived points of view created a certain "comfort zone" and were rarely reconsidered.

5. (c)   Consistent. Bacon viewed *concrete* to be synonymous with *practical* and therefore applicable to the human condition.

Exercise 4.6

Through this highly integrated learning experience, Mrs. Warner provides a number of activities that allow the students to arrive at conclusions. The most obvious is that the children are interacting, in her learning center, with examples of food and are arriving at conclusions with regard to "healthy teeth." These conclusions are also being facilitated by specifics in the science and art learning centers.

Exercise 4.7

This quotation suggests that we do not have to taste the water of all the seven seas in order to "experience" the taste of water. Additionally, to observe the reflection of the moon on one river would be sufficient in terms of "experiencing" that phenomenon. Limited observations do not necessarily lessen the acquisition of general knowledge.

Exercise 4.8

1. (c)   Consistent. This statement represents the central theme of Locke's work.

2. (i)   Inconsistent. This expression means a "clean slate," which negates the idea of innate knowledge.

3. (i)   Inconsistent. Locke was a philosopher who was shifting the philosophical focus from the *what* (metaphysics) to the *how* (epistemology).

4. (i)   Inconsistent. Empirical knowledge, for Locke, is more reliable because it is observable.

5. (i)   Inconsistent. For Locke, absolute knowledge is not obtainable.

Exercise 4.9

In Ms. Pechonik's class, the students are employing their sense of sight and, without knowing the term, are learning about capillary effect. By observing, over a period of a few days, the water level in the glass and the red dye traveling up the veins in the celery, the students are experiencing how plants obtain water from the soil.

CHAPTER FIVE

KNOWLEDGE AND THE SELF: ROUSSEAU AND KANT

After completing Chapter 5, you should be able to accomplish the following objectives:

1. You will become familiar with Jean-Jacques Rousseau's view of the nature and educational needs of the individual by identifying statements as being consistent or inconsistent with his philosophy.

2. You will increase your awareness of Rousseau's philosophy by briefly discussing two ways his methods are employed in the classroom in an actual teaching scenario.

3. You will become familiar with the philosophical positions of Immanuel Kant by identifying statements as being consistent or inconsistent with his philosophy.

4. You will increase your knowledge of Kant's focus on moral excellence by briefly discussing the nature of his categorical imperatives.

As we saw in the last chapter, the Enlightenment was characterized not only by challenges to existing intellectual traditions but also by an interest in alternative methods of acquiring knowledge. These developments have practical implications for contemporary classrooms. Based on the philosophical contributions of Descartes, Bacon, and Locke, teachers can provide classroom experiences that allow students to gain new knowledge by building on previous knowledge, by using inductive reasoning, and by employing empiricism.

In Chapter 5, you will meet two other philosophers who were concerned with the nature of knowledge and the way we learn but who also believed that formal philosophizing ought to be based on human needs rather than reflecting intellectual curiosity alone. These two philosophers are Jean-Jacques Rousseau and Immanuel Kant.

Rousseau, like Bacon, believed in the need to improve social conditions. Bacon viewed science as the mechanism that would achieve this goal. For Rousseau, the key was to be found in the individual, whose morality was based on a combination of human goodness and knowledge acquired through practical interaction with the natural world. He assumed that these knowledgeable, mature individuals would then have a positive impact on society. Because of

Rousseau's passionate advocacy of this theory, Kant saw him as the Newton of the moral world (Gay, 1966). Additionally, Rousseau's work on the nature of the individual provided the foundation for one of Kant's major positions—the idea that we should be concerned not so much with what people appear to be but with what they ought to be.

Kant's life spanned much of the 18th century, and he is often referred to as one of the last notable philosophers of the Enlightenment. In part, this is attributed to the fact that he attempted to synthesize much of what had come before him. Among other things, Kant's philosophy includes the a priori postulate of Aristotle, with specific regard to morality; the rationality of Descartes; the empiricism of Locke; and the naturalism of Rousseau. As you will see, Kant devoted his life to the philosophical quest for moral excellence, which he believed could be attained through a synthesis of goodwill, practical reason, and experience.

JEAN-JACQUES ROUSSEAU, 1712–1778

Locke's idea of the tabula rasa challenged the theory of a predetermined knowledge base in the individual at birth. As we have seen, he believed that sensory experience "wrote on the clean slate." His position, therefore, implies a certain neutrality regarding human nature. Rousseau's approach was not neutral, because he began with the proposition that human beings are individually good from the outset. Whereas Locke answered the epistemological question "How do we know?" by emphasizing sense experience, Rousseau began with his metaphysical position ("What is real?") that individual goodness is real, then moved on to epistemological considerations. Here we find the value of his work in terms of classroom applications, for Rousseau believed that education should be founded on a personal exploration of and contact with nature, people, and things.

Rousseau laid bare the defects and abuses of the society and education of his time, demanding reforms in the direction of truth and simplicity (Davidson, 1971). His rejection of many religious and secular fundamentals resulted in his banishment from France and in a feeling of persecution that plagued him throughout his life.

Life and Times

Rousseau was born in 1712 in Geneva, Switzerland, and was descended from a line of clock makers. However, his father was not a disciplined man and avoided the rigorous world of the artisan. Because his mother died from complications in giving birth to him, the task of raising Rousseau was left to his aunt and wandering father. Although Rousseau's early years appear to have been bleak and lacked the formal educational experiences that Descartes, Bacon, and Locke had, his father not only taught him to read but was wise enough to promote reading as a wonderful, mind-expanding experience. Fortunately, Rousseau's mother had accumulated a substantial number of romance and adventure books, which promoted his desire to read and helped whet his appetite for exploring his world through words.

*Education protects people from
the corruptions of civilization.*

Jean-Jacques Rousseau

During Rousseau's adolescent years, a number of incidents took place that had a major impact on his life. The first is that, at the age of ten, he was abandoned by his father, who fled from Switzerland as a result of fights and other conflicts. Rousseau was apprenticed to a relative who was an engraver, but he found this life tedious and restrictive, and so he struck out on his own when he was about 16. In this period he received some formal education through the use of tutors or paid teachers as opposed to institutions of learning. However, this experience was cut short when Rousseau's teachers allegedly stamped him as a thief, and, like his father, he ended up with a peripatetic lifestyle.

Though Rousseau's life could be characterized as restless, he did have some anchors. He never married but had significant relationships with a number of women. The first was Mme. de Warens, who lived in Savoy and provided an environment of friendship and security. During this time, Rousseau became committed to self-education, engaging in more formal study of Latin and other subjects. He also converted to Catholicism, although he eventually returned to his Protestant roots.

Rousseau then set out to do something with himself. One of his earliest positions was as a tutor in Lyons, France, in 1740. This effort was most likely bittersweet, in that his tenure as a teacher was brief. However, the whole notion of education captivated Rousseau. His influence became powerful beyond measure; he was one of the first, with fiery rhetoric, to make the subject of education a burning question, underscoring its connection with almost every aspect of human welfare (Davidson, 1957).

Rousseau's next venture, in Paris, took him into the world of music. Again, something came from nothing. Apparently, Rousseau's love of music did little to foster success in this field, but it did allow him to meet many Parisian "movers and shakers" who assisted him in various ways over the years. One such acquaintance was instrumental in securing a position for Rousseau as a secretary to the French ambassador at Venice.

In 1745, at the age of 33, Rousseau began living with Thérèse Le Vasseur, a servant who was considered kind, able, and understanding. Although there were occasional separations, Rousseau spent most of his life with this woman, who may have had as many as five children by various fathers.

During these years, Rousseau spent much of his time as an "amusement" for the well-to-do, since he alternated between the roles of intellectual and nonconformist. His trademark Bohemian fur hat, often shown in many illustrations, was a way of setting himself apart from his upper-class companions. Rousseau saw in the world around him a superficial society and a weakening of human relationships, and he began to express these views with the written word.

In 1749, he entered an essay in a contest sponsored by the Dijon Academy in France. The essay argued that human beings are by nature good and that if they become bad, it is due to the influence of corrupt social institutions. He won the contest, which undoubtedly provided motivation for pursuing the literary career that took off with the publication of the *Discourse on the Sciences and the Arts* in 1750. However, like other philosophers you have encountered in earlier chapters, Rousseau alienated significant and powerful groups. Thus, he returned to Geneva in 1756 to continue his writing. But religious and political controversy followed him, and so he traveled to Prussia in 1762 and then moved to England in 1765.

Le Vasseur accompanied Rousseau throughout these years and in England lived quietly with him and his dog at the home of the English philosopher David Hume. The philosophers did not get along very well; in 1767 Rousseau and his companion returned to France, where he wandered around for a number of years before settling again in Paris. As had been the case often in his life, Rousseau's last year was spent living off the generosity and hospitality of a nobleman. Le Vasseur remained with him but eventually married the nobleman's gardener.

Due to the suddenness of his death on July 2, 1778, there was speculation that Rousseau may have committed suicide. But the more commonly accepted explanation was that he died of a cerebral hemorrhage. This event brought to an end 66 years of little in the way of permanent family, home, or even country, which might be considered ironic in that a cornerstone of Rousseau's philosophy was on the need to search for the good life. This life, by the standards of his day, apparently eluded him.

Philosophical Contributions

Rousseau, as you now know, experienced the smallness of Geneva, negative experiences with teachers, and the corruption of the French nation-state. These perceptions, among others, supplied the bedrock for his philosophy, by convincing him of the need for simplicity, personalized education, and a just society founded on individual responsibility.

Rousseau based his work on two assumptions. The first assumption is that all humans beings are born innocent and are fundamentally good. If the people we see around us are corrupt, society is responsible for their corruption. Therefore, children should be educated as far away from society as possible (Cranston, 1991). The second assumption is an outgrowth of Locke's thinking, in that Rousseau believed that all knowledge reaches the mind through the senses. Where he differs from Locke is in his belief that education should be (as we say today) individualized, with a focus on the acquisition of knowledge and understanding through personal experience. For Rousseau, this experience involves children's direct interaction with nature. This position, put forth in his classic work *Émile*, reveals Rousseau's tendency to appreciate childhood for its own sake rather than viewing it as a training period for future adults (France, 1987).

Rousseau championed experiential learning, for he believed that if we are to grow in the direction of goodness, we must be in harmony with and aware of the needs of nature. He moved away from Locke, asserting that this is not accomplished solely through the empirical examination of facts. Although the tabula rasa idea influenced Rousseau, he believed that the world was one of verifiable constants, or order, established through the intelligence of a Supreme Being. He further believed that this knowledge was observable and need not be limited to knowledge acquired through reason. Unlike those who considered human reason capable of finding answers to the important questions about the nature of the universe, Rousseau pointed to the limits of the human intellect (Viroli, 1988). He also believed that intuition, sensation, and imagination could allow people to establish conceptual relationships facilitating an intellectual awareness of nature.

As you can readily see, Rousseau was a proponent of naturalism, for he believed that knowledge was derived from nature, that reality was determined by collecting information through the senses and validated by constructing relationships, and that human beings learned gradually and constantly throughout their lives. When undertaken in a positive and controlled fashion, this process benefited both the individual and society. He thought that understanding nature and living in harmony with it allow one to attain satisfaction with self, which was, for him, the key to happiness.

As for society, in his scheme of things, Rousseau would have good and happy and moral individuals coming together to form a commonwealth of people:

> The fact that man needs to live in an organized society could not be denied. Just as primitive man has to respect the laws of nature, so must the citizen reckon with the interdependence of freedom and political order: without the law there can be no equality of right, and without the equality of right, there can be no true political freedom. (Grimsley, 1973a).

For Rousseau, as he argued in his *Social Contract*, participation in social life for the purpose of freely imposing an organizational (political) structure and achieving a common unity was necessary if a human being was to attain complete self-realization.

In spite of everything, I still believe that people are really good at heart.

Anne Frank

Exercise 5.1

Taking into consideration Rousseau's assumptions with regard to human nature, briefly discuss how his philosophy might be used to support the statement from the *Diary of Anne Frank*. Then compare your thoughts with the feedback at the end of the chapter.

From *Émile*, Book I, Rousseau

Everything is good as it leaves the hands of the Author of things; everything degenerates in the hands of man. He forces one soil to nourish the products of another, one tree to bear the fruit of another. He mixes and confuses the climates, the elements, the seasons. He mutilates his dog, his horse, his slave. He turns everything upside down; he disfigures everything; he loves deformity, monsters. He wants nothing as nature made it, not even man; for him, man must be trained like a school horse; man must be fashioned in keeping with his fancy like a tree in his garden.

Were he not to do this, however, everything would go even worse, and our species does not admit of being formed halfway. In the present state of things a man abandoned to himself in the midst of other men from birth would be the most disfigured of all. Prejudices, authority, necessity, example, all the social institutions in which we find ourselves submerged would stifle nature in him and put nothing in its place. Nature there would be like a shrub that chance had caused to be born in the middle of a path and that the passers-by soon cause to perish by bumping into it from all sides and bending it in every direction.

It is to you that I address myself, tender and foresighted mother, who are capable of keeping the nascent shrub away from the highway and securing it from the impact of human opinions! Cultivate and water the young plant before it dies. Its fruits will one day be your delights. Form an enclosure around your child's soul at an early date. Someone else can draw its circumference, but you alone must build the fence.

(continued)

Plants are shaped by cultivation, and men by education. If man were born big and strong, his size and strength would be useless to him until he learned to make use of them. They would be detrimental to him in that they would keep others from thinking of aiding him. And abandoned to himself, he would die of want before knowing his needs. And childhood is taken to be a pitiable state! It is not that the human race would have perished if man had not begun as a child.

We are born weak, we need strength; we are born totally unprovided, we need aid; we are born stupid, we need judgment. Everything we do not have at birth and which we need when we are grown is given us by education.

This education comes to us from nature or from men or from things. The internal development of our faculties and our organs is the education of nature. The use that we are taught to make of this development is the education of men. And what we acquire from our own experience about the objects which affect us is the education of things.

Each of us is thus formed by three kinds of masters. The disciple in whom their various lessons are at odds with one another is badly raised and will never be in agreement with himself. He alone in whom they all coincide at the same points and tend to the same ends reaches his goal and lives consistently. He alone is well raised.

Boyd, W. (Ed. and Trans.). (1956). *Émile for Today.* Essex, England: World Education Fellowship, pp. 11–12. Reprinted with permission of World Education Fellowship.

Rousseau in the Classroom

Rousseau's educational philosophy follows from his belief that education should involve the development of capacities rather than an imposition of ideas, and that is should be nurtured by love and understanding, not compulsion (Feibleman, 1973). Rousseau offers suggestions on how to achieve this goal in *Émile,* which presents two of his most critical philosophical positions: (1) all knowledge finds its way into the mind through the senses, so that we learn through our individual experiences, and (2) human beings are born good and innocent.

For Rousseau, therefore, early education should be based on the senses, should be individualized, and should be protected from the negatives of societal institutions. These needs are addressed through a series of stages that include the following:

Stage 1: Needs and moral education during childhood. Key features include interaction with the environment and positive role modeling by a tutor, which promotes the incorporation of positive traits into child behavior. The tutor respects the freedom of the student but guides learning experiences, stimulates curiosity, and promotes the cultivation of the senses through observations and simple experiments.

Stage 2:   Intellectual/practical applications during early adolescence. The key features here are comparing and reasoning with an emphasis on real-world problems and hands-on solutions, as opposed to book learning or other forms of teacher-centered instruction mostly through spoken and written words.

Stage 3:   Academic disciplines/intellectual education during middle and later teens. The primary concern here is the facilitation of the transition toward social living—that is, a student moves from the study of a world of things to a study of societal considerations.

Rousseau believed the best way to educate a human being was in a tutorial situation. Undoubtedly based on his own experiences, this approach would shield the immature and developing child from the corruption of societal institutions and influences. Some key characteristics of this individualized approach include:

- Removing obstacles that might hinder positive development
- Addressing the special needs of the individual
- Employing as natural an environment as possible
- Leading as opposed to forcing children during the learning process
- Directing experiences, activities, and projects
- Facilitating children's basic interest and need to explore and discover the world in which they live
- Facilitating the transition from individual immaturity to social maturity

Although Rousseau's primary educational focus involves tutor-student interactions, he was one of the first influential persons of his time to emphasize the critical role a mother plays in the development of her child prior to the tutorial age of five. He also believed in the world of work or a concrete world in which learners are motivated to learn because they want to be practical people who solve their own as well as more general social problems. Rousseau greatly admired Robinson Crusoe's inventiveness and made him Émile's hero and model (Cranston, 1991).

Now let's take a look at how some of these characteristics are employed in the classroom, with the goal of exploring the natural world in a practical way.

 ## Scenario 5.1

Ms. Kristen Mittelstadt, a second-grade teacher at Ponte Vedra Palm Valley Elementary School, sat in front of the board and had the children sit on the floor close to her in semicircles. She began her lesson by saying, "Let me see a show of hands of

With permission. Ponta Vedra Palm Valley Elementary School. Ponte Vedra, Florida. Mr. Michael Parrish, Principal.

who goes to the beach during the summer break." Because the beach was less than a mile from the majority of the children's homes, all of them raised their hands.

"What are some of the things you like to do at the beach?" Ms. Mittelstadt asked.

"I swim," Darlene answered.

"I like to build things in the sand," Cheryl added.

"My dad got me a boogie board, and I like to play in the waves," Robert said.

"Wow! You all like to do many different things, and they all sound like fun. Now, what happens if you get hungry?"

"My mom usually brings a picnic basket with sandwiches and stuff," Marna said.

"Yeah, and my mom brings a cooler with soda cans," Donald added.

"That's fine," Ms. Mittelstadt said. "What happens if it gets really hot in the middle of the afternoon?"

"We leave," Daniel said, and the class giggled.

"That's a good idea," Ms. Mittelstadt said, "but what if you didn't leave? What would you do, Daniel?"

"Well, I see lots of people with umbrellas, so I guess that would be a good idea."

"And that's a good answer," Ms. Mittelstadt said with a smile. "Now," she continued, "we're going to do one of our exploration exercises, and what I want you to do today is to use lots of imagination and also think about some of the things we have been learning with some of our science projects. Okay, here we go. We have been talking about going to the beach and having a good time, but what would you do if you and your family were on a ship that sank and you were stranded on the empty beach?"

"Ms. Mittelstadt, what is *stranded?*" Lizzie asked.

"That means that you and your family are on the beach and as far as you know, you are on your own and no one is around to help you. Is that okay?"

"Yes," Lizzie answered.

"Good. Now, what are the things you have to worry about? (Pause.) Theresa?"

"I'm worried about getting home."

"That's a good idea, but let's say for the time being you can't get home, so what do you need to do? (No response.) Well, what happens if you get hungry?"

"Oh, I see," Theresa said. "I need to worry about eating something."

"Fine, Theresa. Okay, group, how are we going to solve that problem?"

"We could catch fish and look for oysters and clams and things like that," Sunni said.

"Maybe we could find some coconuts in the trees like they have here," Candice added.

"And we might be able to find berries and other things out of the ground."

"All good answers. Great job! What else would we have to worry about? (Pause.) Jeffrey?"

"I don't like it when it thunders and rains when I am at the beach, so I would worry about being someplace where I was safe."

"And where might that be, Jeffrey?"

"Well, if it was a beach like ours, I would go up over the dunes and down into the trees and build something."

"Like a shelter?" Ms. Mittelstadt asked.

"Yes," Jeffrey replied.

"And what might you use to do that?"

"I could use branches and sticks and stones and big leaves and things like that."

"Good ideas, Jeffrey. Now what I would like all of you to do is to return to your desks. John, I would like you to make sure everyone gets one piece of white poster paper, and I would like you to make sure everyone gets crayons, Kim. What I want all of you to do is think about our beach, what it looks like and what is on it, and draw and color a shelter you would build if you were stranded here. And what is *stranded*, Lizzie?"

"I'm on the beach with my family and we can't get off it."

"Good going, Lizzie. Okay, group, let's spend about 20 minutes on this task, and then we will all come back to the floor and I will show you the big book of Robinson Crusoe. Has anyone ever heard of him? (About half the hands go up, including Lizzie's.) What happened to him, Lizzie?"

"He got stranded," she said with a big smile

"Yes, he did," Ms. Mittelstadt said, "and when we all sit back down on the floor we will see what kind of shelter he built and then share our drawings. Okay, off to your desks."

In this lesson, Ms. Mittelstadt has employed a number of techniques Rousseau believed to be critical to an individual's education. Among other things, she utilized the local surroundings—that is, the beach, which provided a familiar environment. She also directed the activity by leading the students during the problem (worries) development component of the lesson. In addition, we can assume from her statements about early science activities that she intends to have the students apply prior knowledge to this practical, problem-solving activity. This lesson also obviously explores the immediate world in which the students live, which was one of the most critical facets of Rousseau's application of philosophy to education.

Because of Rousseau's emphasis on this exploration, which he thought would lead to a better world, and because of his belief in the goodness of human beings, he is often considered a moral philosopher. His theory was a theory not of "what exists but what should be, not . . . an account of what has been but . . . an expression of what ought to be, not . . . a retrospective elegy but . . . a prospective prophecy" (Cassirer, 1963, p. 10).

Exercise 5.2

Examine the following statements and determine if they are consistent (c) or inconsistent (i) with Rousseau's philosophy. Then compare your answers to those at the end of the chapter.

_____ 1. Human beings are born with a vast storehouse of innate knowledge.

_____ 2. Individuals corrupt society.

_____ 3. The most useful education involves the exploration of one's environment.

_____ 4. Children are little adults.

_____ 5. The most effective education should be undertaken in formal, institutional environments.

Exercise 5.3

Read the following scenario and determine two of Rousseau's methodologies or techniques that are applied in this classroom lesson. Then consult the feedback at the end of the chapter.

Mrs. Dolores Salazar, a chemistry teacher at Rio Grande High School, began her lesson by asking her students to take out their notes in order to review yesterday's work. The 20-plus students enrolled in this "Chemistry in the Community" class were seated in a U-shaped arrangement with the laboratory stations lining the walls of the classroom. Her method of soliciting involvement in a question-and-answer session was to toss a koosh to students when they raised their hands. Toni made the first catch of the day!

"We have been working on water purification and we said that back in the 1800s people obtained their water in three different ways. What was one of those ways, Toni?"

"Wells," Toni said.

"I couldn't quite hear you."

"Wells!"

"Wells. Good. Rob, a second way?"

"Ponds."

"Good. Along with ponds, what else?"

"Rivers, oceans, stuff life that," Bianca added.

"Great," Mrs. Salazar said. "And the third source?"

"Rain," Paul said.

"Right, so those were basically the sources of water. Now, water has to be discarded, so what were three ways they got rid of wastewater?"

"Cesspools," Nancy answered.

"Okay, what are cesspools?"

"Pits."

"Good, and what were they lined with?"

"Stones or rocks," Nancy added.

"Okay. Now a second way water was discarded . . . Alina?"

"How about just using the ground," Alina said.

"Right. A lot of times people just dumped it outside so it went into the ground. And finally, a third way?" Mrs. Salazar asked as she tossed the ball to Gabe.

"A dry well."

"And what is a dry well, Gabe?"

With permission. Rio Grande High School, Albuquerque, New Mexico. Mrs. Judith K. Martin, Acting Principal.

"A well that doesn't have any water in it."

"Exactly, Gabe. Simply a well that has dried up. Now, what happened if somehow discarded water or wastewater got into the wells or rivers, meaning the drinking water? Josie?"

"It got contaminated," Josie said.

"Which means?"

"If you drank it you got sick."

"Right. Now today, what are two things we can do with water to prevent sickness or other negative effects?"

"We can filter it," David replied.

"Okay," Mrs. Salazar said, "but what does filtering do? When we filter something out, what are we actually doing?"

"Taking stuff out," David said.

"How?"

"By holding back the stuff that is too big to pass through the filter," David added.

"Great, so filtering is one method. What is a second, Melissa?"

"Chlorinating," Melissa answered.

"Chlorinating. Why do you think we need to chlorinate water?"

Vince caught the ball. "To kill bacteria," he said.

"Okay. Good," Mrs. Salazar said. "We also talked about the way nature purifies water if left alone and given enough time. However, we don't have that kind of time because we are using water quicker than the time it takes to naturally replenish itself. In addition, we talked about hard and soft water and that hard water has an excess amount of calcium, magnesium, or ions. Therefore, water purification can also involve the removal of these excess minerals.

"In today's lab, I am going to give you a sample of hard water that has an excess amount of calcium ions. Your job is to soften or purify this water using filtering techniques."

Mrs. Salazar then provided the students with a filtration procedure handout and demonstrated the placement of filters in test tubes. She went on to briefly discuss how the test would show whether they had gotten rid of the calcium. For the remainder of the class, Mrs. Salazar assisted the students at their laboratory stations.

IMMANUEL KANT, 1724–1804

As noted in the introduction to this chapter, Kant's goal was to combine reason and experience because he found weaknesses in both. Philosophers like Aristotle tried to establish universal truth and then employ deductive reasoning to attain knowledge; Kant believed this approach to be too abstract. On the other hand, empiricists such as Locke prioritized sensory experience and exploration of the practical world as the ideal method for obtaining knowledge; Kant rejected this approach because he believed it to be too personal or individualized.

In Kant's view,

> the key was the human mind, which had the power to draw from intuition as well as experience in order to determine reality. Therefore, knowing was dependent upon an active mind, which not only collected information through the senses but contributed to those experiences as well by shaping sensory material. Although Kant believed all knowledge began with experience, he also believed the foundation of knowledge to be a priori, and his goal . . . was to rectify the deficiencies in rationalist and empiricist metaphysics by adapting the scientific method to philosophical investigations. (Hahn, 1988, p. 120).

Life and Times

Kant was born in Königsberg in East Prussia on April 22, 1724. He was the fourth of nine children born to Scottish parents who lived in what is today Kaliningrad, Russia. His father was a saddle maker and, based on the standards of the day, the family was of limited means and lived in humble conditions. Kant's childhood was extremely strict and rigorous, because his mother was a member of a religious sect that immersed its followers in rituals from morning to night. She died when Kant was only 14, but her presence was significant in his earlier childhood, since she provided discipline, an emphasis on personal responsibility, and a basic education, which enabled him to enter the University of Königsberg.

For the next six years, Kant, along with the other 300 members of the student body, studied classics, physics, and philosophy under the faculty of 16. He is believed to have put himself through school through his prowess with a cue stick and a deck of cards, although he did tutor many of his wealthy classmates. After graduating, Kant earned his living for eight years as a family tutor, before he managed to obtain a lecturing position at the University of Königsberg in 1755. He held this post for 15 years, with his income coming from the students, since this was a nonsalaried position. In 1770, Kant secured the philosophy chair at Königsberg and was so devoted to his students that his scholarly work did not appear until his later years.

As for the nonacademic part of his life, there is little to say. He was small and frail—factors that may have contributed to a quiet and unassuming lifestyle. Kant's life, according to one biographer, "passed like the most regular of regular verbs . . . rising, coffee-drinking, writing, lecturing, dining and walking" (Durant, 1953, p. 200). This lifestyle was clearly reflected in his walking, which began daily at 3:45 P.M. sharp and involved eight laps on a street that to this day is called "Philosopher's Walk." He was up at 5:00 A.M. and went to bed at 10:00 P.M. Although he was said to be pleasant, he maintained no significant social or political connections. As for marriage, he defined this relationship as the "mutual lease of sexual organs ignoring all the emotion and sentiments which play so large a part" (Feibleman, 1973. p. 146).

Kant established for himself specific goals and a sense of morality that could not be compromised. The latter was best exemplified when some of his views

Knowledge comes from the mind's interaction with the world.

Immanuel Kant

found displeasure with the reigning sovereign of Prussia, Frederick Wilhelm II. Although Kant was a champion of freedom of thought and expression, he remained silent on these issues, believing the will of the king to be more important than his inalienable rights.

As for his goals, Kant's focused nature was clearly expressed at the age of 22 when he wrote: "'I have already fixed upon the line which I am resolved to keep. I will enter on my course, and nothing shall prevent me from pursuing it'" (in Durant, 1953, pp. 200–201). This tendency to not deviate from his chosen lifestyle was also apparent in his work, and Kant is "revered for his unswerving defense of human freedom and respect for persons, and for his insistence that reason can guide action" (O'Neill, 1989, p. ix).

Philosophical Contributions

Let's begin with the notion that part of the foundation of Kant's thinking was somewhat eclectic. He claims to have been "aroused from his slumber" by David Hume, John Locke, and the British empiricist movement, which championed the theory that all knowledge is derived from experience. The rationalist point of view stressed the attainment of knowledge independent of experience, with human beings sequentially building one piece of information on another.

Finally, Rousseau's *Émile* emphasized "the exploration of nature, which Rousseau felt was conducive to moral development. Apparently "the only time Kant missed starting his ritual walk 'on time' was when he refused to put down Rousseau's book until he finished it" (Wolff, 1989, p. 154.)

To shed light on how a priori knowledge is possible and how knowledge is acquired, Kant posed three fundamental questions:

- What can I know?
- What can I do?
- What may I hope?

He addressed the first question by examining opposing metaphysical theories, because dualism (for example, the distinction between intuition and concept and between appearance and the thing itself) was central to his philosophy (Guyer, 1992). Kant referred to these descriptions of reality, such as permanence versus change, as *categories,* and he believed the mind imposed its own categories on the sensory experience of the individual. Kant further defined categories as innate, as opposed to being learned. Therefore, Aristotle's universals can be a priori, and Kant was concerned about the inclination of human beings to adopt dogmatic positions based solely on knowledge derived from a single source.

As a result, Kant's dualistic approach also included *a posteriori* knowledge, which is not innate but comes through experience. By accepting the validity of both sources of knowledge, he concluded that reality is a combination of abstract ideas and information obtained through the senses. He called the components of this combination *noumena* ("things in themselves") and *phenomena* ("the appearance of things") and believed that the more we know about phenomena, the closer we come to noumena.

However, like Locke, Kant thought that through sensory experience, we can only come to know the characteristics and properties of a physical object, while the "essence" of the object remains unknown. Therefore, we cannot attain concrete knowledge of reality, because the totality of the universe lies beyond human experience, and knowledge is limited when experience comes to an end. In overcoming this limitation, Kant turned to the mind. For example, from the standpoint of universalism, it is generally held that God exists, but this conception certainly lies beyond the realm of experience. Kant's answer is that we need God, so we must think of him as existing (Feibleman, 1973). In the *Critique of Pure Reason,* Kant "tries to prove his contention that we can anticipate the form, although not the content, of a possible experience and hence make valid judgments a priori about experience in general" (Schaper and Vossenkuhl, 1989, p. 5).

This answer is characteristic of Kant's theory that ideas or knowledge are inherent in the mind and not necessarily learned. For instance, with regard to space, we see things in spatial relation to one another, so space must have existed before we saw the objects in it (Runes, 1963). This point is fundamental to Kant's answer to his first question, for "What can I know?" is determined by an active, rational mind that begins with physical experiences and shapes them automatically throught innate principles that, in turn, results in the establishment of individual beliefs and views of the world.

Kant developed this idea of innate or a priori knowledge around what he referred to as *imperatives*, which provided a foundation for the answer to his second question, "What can I do?" Imperatives are statements or rules about what people ought to do. If we think specifically of education, imperatives are statements or rules about what parents, teachers, school administrators, and children should do (Frankena, 1965). According to Frankena (1965, p. 82), Kant identified two kinds of imperatives:

1. Hypothetical imperatives, which address specific and individual ends or results, i.e., what to do in order to be happy.
2. Categorical imperatives, which transcend individuals and serve as universal laws of behavior.

Categorical imperatives provided the foundation for Kant's philosophical focus on moral behavior, for, unlike Aristotle, Kant ranked moral excellence above intellectual excellence. If the human condition was to be improved, it would have to be based on contentment with self, goodwill, honesty, and the willingness and obligation of rational beings to adhere to universally valid moral laws, which, for Kant, was implicit in his definition of categorical imperatives. Though he believed people exercised freedom of behavior, in his *Critique of Practical Reason*, Kant stated that individual judgment, in general, is the faculty of thinking the particular as contained within the universal—for example, morality is universal because it satisfies universal societal needs as opposed to individual desires. This theory provided the bedrock for Kant's concept of "duty" when he "separated obligation from fulfillment in that duty is the focus, not happiness" (Bernstein, 1980, p. 155).

The third question, "What may I hope?", is addressed in the following discussion of Kant's philosophy of education. Regarding the education of individuals, the virtue found in all three of Kant's cardinal questions (and value to us as educators) is that of challenging dogmatic and prejudicial thinking (Norris, 1993).

Life was meant to be lived. Curiosity must be kept alive. The fatal thing is the rejection. One must never, for whatever reason, turn his back on life.

Eleanor Roosevelt

Exercise 5.4

Reread the Eleanor Roosevelt statement and briefly discuss one component in light of Kant's philosophy. Then check the feedback at the end of the chapter.

From *The Critique of Pure Reason*, Kant

That all our knowledge begins with experience there can be no doubt. For how is it possible that the faculty of cognition should be awakened into exercise otherwise than by means of objects which affect our senses, and partly of themselves produce representations, partly rouse our powers of understanding into activity, to compare, to connect, or to separate these, and so to convert the raw material of our sensuous impressions into a knowledge of objects, which is called experience? In respect of time, therefore, no knowledge of ours is antecedent to experience, but begins with it.

But, though all our knowledge begins with experience, it by no means follows that all arises out of experience. For, on the contrary, it is quite possible that our empirical knowledge is a compound of that which the faculty of cognition supplies from itself (sensuous impressions giving merely the occasion), an addition which we cannot distinguish from the original element given by the sense, till long practice has made us attentive to, and skillful in separating it. It is, therefore, a question which requires close investigation, and not to be answered at first sight, whether there exists a knowledge altogether independent of experience, and even of all sensuous impressions? Knowledge of this kind is called *a priori*, in contradistinction to empirical knowledge, which has its sources *a posteriori*, that is, in experience.

But the expression *a priori* is not as yet definite enough adequately to indicate the whole meaning of the question above started. For, in speaking of knowledge which has its sources in experience, we are wont to say, that this or that may be known *a priori* because we do not derive this knowledge immediately from experience but from a general rule, which, however, we have itself borrowed from experience. Thus, if a man undermined his house, we say, "he might know a priori that it would have fallen"; that is, he needed not to have waited for the experience that it did actually fall. But still, *a priori,* he could not know even this much. For, that bodies are heavy, and, consequently, that they fall when their supports are taken away, must have been known to him previously, by means of experience.

By the term "knowledge *a priori,*" therefore, we shall in the sequel understand, not such as is independent of this or that kind of experience, but such as is absolutely so of all experience. Opposed to this is empirical knowledge, or that which is possible only *a posteriori*, that is through experience. Knowledge *a priori* is either pure or impure. Pure knowledge *a priori* is that with which no empirical element is mixed up. For example, the proposition, "Every change has a cause," is a proposition a *priori,* but impure, because change is a conception which can only be derived from experience.

The question now is as to a criterion, by which we may securely distinguish a pure from an empirical cognition. Experience no doubt teaches us that this or that object is constituted in such and such a manner, but not that it could not possibly exist otherwise. Now, in the first place, if we have a proposition which contains the idea of necessity in its very conception, it is a judgement a *priori;* if, moreover, it is not derived from any other proposition, unless from one equally involving the idea of necessity, it is absolutely a *priori.* Secondly, an empirical judgement never exhibits strict and absolute, but only assumed and comparative universality (by induction); therefore, the most we can say is . . . so far as we have hitherto observed, there is no exception to this or that rule. If, on the other hand, a judgement carries with it strict and absolute universality, that is, admits of no possible exception, it is not derived from experience, but is valid absolutely a *priori.*

Empirical universality is, therefore, only an arbitrary extension of validity, from that which may be predicted of a proposition valid in most cases, to that which is asserted of a proposition which holds good in all.

Hutchins, R. M. (Ed.) (1952). *Great Books of the Western World: Kant.* Chicago: Encyclopaedia Britannica., pp. 14–15. Reprinted from Great Books of the Western World. ©1952, 1990 Encyclopaedia Britannica, Inc.

Kant in the Classroom

Kant believed that human beings are the only beings who need education and that we can only become human through education. We are merely what education makes of us, and the primary goal is to make us good and promote or foster desired dispositions of intellectual skill and moral traits, which in turn would allow us to know and to do our duty (Frankena, 1965).

To achieve this goal, Kant proposed two kinds of education: natural education and practical education. The former primarily involves the acquisition of information, while the latter focuses on decision making with specific regard to moral behavior. Some educators might also distinguish between the two by labeling acquisition *passive learning* and decision making *active learning.* However, Kant would take issue with this notion, in that acquisition of knowledge requires the student to be covertly active. That is, as teachers, we cannot observe or certify "listening," which requires student activity. In other words, Kant is alerting us that educators might equate passive behavior with doing nothing at all.

To achieve the preceding goals, Kant proposed two negative and three positive educational needs (Frankena, 1965, pp. 84–85):

1. Education needs to physiologically nurture the individual. The negative aspect of this need involves the prevention of bad habits, for Kant believed that habit formation, even possibly good ones, delimited the degree of human freedom.

2. Education needs to provide discipline, the negative aspect of which involves extinguishing undesirable dispositions and off-task behaviors. Discipline in the classroom promotes obedience and respect for others and self and lays the foundation for the acquisition of knowledge and cultivation of skills.

3. Education needs to enculturate the individual through the positive promotion of intellectual excellence and understanding, which, unlike judgment, Kant believed could be taught. Specific methods include employing reason based on a memorized storehouse of information; providing direct instruction with examples and discussions; and formulating rules, concepts, and generalizations.

4. Education needs to promote prudence, which goes beyond the acquisition of information and the process of reasoning in that it requires the individual to put into practice those desirable and relevant behaviors founded upon the enculturated body of knowledge.

5. Education needs to promote desired moral behavior, which requires a focus on positive self concept, high self-esteem, and the Hebrew concept of *tsdekah*, which embraces doing one's duty for its own sake as opposed to calling attention to or glorifying one's self. Specific methods here would include calling attention to morally good dispositions through case studies, examples, role modeling, and the occasional use of Plato's guided discovery.

The needs just described provide the foundation, tools, and direction in response to the third question, "What can I hope?" These needs also provide us with Kant's view of the classroom (behavioral) environment, because to achieve the desired ends as stated, education should consist of work, not play; it should be serious and involve restraint and compulsion; it should be uniform; it should differentiate between knowledge and opinion; and it should always be related to application and practice (Frankena, 1965). Now let's take a look at how some aspects of Kant's philosophy and specific strategies are employed in the classroom.

Without discipline, there's no life at all.

Katharine Hepburn

 ## Scenario 5.2

After the daily announcements and the presentation of two student awards through the medium of closed-circuit television, Mrs. Pat Watson, a ninth-grade language

With permission. John McKnitt Alexander Middle School, Huntersville, North Carolina. Mr. Jimmy Poole, Principal.

arts teacher at Alexander Middle School, shared with her students her opinion that they had been reading one of the greatest adventure stories ever written.

"Who was the hero of the story?" Mrs. Watson began.

"Odysseus," Sam said.

"And what made him a hero?"

"He was clever," Sam responded

"Yes, and how about when he encountered the Cyclops?"

"He was curious," JaNean added.

"Fine! What else?"

"He had lots of pride," Molly said.

"And strength," Ronald added.

"And lots of courage," John said, joining in.

"Great," Mrs. Watson said, "but every adventurer has these qualities. So, what was there about Odysseus and this work that makes it one of the greatest stories ever?"

"It shows us the qualities of the culture," Mo said.

"Yes. You are right, Mo. He reflects the times when we read of his son, wife, the behavior of the suitors who invaded his home, and his travels and contests. Now, be honest with me. How many of you enjoyed the story? (Large positive response.)

"Well," Mrs. Watson continued, "it is exciting, but let's think beyond the fascinating story, beyond the Cyclops whose name was . . . ?"

"Polyphemus," Sylvana said.

"Yes, and Circe and the others, but there is much more to this adventure, and we need to dig in if we are to understand why this work is worth reading."

Mrs. Watson then directed the students to break into five groups and assigned one discussion problem to each. She instructed them to take notes and identify a reporter. The problems were as follows:

1. Compare the behavior of the hero Odysseus with that of modern heroes.
2. What Greek values or ideas are present in the *Odyssey?*
3. Discuss the place of women in the *Odyssey.*
4. Discuss the relationship of men and gods in the *Odyssey.* Men and nature.
5. Discuss other themes of the *Odyssey.*

After 10 to 15 minutes, Mrs. Watson reconvened the class. "You've worked very well and we only have a few minutes, so let's hear just one or two things from each group. How about today's heroes compared to Odysseus?"

"It seems as if most of today's heroes are in the comic books and are super heroes, but Odysseus seemed more like a real person," said Terri, the spokesperson for Group 1.

"Super meaning . . .?"

"Kind of perfect," Terri added. "We think Odysseus was exceptional in lots of ways but he wasn't perfect."

"Fine. How about values, Group 2?"

"There seems to be the desire to achieve, to be excellent. Maybe to move toward perfection," Jim said.

"Great . . . and we'll say more about that. Group 3. What was the place of women?"

"This was tough because different women seemed to have different roles. Some were loyal, while some were subservient and others were even dangerous," Colleen said.

"Okay. Nice list," said Mrs. Watson. "Also, in those ancient times, Plato had some positive views about equality, and we will explore what happened then compared to what is happening today. Next group?"

"We talked about human beings, God, and nature," Bo said. We think the gods could be helpful or harmful, but either way, people had no control."

"The gods overpowered human beings?" Mrs. Watson inquired.

"Yes," Bo answered. "Just like nature does sometimes now."

"Example please?"

"Like when Hurricane Hugo hit our outer banks a few years ago."

"Fine. Okay, Group 5. How about a few themes?"

Stephanie said, "We came up with 'there's no place like home' and 'what goes around comes around.'"

"That will certainly give us something to talk about," Mrs. Watson said. "We will continue our analysis of the five discussion topics tomorrow and then briefly review a few of the other books we have read that have been called great to see if we can arrive at some conclusion about heroes, among other things.

In this classroom lesson, we see the applicability of Kant's philosophy, both in terms of what is being taught and with respect to some of the teaching strategies employed. First and foremost, Mrs. Watson is laying the foundation for the concept "hero," the nature of which suggests universal moral behavior. The universality of the hero and other cultural behaviors discussed is established with her use of classical literature, which, by definition, has survived the test of time. As a classic, the *Odyssey* provides a vehicle for examples, role models, and provocative discussions, all of which Kant believed to be extremely useful in an educational environment. Furthermore, Mrs. Watson's questions are designed to facilitate comparisons and contemporary considerations, which prevents the dust from settling on the desired moral behavior and duties of Odysseus and the people of ancient Greek culture.

In a practical sense, Kant's value to us in the classroom is found more in the curriculum itself. The relevant areas of universally desired moral behaviors, based on a sense of duty, can be presented and discussed in a wide range of cognitive, knowledge-based units of subject matter. Kant believed these educational experiences, acquired through practice and teaching, were critical in enabling a human being to become a disciplined person of goodwill.

Exercise 5.5

Examine the following statements to determine if they are consistent (c) or inconsistent (i) with Kant's philosophy. Then check your answers against those at the end of the chapter.

_____ 1. All knowledge is derived from experience.
_____ 2. Acquiring knowledge is independent of experience.
_____ 3. Knowledge is inherent in human beings.

_____ 4. A concrete knowledge of reality is not possible.
_____ 5. A body of universal laws regarding moral behavior exists.

Exercise 5.6

According to Kant, knowledge comes from the mind's interaction with the world. Briefly discuss the role categorical imperatives play in this process. Then compare your response to the one at the end of the chapter.

SUMMARY

For both Rousseau and Kant, knowledge of the self involved the acquisition and processing of information for the purpose of seeking the good life, which in turn would produce a better society.

Rousseau's good life was based on a practical, individualized education, with the natural environment serving as the classroom. He believed that a sensitive and imaginative interaction with the physical world, coupled with intuition, would provide a knowledge base that would lead in turn to goodness in human beings. This knowledge base would be incorporated into basic human nature, which Rousseau believed to be inherently good; then individual goodness would lend itself to societal goodness. Therefore, the key to advances in social evolution was found not only in the knowledge of self, but also in the satisfaction of self.

For Kant, knowledge of self should be understood in epistemological terms, for he was more concerned with individual human reason—which involves judgments (based on intuitive knowledge and sensory experience)—than he was with the speculative nature of metaphysical propositions. Kant then connected human reason to moral behavior and was undoubtedly influenced by Rousseau, who believed that the just state and morality itself arose from the exercise of our rational powers (Wolff, 1989). Furthermore, Kant believed that moral imperatives existed that were categorical, or universal, in nature. People arrived at these moral behaviors through a combination of experiences, reason, and a priori knowledge. Kant, however, went beyond knowledge of self in that he believed it was the obligation or duty of each individual to manifest these universal moral behaviors in an effort to better society.

Clearly, both philosophers championed the worth and equality of human beings and believed that it was up to them—rather than society as a whole—to try to create a better world.

Questions for Discussion

1. Bacon believed science would improve social conditions. How would the philosophy of Rousseau promote a better world?
2. On the basis of the excerpt from _Émile_, how did Rousseau envision education protecting people from the corruptions of civilization?

3. In terms of educational ideology, with which of the following statements would Rousseau be more comfortable: (1) education is a preparation for life, or (2) education is life. Why?

4. Rousseau placed little to no value on institutionally educating youngsters but offered much in the way of methodology. What are some of the ways his contributions can be applied to classroom teaching?

5. Among other things, Kant's work focused on not what human beings appear to be but on what they ought to be. With this in mind, how did Kant conceptualize moral excellence?

6. For Kant, reality is determined through a combination of reason and experience. How does this synthesis or dualistic approach take place?

7. Review the long quotation from Kant. How does Kant conceptualize the mind's interaction with the world?

8. What are some characteristics of what Kant called a practical education?

Suggested Field Laboratory Activities

1. Select a curriculum guide, text, or other instructional materials in a discipline of your choice and see if you can find examples of what Rousseau would term naturalism in the classroom.

2. If available, review a directing teacher's plans to determine whether tutorials are being employed in the classroom.

3. Undertake a series of classroom teaching observations and note the presentations that have an element of "discovery" in a student-centered environment.

4. If given the opportunity, prepare and present a lesson that would use the immediate physical environment, locale, and so on to promote a learning objective.

5. According to Kant, "listening" requires student activity. Observe ways the quantity and quality of student "listening" can be determined.

6. Observe selected lessons and note the way selected strategies emphasized by Kant (case studies, use of examples, and role modeling) are implemented in the classroom.

7. If given the opportunity, design and implement a lesson that allows you to model some aspect of the learning objective.

Exercise Feedback

Exercise 5.1

Regardless of the horrors perpetrated on her during her brief lifetime, Anne Frank still believed in the basic goodness of human beings, a belief expressed in the work of Rousseau two centuries earlier. Rousseau thought that human beings were good by nature and if they were allowed to individually, through tutorial guidance, explore and construct their environments, society in turn would reflect their goodness.

Exercise 5.2

1. (i) Inconsistent. Rousseau did not accept the theory that human beings were born with a predetermined body of knowledge.

2. (i) Inconsistent. The other way around! Society corrupts individuals.

3. (c) Consistent.

4. (i) Inconsistent. Rousseau believed that children were children and as such went through a series of stages and experiences that allowed them to become mature and socially responsible adults.

5. (i) Inconsistent. Rousseau did not want to work within existing social structures, and education was no exception.

Exercise 5.3

A number of components of Rousseau's philosophy are applied in Mrs. Salazar's classroom. The first, and possibly most important, is hinted at by the title of the course, "Chemistry in the Community," which suggests a practical application of science in the student's physical environment. In this particular lesson, you could discuss her utilization of actual practices in obtaining water from such sources as wells, ponds, seas, and rain; the methods of getting rid of water with an eventual focus on filtering processes; and the hands-on experiment involving filtration—specifically, the removal of excess minerals from water.

Exercise 5.4

Eleanor Roosevelt's focus on the desirability of continually living and seeking new and enriching experiences supports Kant's concern about the problem of habit formation. To live is to grow, and habitual behavior clearly has the ability to stunt growth. Also, Roosevelt's recommendation that we seek eagerly without fear of rejection suggests a need to curtail dogma. The belief that dogmatic thinking stifles human growth through such things as blind faith, in-doctrination, or possibly the fear of challenging commonly accepted knowledge was a serious concern of Kant's and would obviously be inconsistent with Roosevelt's emphasis on "living life."

Exercise 5.5

1. (i) Inconsistent. Although Kant valued experience and incorporated it in his epistemological positions, he did not believe, as did the empiricists, that *all* knowledge was derived from experience.

2. (i) Inconsistent. Human or sensory experience contributes to human knowledge.

3. (c) Consistent. Although Kant did not believe that *all* knowledge is inherent, he did subscribe to the theory of a priori knowledge.

4. (c)   Consistent. Not all things can be factually ascertained.

5. (c)   Consistent. This statement is foundational with regard to Kant's philo-
          sophy and may be his most critical example of the a priori knowledge
          referred to in point 3.

Exercise 5.6

Kant's theory regarding the acquisition of knowledge through the mind's interaction with the world is multifaceted. The initial interaction is physical and
is found through experiencing the material world. Then the mind processes
this information through the use of reason. Reason, however, is affected by
categorical imperatives, which Kant defines as a priori knowledge that does
not arise from experience and that is in the form of universal moral statements or rules.

CHAPTER 6

LOGIC AND HUMAN BEHAVIOR: HEGEL AND MARX

After completing Chapter 6, you should be able to accomplish the following objectives:

1. You will become familiar with G. F. W. Hegel's view of reality, so that you will be able to identify a number of statements as being consistent or inconsistent with his philosophy.

2. You will acquire a knowledge of the dialectic, so that you will be able to discuss, in writing, the three steps of this process.

3. You will become familiar with Karl Marx's philosophy, so that you will be able to identify a number of statements as being consistent or inconsistent with his views.

4. You will increase your knowledge of Marx's work so that you will be able to briefly discuss two significant differences between his and Hegel's use of the dialectic.

In Chapter 5, you became acquainted with the work of two philosophers who believed the pursuit of knowledge, on an individual basis, would result in a better world. For Jean-Jacques Rousseau, this pursuit was undertaken though an interaction with the natural, or physical, or material world by students whose education protected them from the negative impact of an imperfect society. Kant believed knowledge led human beings to an understanding of what they ought to be through a process of conceptualizing universal, moral imperatives. Both philosophers focused on the individual and the betterment of society and so contributed to the foundation on which Georg Wilhelm Friedrich Hegel and Karl Marx developed their theories.

Hegel was influenced by Kant in arguing that human reason raises questions that cannot be sloughed off or proven in fact. Some things are simply beyond the scope of human reason. Kant viewed this limitation as a negative, but Hegel set out to formulate a method that would employ contradiction as a positive force, which, in turn, would bring human beings closer and closer to ultimate truth. He also differed with Kant, as well as Rousseau by emphasizing the societal rather than individual nature of this movement.

This approach was also shared by Marx, who utilized aspects of Hegel's method in an attempt to theorize society's inevitable march toward an economic utopia. Though Hegel and Marx both believed that societies, not individuals, would produce a better world, there were significant differences between these two 19th-century philosophers, as you will see.

GEORG WILHELM FRIEDRICH HEGEL, 1770–1831

As you know from Chapter 4, Socrates and Plato were considered idealists, because they argued that ideas and concepts were real rather than taking the position that reality manifested itself in the physical or material world. Additionally, both ancient philosophers believed that a body of ultimate, absolute truth existed. Hegel, too, adhered to these positions and, like Plato, was constantly endeavoring to see, not merely . . . like all the other philosophers . . . what the truth is, but also how it is to be reached and appropriated by a mind to which it is naturally remote and foreign. One difference is that Hegel was more concerned with the education of the human race, as opposed to Plato's education of the individual, because the goal of individual (thought) growth is to promote human or world growth.

For Socrates, the growth or movement toward absolute knowledge was accomplished through the application of the Socratic method. Hegel developed a theory of logic called the *dialectic,* which provided the process by which

> the spirit was driven forward by the movement of its own analytical thought to a higher comprehension of truth. However, for Hegel, the dialectic was more than a theory of logic, it was a theory of reality. The dialectic did not merely describe the path of the spirit, it was the path of the spirit. (Brazill, 1970, pp. 37–38).

Using the dialectic and historical theory, Hegel attempted to lay the groundwork for definite knowledge. In his words:

> "This is the vocation of our own and every age: to grasp the knowledge that already exists, to make it our own, and in doing so to develop it further and raise it to a higher level; in thus appropriating it to ourselves we make of it something different from what it was before." (In Brazill, 1970, p.1)

Life and Times

Georg Wilhelm Friedrich Hegel was born in Stuttgart, Germany, on August 27, 1770. His father was a minor government official who was able to provide an economically modest, middle-class lifestyle for his wife and three children. Hegel's mother was commited to the need for education and stimulated his interest in his studies and in intellectual development at an early age. Due in part to his early education, Hegel entered what was called a Latin school at age five and began his pursuit of knowledge through Latin and Greek literature, history, and eventually theology. He was considered a quiet and proper lad, reflecting behavior deemed appropriate at that time in Germany. When he was

What is real is rational; what is rational is real.

G. W. F. Hegel

13, the death of his mother produced an even more sober personality, which, along with the Germanic emphasis on discipline and obedience, would characterize him for the remainder of his life.

Hegel entered the Tübingen Seminary at age 18 and graduated in 1793, having focused on theological studies. He was apparently not a proficient public speaker and was, of all things, weak in philosophy. Furthermore, he was not overly enthused about the prospect of a theological career, so he accepted the position of a resident tutor for three wealthy children in an aristocratic home in Berne, Switzerland. Although he did not find this experience appealing, he continued to be a tutor after he returned to Germany.

In 1800, Hegel's father died and left him a modest inheritance, which the conservative, well-dressed young man used to go to Jena to start a formal career as a schoolteacher. Although he did not consider himself highly successful, he found schoolteaching indispensable to his eventual success at the university level. This was partly because it was necessary at the school level to attempt to simplify philosophical ideas in order to get them across to immature minds. This teaching experience was also valuable in clarifying his own views and in enabling him to establish firm foundations for his philosophy (Mackenzie, 1970). Hegel began his formal writing and completed his first major work, *Phenomenology of the Mind,* in this period.

Previously, he had been greatly influenced by ancient Greek culture, which emphasized the collective fate of the "nation." But he eventually realized he could not overlay a past culture on a contemporary society, which was being influenced by the onset of the Industrial Revolution and the emergence of capitalism. During his stay in Jena, Hegel fell under the influence of the French Revolution and the romanticism of the concept of citizen participation, which ended with the Reign of Terror. This era eventually gave rise to the embodiment of the state in the person of Napoleon, whom he actually saw during the triumphant French march through Jena. The fall of that city brought an end to Hegel's seven-year stay.

Hegel's travels then took him to Bamberg, Bavaria, where he became the editor of the *Bamberg Zeitung*. He did not find newspaper journalism overly rewarding or stimulating; within a year he accepted the position of headmaster at a *Gymnasium* (school) in Nuremberg, a post he held for eight years. During this time, the forty-one year old Hegel married a wonderful and charming woman half his age. Like his father before him, Hegel lived a somewhat quiet, cautious life and had a relatively small family (two sons). He completed his second major work, *Science of Logic* (1812), which brought him to the attention of a number of universities in Germany.

In 1816, Hegel launched his university career as a professor of philosophy at Heidelberg University and in 1818 accepted the chair of philosophy at the University of Berlin, a post he held until 1831, when he died of cholera. A year before the epidemic and his death, Hegel was appointed rector of the university and was decorated by Friedrich Wilhelm III of Prussia. More important, through his distinguished career as a professor of philosophy and the impact of his writing during this time, particularly his *Philosophy of Right,* Hegel was able to impress his peers as well as the government. He was declared the official philosopher of Prussia and in fact was considered Germany's leading philosopher.

Philosophical Contributions

As noted earlier, Hegel lived in a nation that placed a high value on discipline and obedience, and both these cultural traits influenced his thinking. However, he also lived during a time in which the world was experiencing dramatic change, reflected in the Industrial Revolution and the emerging capitalist and socialist economic systems. Hegel's response was to develop a highly disciplined approach that would facilitate change-oriented thought through a logical method.

The work of Parmenides and Socrates provides the foundation for Hegel's philosophy. Parmenides believed the whole of the universe to be more real than its parts. Hegel took this position and postulated that the universe was one of absolute ideas that could be revealed through human thought. He did not limit this theory to ideas or knowledge but extended it to include people, for he believed each individual is related to the totality of the cosmos and should never be viewed in isolation (Butler, 1968). The process that he believed could reveal the absolute ideas was based on Socrates' method of two individuals attempting to ascertain truth through a question-and-answer dialogue. With this in mind, let us begin with Hegel's response to the metaphysical question "What is real?"

As noted, Hegel subscribes to the position that ideas are real. Ideas appear in or are formulated by the mind; therefore, reality is composed solely of ideas in the mind. If only the mind is real, does this mean that material things do not exist? For Hegel, the answer is no! To understand this point, we must realize that Hegel believed the mind to be more of a collective self-consciousness engaged in a historical march or process of refining thoughts, which would eventually culminate in the acquisition and conceptualization of absolute knowledge. Conceived as a never-ending search, the mind, therefore, is infinite. On the other hand, Hegel would argue that material things are less real because they have beginnings and ends and are therefore finite. Put another way, physical things such as a chair or a marble bust cannot be absolute (infinite) because, by definition, these objects must come to an end and enter a realm of nonexistence. With this in mind, Hegel says ideas are more real than material things and that it is "the function of the philosopher to make men conscious of knowledge so that the mind (a system of individuals actively developing their potentialities) can extend itself to its utmost range and thus become absolute" (Acton, 1967, p. 436).

In Chapter 4, you saw that Descartes' search for knowledge was founded on something of which he was certain, of which he had no doubt. Hegel, too, believed we have to have a knowledge base on which to construct future knowledge and, as was the case with many of his predecessors, he was concerned about a reliance on sensory perception and information accepted as fact. He believed that everything had to be examined and clearly expressed this by saying that "in this mixture of empirical things and general classes, perceptual consciousness tumbles about, now declaring one side and then again the other side to be essential" (Hegel, 1963, p. 211).

Hegel's response was to begin with an assumption, for the very nature of an assumption is that it does not imply "truth" and so should be scrutinized. With this position as his stepping-stone, Hegel proceeded to develop his theory of logic, which had the following three stages or *doctrines* (Acton, 1967, pp. 440–441):

1. Doctrine of Being (abstract): separate thoughts standing alone without comparison or contrast.
2. Doctrine of Essence (dialectic): a negative self-examination, which limits the essence of an idea by determining what it is not in light of other thoughts.
3. Doctrine of Idea (speculative): a positive reconceptualization of an idea based upon what it was and what it was not undertaken through a unification of the opposing thoughts.

This process or movement of thought has become known as the *dialectic,* which is undertaken by integrating the Doctrine of Being with the Doctrine of Essence, giving rise to the Doctrine of Idea. More commonly, a thesis is "joined" by an antithesis to produce a synthesis. The synthesis represents a new thesis, which stimulates a new antithesis, which in turn produces a new synthesis, and on and on in a never-ending cycle of starting over, pressing, concluding, and pressing some more—thus moving human knowledge closer and closer to the absolute truth. It is important to note that the process involves transcending without discarding. We get closer to truth not by totally rejecting a thesis but through locating, refining, and retaining its speck of value through contradiction (antithesis). This movement, for Hegel, described the process of intellectual development and the search for truth, which he saw as "the basic function of philosophy, although he conceded most people throughout time were satisfied to find truth through religion" (Butler, 1977, pp. 30–31).

The foundation for the acquisition of knowledge was based on thoughts and ideas as well as experience. Hegel viewed the mind as both subjective and objective and, as with the dialectic, believed that the reconciliation of the two was necessary to the pursuit of knowledge. He felt that "as reflective thought loses its subjective aspects it becomes more objective and moves closer to the absolute, resulting in thought and reality becoming one and the same. This "synthesis" marks the final point of knowledge when concept becomes Absolute Idea and the truth of the world stands revealed" (Kenny, 1994, p.202).

Hegel viewed absolute truth as the goal of history, the end toward which all movement was directed. The goal was reached when all partial truth was negated or contradicted. This process produced more accurate knowledge and therefore came closer to the truth. Further, "each step in the progressive movement to the whole was based on the step before it and replaced that preceding step; but the replacement . . . was not a dismissal of the antecedent step, rather it was a preservation of it plus forward movement, a progression" (Brazill, 1970, p. 405). The development or pursuit of absolute truth, therefore, is a rational process founded on the position that assumption or idea provides a knowledge base on which to begin as opposed to an alleged knowledge base of fact.

Hegel makes the phenomenon of negation the "central event of his system" (Vaught, 1989, p. 35) for he believed that we can only arrive at truth through the identification of error or mistake by using a logical process, which includes asking questions designed to reveal inadequacies. Two functions characterize negation: reason and skepticism. Reason calls for the ability to critically examine isolated things in order to generate a more clear conceptualization of the object or idea, whereas understanding, as defined by Hegel, involves the conceptualization of knowledge that is uncritically accepted. Skepticism requires the need to view existing knowledge as flawed—that is to attack dogmatic positions and thinking, which in turn opens up new possibilities and promotes freedom of reason. By employing both the characteristics of negation, we challenge existing knowledge, which allows us to achieve Hegel's goal of better knowing ideas from previous ideas through a process of contradiction—a process which is necessary if we are to move down the road toward ultimate truth.

The *we* in the above sentence needs to be focused on, for Hegel believed his process would be undertaken by *peoples* as opposed to *individuals*. People create the state, which exists for its own sake. The state is not political but a cultural complex that integrates all components of a people into a unified self-consciousness. Thus, "subjective (individual) freedom must find its place within a structured whole . . . the State" (Acton, 1967, pp. 435–436). Hence, the journey down the road of intellectual reason becomes a historical synthesis of human existence leading toward a more perfect world. Hegel's purpose was "to demonstrate that philosophy expresses the highest and most complete truth about reality" (Flay, 1993, pp. 132–133).

Recognizing what we have done in the past is a recognition of ourselves.
By conducting a dialogue with our past, we are searching how to go forward.

Kiyoko Takeda

Exercise 6.1

Revisit the quotation by Takeda and discuss two characteristics of Hegel's work. Then compare your response to the remarks at the end of the chapter.

From *The Philosophy of History*, Hegel

The most general definition {of the philosophical method of treating history} that can be given is: that the philosophy of history means nothing but the thoughtful consideration of it. Thought is, indeed, essential to humanity. It is this that distinguishes us from the brutes. In sensation, cognition, and intellection, in our instincts and volitions, as far as they are truly human, thought is an invariable element. To insist upon thought in this connection with history may, however, appear unsatisfactory. In this science it would seem as if thought must be subordinate to what is given, to the realities of fact; that this is its basis and guide: while philosophy dwells in the region of self-produced ideas, without reference to actuality. Approaching history thus prepossessed, speculation might be expected to treat it as a mere passive material; and, so far from leaving it in its native truth, to force it into conformity with a tyrannous idea, and to construe it, as the phrase is, "a priori." But as it is the business of history simply to adopt into its records what is and has been, actual occurrences and transactions; and since it remains true to its character in proportion as it strictly adheres to its data, we seem to have in philosophy, a process diametrically opposed to that of the historiographer. This contradiction, and the charge consequently brought against speculation, shall be explained and confuted. We do not, however, propose to correct

(continued)

the innumerable special misrepresentations, trite or novel, that are current respecting the aims, interests, and the modes of treating history, and its relation to philosophy.

The only thought which philosophy brings with it to the contemplation of history, is the simple conception of reason; that reason is sovereign of the world; that the history of the world, therefore, presents us with a rational process. This conviction and intuition is a hypothesis in the domain of history as such. In that of philosophy it is no hypothesis. It is there proved by speculative cognition, that reason—and this term may here suffice us, without investigating the relation sustained by the universe to the divine being—is substance, as well as infinite power; its own infinite material underlying all the natural and spiritual life which it originates, as also the infinite form—that which sets this material in motion. On the one hand, reason is the substance of the universe; viz., that by which and in which all reality has its being and subsistence. On the other hand, it is the infinite energy of the universe; since reason is not so powerless as to be incapable of producing anything but a mere ideal, a mere intention, having its place outside reality, nobody knows where; something separate and abstract, in the heads of certain human beings. It is the infinite complex of things, their entire essence and truth. It is its own material which it commits to its own active energy to work up; not needing, as finite action does, the conditions of an external material of given means from which it may obtain its support, and the objects of its activity. It supplies its own nourishment, and is the object of its own operations. While it is exclusively its own basis of existence, and absolute final aim, it is also the energizing power realizing this aim; developing it not only in the phenomena of the natural, but also the spiritual universe—the history of the world. That this "idea" or "reason" is the true, the eternal, the absolutely powerful essence; that it reveals itself in the world, and that in that world nothing else is revealed but this and its honour and glory—is the thesis which, as we have said, has been proved in philosophy, and is here regarded as demonstrated.

Hegel, G. *The Philosophy of History.* Translated by J. Sibree. (1956). New York: Dover Publications, Inc., pp. 8–10. Reprinted with permission of Dover Publications, Inc.

Hegel in the Classroom

In addition to making his philosophical theories available to us, Hegel also provided us with some very concrete notions about curriculum, instruction, and even classroom management. But his most significant contribution is the process he believed would enable us to arrive at a more "real" knowledge of the world and the universe. Although the key to this process was found in the use of negation, we should not view Hegel's method as negative. Rather, we should impress on our students the need to be open-minded, inquisitive, critical, and, yes, even skeptical when pursuing knowledge. All these characteristics should be considered positives in that they can facilitate a clearer conceptualization of all that we think we know. Students will have a difficult time growing if they continually engage in activities that promote a disposition or attitude of certainty and do not allow for the suspension of judgment or the employment of critical thinking.

The dialectic, when used in the classroom, begins on a positive note by introducing an assumption that contains an aspect of truth, no matter how minuscule. Obviously, an assumption does not function at a 100 percent factual or absolute level. Therefore, the utility of an assumption is that it provides a focus or starting point for the students' intellectual exploration, which should include a critical examination, which, in turn, will produce something of an opposing nature—that is, an antithesis. The "introduction of an opposite and the students' unification of it with the original assumption (thesis) will give rise to new knowledge or put existing knowledge in a larger context" (Pinkard, 1988, pp. 19–20). This process of unifying opposites is continual and allows the students to explore the subject matter under study in depth.

When implementing this process, it is essential that you provide specific learning materials that will enable the students to generate an assumption. For some age groups and given your initial use of the dialectic, you could provide a foundational assumption yourself, but it is much more powerful if you employ a guided discovery technique to establish this base information. Then you need to provide the fuel for the fire in the form of learning materials that will allow the students to "shoot down" the original assumption or thesis with statements or positions of an antithetical nature. This of course will culminate in the synthesis of the two, which allows the students to produce a more accurate assumption, or, as Hegel would say, a statement closer to absolute truth.

It is important for you to realize that the successful implementation of the dialectic depends on your ability to facilitate the lesson and to provide a wide range of learning materials that will stimulate and enhance this intellectual pursuit. In addition, you should attempt to vary the materials, incorporating such things as numerous and different printed materials, models, realia (or real things), mediated software, and interactive technology.

Although methodology offers the most practical application of Hegelian philosophy in the classroom, we can glean from his writings some views on the nature of the learner as well as the nature of knowledge. Although Hegel did not specifically address education in a formal work as others had done, he did hold the following views (Mackenzie, 1970, pp. 27–30):

> *The classics should be emphasized not just for the sake of scholarship but for their bearing on life and character, fundamental idea, and ethics, which provides both knowledge and power or the exercise of thought. History and literature serve as the core for this classic curriculum.

*The seriousness of work should be emphasized as opposed to play.

*Thought begins with obedience and education involves obedience to external authority which aims at making him for himself . . . actually what he is at first only potentially in the eyes of parents and teachers.

*The curriculum should be designed to develop the power of thought, which can only be attained by practice in thinking. Teachers should introduce subjects to strengthen and support this effort.

*So-called useful subjects should never be given precedence over subjects that develop the intellect and character.

For Hegel, the school should have a curriculum that today would be considered academically focused and classically based, should employ methods of instruction that promote intellectual reasoning, and should develop a learning environment based on obedience and hard work. Such a school should promote Hegel's overriding goal, which is to allow the individual to move from an egocentric focus to a world focus, thereby reinforcing the collective drive toward the absolute truth. "Keeping this in view, it is easy to understand the further highly characteristic and significant statement that the whole development of the mind is nothing else than its own self-elevation to truth" (Bryant, 1896, p. 91). Let's now look at how the dialectic can be utilized in the classroom.

Scenario 6.1

Mr. Bruce Hughes, a physics teacher at Stanton College Preparatory School, began his class by telling the students that they were going to discuss some things about force and asked them to pay close attention to what they were about to undertake.

"First of all," he began, "I am going to ask for some responses from you, and I'll want to get some answers. I want you to tell me what you feel even if it doesn't sound right. Just give me the information you have. Okay, John, what is force?"

"It's . . . uh . . . how it acts on something," John replied.

"How it acts on something," Mr. Hughes repeated. "Okay, Victor, what do you think force is?"

"The amount of work that is put on an object to make it move."

"The amount of work put on an object to make it move. Okay. Brenda, what is force?"

"It's a push or pull to make something . . ."

"To make it what?" Mr. Hughes urged.

"To make something move," Brenda concluded.

"Okay. Nita, what is force?"

"A vector quantity . . ."

"That causes?" Mr. Hughes urged again.

"An acceleration."

"Okay. Terry, what is force?"

"I'd have to say the push or pull," Terry replied.

With permission. Stanton College Preparatory School, Jacksonville, Florida. Mr. Ed Pratt-Dannals, Principal.

"A push or pull, okay. Then what is the effect of force?" Mr. Hughes added.

"Motion, I guess," Terry answered.

"Okay. Then Greg, what is force?"

"A push or pull on an object that makes it move and causes motion," Greg concluded.

"Okay," Mr. Hughes said with a certain finality. "Force is a push or pull on an object that makes it move, that causes motion. Now, Sam, does that mean that an object does not move unless it is being pushed or pulled?"

"Right," Sam said.

"Okay. It does not move unless it is being pushed or pulled. So what happens whenever you are driving a car and whenever you press the accelerator, that is, what is happening there? Please describe that for me," Mr. Hughes asked of Sam.

"The power of the engine is transferred to the transmission, which pushes the wheels on the ground, which makes the car go forward."

"So," Mr. Hughes inquired, "if you turn off that car engine and that car engine is no longer functioning, will that car stop immediately?"

"No, because the inertia takes over and causes it to stop moving, but it just decelerates."

"Okay. Then what if you were driving a car and cut off the engine. Would it start slowing down immediately? Or, how long would it take it to stop, do you think, Bill?"

"Oh, probably, like, depending on what the road is like, how fast you are going, how much the car weighs and, ah, how much . . ."

"Well," Mr. Hughes interjected, "what is the longest you think the car can go without stopping? In terms of minutes or seconds?"

"Two or three minutes?" Bill guessed.

"Two or three minutes. Okay. What if you were about to stop and suddenly, at the same time, the car hit a piece of ice, nice smooth ice. How long would that car keep moving? Sam?"

"Another five minutes or so," Sam said.

"Five minutes or so?"

"Well, it would depend on how long the ice was," Sam added.

"Yes, so we have to think then about what we mean by acceleration," Mr. Hughes said. "Debbie, think about what Sam just had to say about the ice. In the case of a patch of ice, do you have motion . . . of that car?"

"If it's moving, I guess so."

"Okay. It is moving," Mr. Hughes agreed. "Do you have any force acting on that car? Making it move?"

"Nah," Debbie concluded.

"So you have motion but you have no force acting on the car when it's sliding across ice. Think about that. Does somebody have a remark they would like to make or a question they want to ask?"

"Didn't force make it move in the first place?" Emmy inquired.

"Now, when you say move, what do you mean? Clarify your word *move* please."

"Set it in actual motion."

"Set it in motion. In other words," Mr. Hughes continued, "if you had to use one of our physics words, what would you say happened whenever it was set into motion?"

"Uhm . . . it accelerated," Emmy said.

"Okay. So the force caused a what?"

"An acceleration."

"Very good. Yes! So force causes an acceleration. In other words, you are coming around to the point of view now, if you think about this, that force does not cause motion. What does force cause, Winston?"

"Acceleration,"

"Yes, acceleration, which can be defined as a change in what?"

"Motion," Winston concluded.

"Motion. So, changes in motion are caused by force. Motion occurs without any force acting at all. What principle is involved in that, Jason? That motion occurs even if no force is acting on it?"

"Inertia."

"Inertia. Yes, inertia. That's good. Any questions about this? (Pause.) Okay, then can anyone give me an example of an acceleration caused by a force? Let me see your hands to see how many of you have an example. Go ahead, Maria."

"How about a parked car being hit by a moving car?" Maria inquired.

"So, the original motion of the parked car is what?" Mr. Hughes asked.

"Zero."

"Which is also called what? You say it is at what?"

"At rest," Maria concluded.

"That's correct. Very good. And then a parked car is hit by a moving car, which causes it to . . . ?"

"Accelerate."

"Accelerate. Good. Marika, another example please?"

"A wagon being pushed downhill," Marika said.

"Okay. Now what forces are acting on that wagon?" Mr. Hughes inquired.

"I don't know," Marika replied.

"Okay. If you have a rolling object at the top of the hill and you let it go, what happens if you just release it without giving it a push?"

"It will go down the hill."

"And what is that force called that will make it go down the hill?"

"Gravity."

"Yes. Gravity. It doesn't work as fast," Mr. Hughes added, "but it still works. Gene, do you have an example of your own?"

"Oh yeah," Gene said with a smile. "A football being kicked through an upright."

"Fine. What force is acting on that football?"

"A foot."

"And how long is that foot acting on that football?"

"Oh, for about one second."

"Very good," Mr. Hughes said. "So the force of the foot only acts on that football one second and, after that, what force is acting on it?"

"Inertia and gravity," Gene answered.

"Inertia and gravity," Mr. Hughes repeated. "Gravity is a force. Is inertia a force? Does it cause a change in velocity?"

"No."

"So inertia is not a force. Very good," Mr. Hughes said. "So you have the force of gravity and, for a short period of time, you have the force of the foot on the football but, because of inertia, even though the foot is no longer kicking the football, what happens?"

"It goes 50 yards down the field," Gene said, again with a smile.

"Right," Mr. Hughes responded, also smiling. "Does anyone have any questions about this?" (Pause.) "Okay, then, the idea you need to take away with you is that motion itself is not actually a part of force. Motion is not caused by force. Changes in motion are caused by force." Mr. Hughes showed the students some diagrams that depicted the preceding relationships, then continued the discussion.

In reflecting on this presentation, it is important to note that Mr. Hughes begins by facilitating a process that allows the students to verbalize a consensus regarding their collective thoughts about a cognitive concept, force. He then challenges them by "fueling the fire" through an examination of their conceptualization, which results in (1) an identification of error—that is contradiction, and (2) a conclusion with a (new) reconceptualization.

In taking this approach, Mr. Hughes not only employs the principles of Hegel's dialectic. He also demonstrates the validity of Hegel's assumption that our task is that of facilitating change-oriented thought through a logical method that allows ourselves and our students to come closer to truth.

Exercise 6.2

Examine the following statements to determine if they are consistent (c) or inconsistent (i) with Hegel's philosophy. Then compare your answers with those at the end of the chapter.

_____ 1. The primary function of every generation is to accept existing knowledge.

_____ 2. Ideas or thoughts are more real than physical objects and material things.

_____ 3. When employing the dialectic, the "thesis" needs to be challenged and totally rejected.

_____ 4. When employing the dialectic, the "antithesis" is used soley for the purpose of rejecting the "thesis."

_____ 5. The nature of an assumption is that it is a statement of fact.

Exercise 6.3

According to Hegel, the pursuit of absolute knowledge involves a logical process known as the dialectic. Briefly discuss the three steps in this process, then compare your response to the one at the end of the chapter.

KARL MARX, 1818–1881

In the late 20th century, we have witnessed the collapse of the Soviet Union and the withering of communism in Central European nations and other countries worldwide. Because of the role of Marxist thought as the foundation of communism, you might be asking why Marx's work is included in this book. The answer is found by concentrating on Marx the philosopher, as opposed to Marx the economic theorist.

First, Marx was a dialectician (before he was a materialist) whose system attempted to comprehend the totality of society and history and whose practice would overthrow it. Further, "it is incorrect to say that Marx's materialist theory is no longer philosophical merely because it has an aim that is not simply theoretical but is also a practical and revolutionary goal. On the contrary, Dialectical Materialism is by its own very nature a philosophy through and through" (Korsch, 1970, p. 75). Thus, "Marx's aim was not to merely interpret the human experience and the world but to change it" (McBride, 1977, p. 12).

Until the 19th century, Western philosophy, in its 2500-year history, exhibited many continuities, including two complementary traditions: dogmatic assertion about the nature of reality and scepticism about knowledge claims (Prokopczyk, 1980). Marx brought an additional dimension to the table: a move from speculation to action.

Life and Times

On May 5, 1818, Karl Marx was born in Trier, Germany, a city of 12,000 people located on the banks of the Moselle River. He was the first son and third of 11 children born to Heinrich Marx, a prestigious lawyer. Although his family was Jewish (the elder Marx's actual name was Herschel Levi), his father adopted the Lutheran religion in the apparent belief that he could practice his chosen profession more freely. Therefore, on the one hand, Marx's early years were colored by liberal Protestantism and an education centered around the classics and human reasoning. This economically comfortable environment often focused on humanitarian ideals, a focus that came to influence his thoughts and writings. On the other hand, his youth was spent in a geographic region of Germany that was considered progressive and enlightened but was controlled and to some degree oppressed by the government in Berlin.

Marx's home schooling ended at age 12, when his father enrolled him in a *Gymnasium* (somewhat more advanced than a U.S. high school). He was a good student and graduated at age 17. Throughout those school years, Marx developed a deepening relationship with a childhood friend, Jenny von Westphalen, and became close to her father, who introduced him to the ideas of Saint-Simon and French socialism. After graduating from the *Gymnasium,* he entered the University of Bonn and began to study law. However, his father's profession could not captivate his dynamic mind, and he began to associate with a kind of liberal bourgeoisie spawned by the Paris July Revolution. In response, his father moved him from Bonn and its small school of 700 students to the University of Berlin with its 2000 students in a city of 300,000 people.

The philosophers have only interpreted the world in various ways: The point is to change it.

Karl Marx

For the next two years, Marx remained true to the wishes of his father regarding his studies. But he became increasingly restless as he experienced, first-hand, the yoke of feudalism, which continued to prevail in Germany. During this time he discovered in Hegel's dialectic the constant process of development and transformation and tried to "formulate the laws that govern the behavior of men in society and create a movement designed to transform the lives of men in conformity with these laws" (Urmson, 1960, p. 248). He became part of the Young Hegelian Movement but became quickly disenchanted with their focus on intellectual speculation and a lack of philosophical application to the real world. Marx's father died around the same time, which resulted in the loss of emotional as well as financial ties and brought to an end his legal studies. He turned to the study of philosophy in earnest and transferred to the University of Jena, where he was awarded a doctorate at age 24 in 1841.

Credentials in hand, Marx had in mind the academic life of a lecturer. But the political conflict between an increasingly liberal populace and a reactionary government produced in him the desire to be an activist, and he began writing political and social articles. This brought him to the attention of other antifeudalists, with whom he founded and edited a newspaper. The government viewed him as a revolutionary democrat and a materialist, and, after countless episodes of censorship, Marx resigned his editorship. His work as editor of the *Rheinische Zeitung*, though for only a short period, had enriched him by way of two significant experiences. He had begun to recognize what a great role material interests play in human society, and he had seen that in the fight for the interests of the dispossessed masses, idealism and bourgeois democracy were inadequate as philosophical and political weapons. That drove him to a fundamental examination of economic and social problems. Furthermore, he came to the unalterable conclusion that history was not determined by ideas, or by the Hegelian "world spirit," but that "the doctrine of historical materialism, the theory that the material conditions of life and specifically the mode of production of the material means of existence determine much else in human consciousness and society" (McInnes, 1967, p. 172).

At age 25, Marx married his childhood sweetheart, Jenny, and moved to Paris, where he continued to publish his ideas in what were viewed as radical periodicals. Regarding his personal life, this was to be the beginning of 40 years of sacrifice and poverty in foreign lands. Within a year, he and Jenny fled Paris and arrived in Brussels, Belgium, where they lived for three years or so. During that time, Marx became affiliated with unions that eventually gave rise to the International Communist League. This group asked him to write a position paper, which became the *Manifesto of the Communist Party*. After trying to return to France, Marx headed for England, where he spent the remainder of his life.

He and Jenny lived in a small apartment in the shoddy area of Soho, within the city limits of London. Marx rarely associated with anyone and lived an isolated life, spending most of his waking hours writing in the British Museum. Like Socrates, Marx was a poor provider and was dependent on small stipends from his friends. Unlike Socrates, however, he did try to provide for his family, though, at one time or another, literally every family possession had to be pawned. Still, there were insufficient funds, and three of his children died at young ages primarily due to a poor diet and a lack of medicine. Eventually, Marx was able to rely on financial assistance provided on a monthly basis by his friend and collaborator, Friedrich Engels. Relieved of some emotional and financial burdens, Marx could fully concentrate on his writing and produced his major work, *Capital*, considered his theoretical masterpiece. Nevertheless, poor health continued and Marx eventually lost his wife and oldest daughter in little more than a year. Within months of this heartbreaking time, at age 63, Marx developed an abscessed lung and died in his sleep. Thus ended the journey of a man who championed the division of wealth and who lived a life of abject poverty.

Philosophical Contributions

It is often said the Marx "turned Hegel upside down." This statement suggests that Marx was diametrically opposed to the philosophical contributions of Hegel. To a large extent, that was the case. However, Hegel's work not only provided Marx with a point of departure but also gave him a foundation on which he would launch his radical theories.

At the onset, Marx credited Hegel with the dialectic and did not disagree with it as a method. However, the problem for Marx was the way Hegel applied this theory of the acquisition of knowledge. Hegel focused on speculative idealism and employed the dialectic, which contradicted or negated a partial truth, which in turn led to new knowledge and brought humankind closer to answering the time-honored metaphysical question "What is real?" Hegel's idealism was founded on the metaphysics of Socrates and Plato, who, as you know, believed that ideas were more "real" than objects. Therefore, the purpose of the dialectic, as employed by Hegel, was to hone ideas in order to move more closely to truth.

Marx's reversal of Hegel is found in the forces that drive the dialectic. For Marx, these forces are not idealistic; they are materialistic. He did not view the dialectic as an exercise in reflecting on metaphysical questions. He saw the dialectic as a dynamic method that brought together economic factors—that is, the class struggle and other economic conditions, which were the sole causal determinants of both history and thought (McBride, 1977). Marx clearly viewed this "coming together" as the key to transforming the external world and changing human nature (Sarup, 1989). Thus, the practical activity or work of individuals collectively affects society, which in turn creates a different world. The reason Marx focused on work as the most essential activity in which human beings engage was that he believed the way people met their needs for food, shelter, clothing, physical safety, and other requirements, and how they cooperated with their fellow human beings for these ends, had great influence on their religious, philosophical, and political beliefs. Furthermore, Marx rejected the assumption that each of us should simply seek our own good; "only the service of a life concerned for all life furnishes the ultimate end" (Hartshorne, 1983, p. 222). This "end" was viewed as the positive resolution of the human condition.

Marx employed the dialectic as a method that would achieve this end. However, unlike Hegel, he viewed the dialectic as a practical, dynamic, and material process as opposed to a logical activity. Both agreed that the key force for human advancement in the dialectic was found in negating existing thought or practice. Beyond this, they had some disagreements: "For Hegel, negations or contradictions were found in ideas, but Marx believed contradiction was found in society and therefore set Hegel on his feet by replacing idealist metaphysics with its materialistic negation" (Kenny, 1994, p. 206). Thus Marx's aim was to develop the philosophy of history into a theory of class struggle and to offer mass movements and economic forces as the basic causes of fundamental change, whether in the world of things or in the life of thought (Durant, 1953).

By combining his views on the foundation of political, social, and intellectual life with Hegel's methodology, "Marx's theory of dialectic materialism was not esoteric philosophy but empirical science" (Hudelson, 1990, p. 145). He believed that "a philosophy of action could change existing laws and institutions and enable men, i.e., the proletariat, to fully satisfy their needs and worldly conditions. Therefore, Marx viewed the job of philosophy as negative: it worked to remove obstacles from the paths of inquiry" (Suchting, 1986, p. 52). At the point at which dialectical materialism would have removed all such obstacles and the proletariat arrived at its desired and final destination, the function of philosophy would cease to exist.

Dreams pass into the reality of action. From action . . . stems the dream again;
and this interdependence produces the highest form of living.

Anais Nin

Exercise 6.4

Return to the quotation by Anais Nin and briefly discuss two thoughts that
could also be found in Marx's work. Then compare your response to the feedback at the end of the chapter.

From *Alienated Labour*, Marx

Man is a species-being not only in the sense that he makes the community (his own as well as those of other things) his object both practically and theoretically, but also (and this is simply another expression for the same thing) in the sense that he treats himself as the
present, living species, as a universal and consequently free being.

Species-life, for man as for animals, has its physical basis in the
fact that man (like animals) lives from inorganic nature, and since man
is more universal than an animal so the range of inorganic nature from
which he lives is more universal. Plants, animals, minerals, air, light,
etc. constitute, from the theoretical aspect, a part of human consciousness as objects of natural science and art; they are man's spiritual inorganic nature, his intellectual means of life, which he must first
prepare for enjoyment and perpetuation. So also, from the practical
aspect, they form a part of human life and activity. In practice man
lives only from these natural products, whether in the form of food,
heating, clothing, housing, etc. The universality of man appears in
practice in the universality which makes the whole of nature into his
organic body: (1) as a direct means of life; and equally (2) as the material object and instrument of his life activity. Nature is the inorganic
body of man; that is to say nature, excluding the human body itself. To
say that man lives from nature means that nature is his body with
which he must remain in a continuous interchange in order not to die.
The statement that the physical and mental life of man, and nature, are
interdependent means simply that nature is interdependent with itself,
for man is part of nature.

Since alienated labour: (1) alienates nature from man; and (2) alienates man from himself, from his own active function, his life activity; so
it alienates him from the species. It makes species-life into a means of

individual life. In the first place it alienates species-life and individual life, and secondly, it turns the latter, as an abstraction, into the purpose of the former, also in its abstract and alienated form.

For labour, life activity, productive life, now appear to man only as means for the satisfaction of a need, the need to maintain his physical existence. Productive life is, however, species-life. It is life creating life. In the type of life activity resides the whole character of a species, its species-character; and free, conscious activity is the species-character of human beings. Life itself appears only as a means of life.

The animal is one with its life activity. It does not distinguish the activity from itself. It is its activity. But man makes his life activity itself an object of his will and consciousness. He has a conscious life activity. It is not a determination with which he is completely identified. Conscious life activity distinguishes man from the life activity of animals. Only for this reason is he a species-being. Or rather, he is only a self-conscious being, i.e., his own life is an object for him, because he is a species-being. Only for this reason is his activity free activity. Alienated labour reverses this relationship, in that man because he is a self-conscious being makes his life activity, his being, only a means for his existence.

The practical construction of an objective world, the manipulation of inorganic nature, is the confirmation of man as a conscious species-being, i.e., a being who treats the species as his own being or himself as a species-being. Of course, animals also produce. They construct nests, dwellings, as in the case of bees, beavers, ants, etc. But they only produce what is strictly necessary for themselves or their young. They produce only in a single direction, while man produces universally. They produce only under the compulsion of direct physical needs, while man produces when he is free from physical need and only truly produces in freedom from such need. Animals produce only themselves, while man produces the whole of nature. The products of animal production belong directly to their physical bodies, whilst man freely confronts his product. Animals construct only in accordance with the standards and needs of the species to which they belong, while man knows how to produce in accordance with the standards of every species and knows how to apply the appropriate standard to the object. Thus man constructs also in accordance with the laws of beauty.

It is just in his work upon the objective world that man really proves himself as a species-being. This production is his active species-life. By means of it nature appears as his work and his reality. The object of

(continued)

labour is, therefore, the objectification of man's species-life; for he no longer reproduces himself merely intellectually, as in consciousness, but actively and in a real sense, and he sees his own reflection in a world which he has constructed. While, therefore, alienated labour takes away the object of production from man, it also takes away his species-life, his real objectivity as a species-being, and changes his advantage over animals into a disadvantage in so far as his inorganic body, nature, is taken from him.

Just as alienated labour transforms free and self-directed activity into a means, so it transforms the species-life of man into a means of physical existence.

Consciousness, which man has from his species, is transformed through alienation so that species-life becomes only a means for him. Thus, alienated labour turns the species-life of man, and also nature as his mental species-property, into an alien being and into a means for his individual existence. It alienates for man his own body, external nature, his mental life, and his human life. A direct consequence of the alienation of man from the product of his labour, from his life activity and from his species-life, is that man is alienated from other men. What is true of man's relationship to his work, to the product of his work and to himself, is also true of his relationship to other men, to their labour and to the objects of their labour.

In general, the statement that man is alienated from his species-life means that each man is alienated from others, and that each of the others is likewise alienated from human life.

Marx, K. (1964). *Economic and Philosophic Manuscripts of 1844.* (D. Struik, Ed.). New York: International Publishers, Co., pp. 112–113. Reprinted with permission of International Publishers, Co.

Marx in the Classroom

In Unit 1 you became familiar with the three functions a school curriculum can satisfy: the conservative role, the evaluative role, and the transforming role. Marx the philosopher would champion the transforming role, presumably arguing that schools should not brainwash students but should try to provide them with empowering knowledge and skills that would allow them to transform society. You also know from your earlier reading that the goals of the curriculum are founded on the needs of the individual, the needs of society, and a body of existing or traditional knowledge. Marx would further argue that schools should focus on the needs of the individual, for only in this way could an educational experience provide students with the intellectual ability and the freedom necessary to bring about societal change.

To accomplish these goals, Marx emphasized a technologically grounded curriculum. Here he was not referring to a narrow skills experience but one more akin to what Adler espoused in the *Paideia Proposal,* stressing the more general world of work as opposed to the ins and outs of specific jobs. It is useful to note that we often hear that the success of individuals as well as nations in the 21st century will depend on their ability to compete in a global economy. In line with that thinking, Marx was interested in having students understand the economic system in which they would have to live—and the one they would have to change. His economic focus coupled with contemporary concerns strongly points to the need for the presentation of economic issues in today's classrooms.

Marx did not believe education should merely reproduce the status quo. If young people were to eventually become adults capable of changing the world, the schools would have to provide them with insights and critical inquiry skills that would enable them to transform the dominant culture (Pinkevich, 1929). The dialectic would be an extremely useful tool in that effort, since its application in the classroom would challenge existing perceptions. Marx saw the need for students to become more knowledgeable about the world they lived in by using the dialectic to challenge traditional assumptions, seek alternatives, and elevate themselves to higher levels of awareness. The key to the dialectic is negation, for every contradiction contains a tension that compels its resolution and requires students to address the following questions (Urmson, 1960, p. 118):

1. How does a contradiction come about?
2. To what extent is a new unity formed?
3. How does a new contradiction arise?

A focal point for Marxist philosophy, particularly as it relates to the school curriculum, is that of *praxis*, which can be defined as human activity of a customary or practical nature. Note that "the logic of the philosophy of praxis in Marxism is first and foremost a commitment to 'doing' something, namely to be realizing, or helping to realize, a certain vision of human liberation. Everything [Marx] did was designed to assist in this realization" (Kitching, 1988, pp. 26–27). As for philosophy itself, Marx believed it was not "sovereign but [was] the servant of worldly concerns. Philosophy often asserted the notion that worldly conditions derived from timeless and universal abstract truths . . . rather than being dependent upon social and political conditions" (Mah, 1987, pp. 1–2). Since Marx believed those conditions in his time reflected an economic sickness and that individual, intellectual action could change society, the primary function of the school would be that of facilitating the ability to transform the existing human experience. If the purpose of Hegel's use of the dialectic in the classroom was that of intellectual reflection, Marx's employment of the dialectic was that of practical action. Therefore, the difference between the two with regard to classroom application is not that of the mechanics of the dialectic but rather the end result of its utilization. With that in mind, let's take a look at Marx the philosopher in the classroom.

Scenario 6.2

Mr. Bill McLin, a fifth-grade social studies teacher at Lakeside Elementary School, began his lesson by using an overhead projector to show his students a transparency of the Middle East during the time of the First Crusade. He spent the first few minutes of the class having the students orally identify the nation-states, major trade routes, and significant military campaigns, all of which were clearly shown on the projected map. He then asked the students to share what they had learned about why the Crusades took place.

"The reason for the Crusades was all about religion," Maryelle said.

"Can you tell us what you mean by that, Maryelle?" Mr. McLin asked.

"Lots of people, like the English, wanted to travel and maybe even live where Jesus had been."

"And where was that, Maryelle? Come up to the overhead and point it out for us." Maryelle approached the overhead and with the tip of her pencil pointed to Jerusalem.

"And what part of the world today do we call that, Maryelle?"

"It's the Middle East."

"That's correct," Mr. McLin said as Maryelle returned to her seat. "Can anyone add to what Maryelle has told us?"

"The Christian people who lived around there may not have been treated okay by the Arabs," Edrie added.

"What was the religion of those Arab peoples, Edrie?"

"I think they are Muslims."

"And you are right. So, Maryelle and Edrie are telling us that the Crusades were fought about holy places and persecution. Does everyone know what persecution is? (Positive nods.) Does everyone agree?" (Again . . . positive nods.) "Okay then, who can tell us something about what Europe was like just before the Crusades began?"

"I think that things were going pretty good," Josh volunteered.

"What do you mean by that, Josh? Can you be specific?" Mr. McLin asked.

"Well, for one thing, there had been a lot of wars and stuff, you know, like the Vikings, but then the big countries seemed to be pretty peaceful."

"Which big countries, Josh?"

"England."

"And another one?"

"France," Josh added.

"Fine," Mr. McLin said, smiling. "Now, can you be more specific about what you mean by peaceful?"

"Well, we learned that the people were okay."

"What was okay?" Mr. McLin urged.

"Well, people were safer and they had more to eat."

With permission. Lakeside Elementary School. Orange Park, Florida. Ms. Carol Eberhart, Principal.

"Good examples, Josh. By more to eat, do you mean they were growing more on their own lands?"

"Yes."

"Were there other sources of food?"

"Oh yeah," Josh said. "One of the things about being safer was that people could trade more and get food and things from other towns and cities."

"Did this mean these countries were growing or expanding?" Mr. McLin asked.

"Oh yes," Josh agreed.

"And their families were growing too," Carla added.

"That's a fact, Carla," Mr. McLin said. "Due to the fact that, as Josh told us, times were pretty good, moms and dads were having increased numbers of children. Can anyone tell us, at that time, what the deal was with inheritance?"

"You mean like who got what?" Roy asked.

"Yes."

"I think the oldest got it all, which is okay with me," Roy said with a grin, "because I have three little brothers."

"You've got it right," Mr. McLin said, also grinning, "and back then, what would have happened to your three little brothers?"

"I guess I was nice to them or they took a walk."

"To where?"

"Another town or farm or land somewhere, I guess."

"All three of them?"

"Sure."

"Okay, now we mentioned expansion and Josh had identified two main European countries, England and France. Look at the map and tell us some of the countries Roy's brothers might have gone to in order to find land and start new homes."

"I think maybe Spain," Debby said.

"And I think Italy . . . and maybe Greece," Tom added.

"All three are on the money," Mr. McLin said. "Tom, you said two of them, Italy and Greece. What do you notice about the trade routes on the map?"

"Lots of them seem to be starting there."

"And why do you think that is so?"

"Ships?" Tom asked

"Do you mean the routes originate from cities that had seaports?"

"Yes."

"Okay, Tom. Now, everyone take another look at the map and see if there is some relationship between the trade routes and the military campaigns of the Crusades. (Pause.) Do you see anything?"

"They pretty much go along together," Paula said.

"Anyone have the math term for that?" Mr. McLin asked.

"They parallel each other," Jim responded.

"Yes, they appear to parallel each other. What if anything might we conclude from this?"

"The Crusades made it possible for, ah . . ."

"Merchants?" Mr. McLin interjected.

"Yeah, merchants to open up their trade in that part of the world."

"Open up?" Mr. McLin inquired.

"Ah, expand," Jim said.

"And, class, Josh told us things were pretty good, so how were expanded trade routes going to affect people in Western Europe?"

"They would have even more stuff," Josh said.

"Right, Josh, and a lot of the 'stuff' you are referring to were things the Western Europeans had not seen like rice and apricots and melons and perfumes and spices and silk. But in addition to just getting these and other things, what else do you think happened in Western Europe?"

"I'm pretty sure they got seed and stuff and starting growing their own food just like the Pilgrims," Pete said.

"Well, the Pilgrims came 400 or so years later but you are right, Pete, they planted new crops . . . but you can't plant silk. How about that . . . anyone?"

"They could learn how to make silk and other things," Julie said.

"They can and they did. Now," Mr. McLin said and paused, "we began with Maryelle telling us that the Crusades were fought for religious purposes and we all agreed. Do we all still agree?"

"Our book says it was a holy war," Kathe began, "and I still think that was what it was all about, but then maybe there were other things that might have had something to do with it."

"Me too," Jeremy said. "I think it really was a religious thing, but then in our current events we hear so much about trade and stuff that I think it must have been pretty important."

"In what way, Jeremy?"

"Well like I said with current events, we are always being told that if we can't do good in trade around the world, we are going to be in big trouble. Maybe, I think, it was the same way back then."

"Okay class, let's take a closer look at what some of you are saying here," Mr. McLin said. He then engaged the class in a discussion and analysis of how economic, as well as religious, factors may have contributed to the launching of the Crusades.

Focusing on Marx's *philosophical* contributions to the classroom, we can see in the preceding presentation that Mr. McLin has employed the dialectic in terms of an economic, practical issue. The possible controversy, or critical component of negation, arises with the notion that religion might not have been the only factor that brought about the Crusades and that what may have appeared to be accurate knowledge could be far more complicated. A "new unity" is being formed as the students appear to simply "prioritize" religion as the prime force behind the Crusades. To what depth the students take this issue remains to be seen, yet there can be little doubt that the dialectic has been employed and that important questions have arisen. Additionally, the contemporary global competition issue has been introduced, which could give Mr. McLin a chance to connect the past, the present, and the possible future. Finally, this last observation opens the door for an elementary discussion of Marx's theory of economic determinism.

Exercise 6.5

Examine the following statements to determine if they are consistent (c) or inconsistent (i) with Marx's philosophy. Then check your answers against those at the end of the chapter.

_____ 1. The "steps" in Marx's dialectic were the same as those employed by Hegel.

_____ 2. Marxist philosophy and Hegelian philosophy are in agreement regarding the end result of the use of the dialectic.

_____ 3. Marx the philosopher was preoccupied with metaphysical questions.

_____ 4. Marxist philosophy is founded on the theories of Socrates and Plato.

_____ 5. Marxist philosophy is only concerned with the betterment of the individual worker.

Exercise 6.6

In the quotation on page 173, Marx implied that the role of his philosophical predecessors was purely speculative. But he viewed the purpose of philosophy in a different light. Briefly discuss that difference and then check your response against the one at the end of the chapter.

SUMMARY

Like Rousseau and Kant, Hegel and Marx focused on the individual pursuit of knowledge. However, as you have seen, there were differences. Hegel perceived cognitive societal development as the objective; Marx perceived material societal development as the goal. Rousseau's work focused on the individual and on what he saw as the debilitating effect of society on human beings. Kant concerned himself with the mind and the speculative process in terms of desired individual behavior.

Building on Kant, Hegel used the dialectic to bring the "is" and "ought" into harmony, whereas Marx went in a totally new direction. In the 17th and 18th centuries, philosophers assumed that "the behavior of man was subject to rules and principles identical with or analogous to those which governed the material world, individual as well as environmental" (Walker, 1989, p. 102). Marx's action-oriented philosophy challenged that premise by suggesting that individual/mass movements could significantly change the material world in which human beings lived.

As for the use of the dialectic, Hegel saw the need to negate existing concepts for the purpose of explaining, understanding, and eventually discovering truth. Marx was not preoccupied with conceptual truth and used Hegel's employment of the dialectic as a springboard to provide a mechanism that would allow for the contradiction and eventual change of the material world. It is often observed that "Hegel spiritualized action, where Marx materialized it"

(Hyppolite, 1969, pp. 93–94). Put differently, Hegel believed the world could be possessed through knowledge, whereas Marx believed the world could be possessed by working on it.

Questions for Discussion

1. Having read the long excerpt from Hegel earlier in the chapter, what is the relationship Hegel develops between history and reason?
2. It is often said that Marx turned Hegel upside down. What is meant by this statement?
3. In general, "alienation is thought of as a condition wherein man is removed from activities or decisions that affect his life" (Kneller, 1971, p. 185). For Hegel, alienation means that consciousness must become foreign to itself in order to put itself back together in an increased level of self-awareness. How does Marx's view of alienation differ from that of Hegel's?
4. It was noted earlier that Marx would favor the transforming role of the school. With which of the three roles—conservative, evaluative, and transforming—do you believe Hegel would be most comfortable?
5. What is the role played by logic in the philosophy of Hegel? In the philosophy of Marx?
6. What did Marx mean by the following statement: "Life determines consciousness, not consciousness life."
7. How would the dialectic be employed in the classroom by Hegel? By Marx?

Suggested Field Laboratory Activities

1. Review curriculum guides, texts, or other available instructional materials in terms of "if" or "how often" Hegel's dialectic is being employed. If you cannot find examples of the complete process, see if you can find lessons that included the component of negation or introduced controversy that led to resolution.
2. Select a topic or objective in a text or teachers' guide that is founded on an alleged factual statement. Then generate some ways you might negate the statement. Finally, resolve the controversy.
3. Repeat the preceding suggestion with the addition of searching for lessons of an economic nature.
4. Given the opportunity, observe lessons in your field site that have an element of controversy. How was the material introduced, manipulated, and resolved?
5. Review selected guides and lesson plans and see if you can identify materials that would facilitate a "transforming" experience—that is, something that is action oriented as opposed to reflective.
6. Develop and present, if possible, a knowledge-based lesson that utilizes the dialectic as employed by Hegel.
7. Develop and present, if possible, an action-oriented, economic-based lesson that utilizes the dialectic as employed by Marx.

Exercise Feedback

Exercise 6.1

One commonality between the thoughts of Takeda and the philosophy of Hegel is the notion of a never-ending cyclical process. For Hegel, we have thesis versus antithesis, which gives rise to synthesis, which becomes a new thesis. For Takeda, we have looking at the past, conducting a dialogue (present), and moving toward the future. Eventually, the future becomes the past and the process repeats itself. A second commonality is found in the result of these processes; both lead to a more perfect self or a more perfect world.

Exercise 6.2

1. (i)   Inconsistent. Each generation needs to take existing knowledge, critically examine it, and revise it to approach absolute truth.
2. (c)   Consistent. Hegel adheres, in this sense, to the classical position of idealism.
3. (i)   Inconsistent. Hegel suggests each thesis has a kernel of truth within it that must be located, preserved, and utilized.
4. (i)   Inconsistent. As with the thesis, the antithesis also possesses value and, when united with the thesis, gives rise to a synthesis.
5. (i)   Inconsistent. Assumptions are not statements of fact and are the foundations on which the dialectic is developed because by nature they lend themselves to refinement.

Exercise 6.3

The first step in the process involves a thesis that entails a statement of existing knowledge. It is assumed that this statement does not represent absolute truth and is therefore flawed. The second step is the appearance of an antithesis, which opposes the thesis and challenges its accuracy, stripping it down to its essence. The third step, synthesis, is a unification of these opposites (thesis and antithesis), which gives rise to a new thesis. The process then begins anew.

Exercise 6.4

Like the quotation from Takeda, the passage from Nin describes a cyclical process. However, more in line with Marx, Nin is addressing a world of reality and implies that the way to move toward a more perfect living (world) is through the direct action on human dreams.

Exercise 6.5

1. (c)   Consistent. The terms *thesis, antithesis,* and *synthesis* apply to Hegel as well as Marx.

2. (i)   Inconsistent. Hegel focused on ideas and reason, while Marx's purpose was to change the material world.

3. (i)   Inconsistent. Marx did not speculate on the ultimate questions of reality; he wanted to change the concrete world.

4. (i)   Inconsistent. Hegel's philosophy was founded on that of Socrates and Plato.

5. (i)   Inconsistent. Marx was concerned with the betterment of the individual worker but believed that only through a mass movement of the proletariat could the institutions and laws of society be changed.

Exercise 6.6

As you have read, Marx thought society was based on a "sick" control of the material world. He therefore was not content to merely espouse theories and speculate on how and when they might alter society. His was a philosophy of action meant to trigger a contemporary mass movement, which would begin the process of changing the world.

CHAPTER 7

PEDAGOGY AND THE MODERNS: HERBART AND SPENCER

After completing Chapter 7, you should be able to accomplish the following objectives:

1. You will become familiar with Johann Friedrich Herbart's theory of ideas by identifying statements as being consistent or inconsistent with his philosophy.

2. You will increase your knowledge of the application of philosophy to classroom teaching by discussing three current practices attributable to Herbart.

3. You will increase your understanding of the work of Herbert Spencer by identifying statements as being consistent or inconsistent with his philosophy.

4. You will increase your appreciation of the contributions of philosophy to classroom teaching by discussing two ways Spencer's work has influenced the role of science in the contemporary curriculum.

In the previous chapters in Unit 2, you may have noticed that certain philosophers discussed were more or less contemporaries. For example, Aristotle was a student of Plato, who was in turn a student of Socrates. Marx was about 13 years old when Hegel died. In the chapter you are about to read, the philosophers' lives reveal a similar chronological overlap, beginning with Johann Friedrich Herbart, who was born in 1776, and ending with Herbert Spencer, who died in 1903. What connects them is their focus on schools as formal institutions of learning, though as with the earlier philosophers, their views were not always compatible. You will recall from Chapter 3 that Socrates and Plato believed reality was found in theories of idealism, while Aristotle championed realism as the path to truth. In Chapter 4, we saw that Descartes focused on the rational powers of the mind but Locke turned to empiricism as the source of knowledge. We observed in Chapter 5 that Hegel employed the dialectic as the vehicle that would carry us to a body of universals; Marx used the dialectic in a far different way. When reading Herbart and Spencer, you will find that for our purposes, they differed primarily in terms of what they believed to be the bedrock of a school's curriculum. For Herbart, the foundation was one of ideas;

for Spencer, it was one of objects. But there is a significant connection between them: their preoccupation with and modern application of philosophical methodology to teaching.

Although Descartes is often credited with ushering in the modern age of philosophy, few philosophers addressed educational practices in detail prior to the late 18th century, for the simple reason that the rise of common educational institutions had not occurred. As used in this chapter, the term *modern* focuses on the pedagogical application and implementation of philosophical methodologies in teaching, which of course is the purpose of this book. Many philosophers, such as Plato, had been unconcerned about educating the masses; others, such as Rousseau, did not believe in the value of educational institutions at all. Unlike them, the philosophers in this chapter concerned themselves with the art of teaching, or pedagogy, and the ways philosophy could positively affect classroom teaching.

Specifically, Herbart devoted much thought to the teaching and learning process and the ways schools could stimulate students' interests and promote self-realization. Spencer was object oriented and was concerned about the utility of knowledge; therefore, he emphasized science as the focus of the curriculum. The collective work of these two philosophers, coupled with the fledgling drive toward the achievement of universal primary/elementary education, had and continues to have the potential to significantly influence contemporary pedagogy, particularly in the areas of organization and methodology.

JOHANN FRIEDRICH HERBART, 1776–1841

The period in which Herbart lived was a time of excitement and change. Kant and Hegel were creating a stir in the philosophical world and Marx was in his period of youthful development. The aesthetic times were being changed by such masters as Mozart and Beethoven, while Napoleon was altering the political face of Europe. These were only some of the dynamic individuals revolutionizing the culture in which Herbart lived, but it is the year he was born that probably caught your attention. Freedom, fireworks, Jefferson and the Declaration of Independence, the Revolutionary War and the Liberty Bell are some of the more common images or ideas that may have surfaced. The origin, nature, and formulation of these and other ideas in a changing world were central to Herbart's work.

In Chapter 4, you were introduced to Descartes and Bacon as well as to Locke's theory of ideas and what he called the tabula rasa (the "blank slate" nature of the mind). Herbart used Locke's hypotheses about the nature or existence of innate ideas as a foundation for developing his theories on ideas and concept formation. One significant area Herbart identified as a factor contributing to concept development was that of human motivation or interest. He believed that formal educational institutions should provide learning environments that would stimulate various kinds of interests in students. For this

The end of education is the building of lifelong traits and interest.

Johann Friedrich Herbart

reason, unlike many of his philosophical predecessors, he gave us a large body of work that directly addresses critical and practical educational considerations, primarily in the areas of organization and methodology. (These considerations are commonly referred to today as pedagogy or the "art" of teaching.)

Life and Times

Herbart was born on May 4, 1776, in the town of Oldenburg near Bremen, Germany. His father was a lawyer and was a somewhat introverted bureaucrat who lived a simple and conservative life. On the other hand, Herbart's mother was a strong, extroverted woman who lived life enthusiastically. Additionally, she was obsessively possessive of her only son, whom she viewed as frail. Therefore, his early years, including his education, were spent at home under the watchful eye of his mother, who was assisted by a tutor who encouraged the young man to focus on the power of philosophical inquiry. At the age of 12, Herbart was allowed to go off to a Latin school—the equivalent of a contemporary elementary school. His teachers saw him as a dedicated and intelligent student, though perhaps due to his cloistured childhood, his peers believed him to be aloof, self-centered, and somewhat obstinate. However, his success as a student could not be denied. After graduating as valedictorian of his class, he returned home, where he remained into his twenties.

In 1794, it was decided that Herbart should return to his studies, and so he was enrolled at the University of Jena. As was the custom of the times, it was assumed he would study law and follow his father in civil work, but philosophy was in his blood and his parents allowed him to pursue his desire, hoping it to be fleeting. Not surprisingly, Herbart's mother went off to school with him. Much to his parents' disappointment, Herbart became increasingly committed to philosophy and was particularly influenced by the work of Kant, who was still alive at that time. His mother's control diminished as Herbart spent most of his time with writers and other intellectuals. Nevertheless, the need to sever his bond with his mother became so important that he dropped out of school and spent the next three years tutoring children for a family in Switzerland. This experience, coupled with his philosophical studies, provided the foundation for the work he would produce in the coming years.

In the early 19th century, a number of key values were shifting in European society. In the first place, this period was marked by the fuller recognition of the worth of the individual and of a person's right to self-realization. Second, a gradual change occurred from mechanical and static to organic and developmental ways of viewing nature and society. These and other views heralded a more dynamic era, which demanded a more practical education, reflected in the work of Johann Heinrich Pestalozzi. Pestalozzi's "interaction with the important economic, political, and social events and changes of his time contributed to a philosophy of natural education that emphasized both cognitive and affective development" (Gutek, 1997, p. 131). Herbart's acquaintance with Pestalozzi's theories, his opportunity to work directly with children, and the changing views mentioned earlier impressed on the young philosopher the importance of focusing on the curriculum that would organize and classify knowledge and address the societal and individual needs of students entering the following century.

In 1800, Herbart returned home and was surprised to find that his mother was about to end her uneventful marriage in order to remarry and live in Paris. Her death two years later resulted in a comfortable inheritance, enabling Herbart to return to his studies and earn a doctorate in 1802 at Göttingen, where he taught for the next half dozen or so years. During this period he became so well versed in Kantian philosophy that he ascended to the master's chair of philosophy at Königsberg, a post he held for the better part of 30 years.

During this time the introspective philosopher finally married. With his wife's financial assistance, he bought a house and began a small school, which made it possible for him to implement his pedagogical theories. This effort became part of his pedagogical seminary, founded for the purpose of preparing and training prospective teachers. Herbart himself presented lectures on methodology and supervised what today would be called student teaching; in doing so, he may have pioneered a forerunner of today's colleges of education. But "Herbart's biggest disappointment was that he never achieved his goal of securing Hegel's seat of philosophy at the University of Berlin. This was probably due in part to Herbart's philosophical leaning toward realism, as opposed to Hegel's idealism" (Dunkel, 1967, p. 481).

It was also at this time, around 1833, that an extremely autocratic and dictatorial ruler came on the political scene and demanded absolute loyalty from all citizens, particularly academicians. Herbart, who was the dean of the philosophy faculty, accepted the situation, but a number of his staff members were disobedient and actually banished from Germany. Having perceived this as his own failure, Herbart resigned his chair and returned to Göttingen, where for the remainder of his life he labored over his significant works. These works included his *Encyclopedia of Philosophy, Outlines of Pedagogical Lectures,* and *Psychological Investigations.* Unlike many of his philosophical predecessors, he had few followers at the time of his death (in 1841), but time would treat him well and his pedagogical theories would have much to say about contemporary classroom practices.

Philosophical Contributions

For centuries, philosophers have been preoccupied with determining how the mind creates or finds or synthesizes ideas. The focus therefore has been one of prioritizing the functions of the mind or theorizing the ways ideas come to be. Herbart believed this process to be inverted; he thought the starting point should be ideas themselves. He apparently thought that every idea is a distinct entity and that ideas spring from two main sources: experience and social interaction.

We might say that ideas are plucked from experience and social interaction and, on being absorbed, influence the mind. Initially, Herbart accepted Locke's tabula rasa concept and the position that the mind does not come into being in possession of innate ideas or any content whatsoever. However, he took issue with Locke's belief that empiricism involves the acquisition of knowledge of an unchanging physical world through the senses. For Herbart, human perception could not be absolute, because when we encounter and internalize an idea, it is mixed into or processed by the ideas we have previously absorbed. The end result is so individualistic that it would be virtually impossible for a group of people to hold exactly the same concept or idea of any one thing. Having established this position, even if the minds of two individuals shared a multitude of common ideas, they would not perceive the same reality because ideas are constantly in a state of flux within the mind and are at different levels of consciousness. They slip in and slip out and the mind is little else than a battleground of contending ideas, always competing for space and supremacy. Some ideas eventually become singular in nature or lack relevance or interest and pass into our unconscious.

Learning theorists tell us that we retain everything we have ever encountered in our minds. For example, who was the first president of the United States? Ah ha! You have it. And you did not even think about it. In possibly a millisecond, "George Washington" flashed before your eyes, and chances are that is exactly the way you saw it. Not "President Washington" or "Mr. Washington" or "General Washington." Bloom and Krathwohl's *Taxonomy of Educational Objectives* would refer to this example as knowledge or recall, which is the lowest of the six levels in the cognitive domain. The other five levels require the processing of information and the employing of critical thinking skills. In the Washington example, there is nothing to process or manipulate; either you can recall it or you cannot. How about this one: Who was the 21st president of the United States? Ah ha! Your millisecond is long gone and chances are, unless you are a presidential scholar, nothing has flashed before your eyes. Undoubt-edly you studied the presidency of Chester A. Arthur, but you have been unable to recall it. Herbart would suggest to us that we could not "regurgitate" Chester A. Arthur because we have rarely had the occasion to do so, and the strength of an idea or thought's presence in the mind is directly related to its frequency of employment. We have recalled Washington—in contrast to Arthur—countless times, and every time we have done so, the strength of Washington's presence in our mind has increased. While singular ideas come and go in our minds, other ideas find commonalities, group together, and become known as what Herbart refers to as *apperception masses*, which allow us to go beyond knowing only the characteristics of objects in the physical world by relating them to larger bodies of knowledge. According to Adams (1899, p. 92),

> Intellectual life involves forming new apperception masses and expanding old ones through the constant interaction of new ideas bombarding the mind. In conceptualizing apperception masses, Herbart identified three classes, all of which lend themselves to the more complex development of a given idea:
>
> 1. Similar apperception masses, which combine ideas resulting in a stronger idea or ideas
> 2. Disparate apperception masses, which combine and form a new idea
> 3. Contrary apperception masses, which oppose and arrest the growth of an idea

As the mind encounters new ideas, these ideas have the potential to influ-ence existing apperception masses and change their conceptual nature, thereby increasing or decreasing their significance. For Herbart, this is a logical process that allows us to rework and clarify our ideas, resulting in a personally more accurate view of the world. This process not only refines concepts. It may enhance our ability to distinguish and order concepts and eventually form them into judgments that promote an inner freedom or virtue, which Herbart views as the perception of what is right or wrong. The sources that provide the raw material for the development of our ideas and concepts are found in what Herbart identified as six kinds of interests (Herbart, 1904, pp. 76–77):

1. Empirical interests: direct appeal to the senses
2. Speculative interests: perception of the relations of cause and effect
3. Aesthetic interests: enjoyment of contemplation
4. Sympathetic interests: family life, human cooperation
5. Social interests: social and civic duties
6. Religious interests: differences of creed and sect

It is important to note that Herbart's concern with individual as well as social needs is addressed by the first three items, which are aimed at individual and subjective interests, whereas the last three interests involve interaction with other human beings.

Herbart viewed interest as self-activity and believed it was the schools' responsibility not only to arouse various interests in students but to provide direction for their thoughts and actions. This process would result in the acquisition of the good and the right or virtue, which Herbart believed expressed the whole purpose of education.

Learning . . . should be a joy and full of excitement. It is life's greatest adventure; it is an illustrated excursion into the mind of noble and learned men, not a conducted tour through a jail.

Taylor Caldwell

Exercise 7.1

Reread the quotation by Taylor Caldwell and discuss how Herbart might champion her words in light of his view of the purpose of education. Then compare your work to the feedback at the end of the chapter.

From *Outlines of Educational Doctrine*, Herbart

Where many diverse means are to cooperate for the attainment of one end, where many obstacles have to be overcome, where persons of higher, equal, and lower rank enter as factors requiring consideration, is always a difficult matter to keep the end itself, the one fixed goal, steadily in view. In instruction the difficulty is increased by the fact that no one single teacher can impart the whole, and that consequently a number of teachers are obliged to depend on one another. But for this very reason, however much circumstances may vary the courses of study, the common end, namely many-sided, well-balanced, well-connected interest, in the achievement of which the true development of mental powers consists, needs to be lifted into prominence as the one thing toward which all details and procedure should point.

No more time, we need to realize at the outset, should be demanded for instruction than is consistent with the proviso that the pupils retain their natural buoyancy of spirits. This must be insisted on and not merely for the sake of health and physical vigor; a more direct argument for our present purpose lies in the fact that all art and labor employed to keep the attention awake will be thwarted by the

(continued)

disinclination to study caused by sitting too long, and even by excessive mental application alone. Forced attention does not suffice for instruction, even though it may be had through disciplinary measures.

It is urgently necessary that every school have not only spacious schoolrooms, but also a playground; it is further necessary that each recitation be followed by an intermission, that after the first two periods permission be granted for exercise in the open air, and that the same permission be given after the third period if there is a fourth to follow.

Still more urgent is the demand that pupils shall not be deprived of their hours of needed recreation by an excessive amount of school work to be done at home. The teacher who loads pupils down with home tasks in order to dispense as much as possible with perhaps uncertain home supervision, substitutes a certain general evil for a possible and partial one. Saving time depends upon our proficiency in presenting a subject and skill in conducting recitations.

From beginning to end the course of study must be arranged so as to provide for each of the main classes of interest. The empirical interest, to be sure, is called forth everywhere more easily than any of the other kinds. But religious instruction always fosters sympathetic interest; in this it must have the assistance of history and language study. Aesthetic culture at first depends on the work in the mother-tongue; it is desirable to have, in addition, instruction in singing, which at the same time promotes the health of the pupil. Later on, the ancient classics contribute their share of influence. Training in thinking is afforded by analytic, grammatical, and mathematical instruction; toward the end, also, by the study of history, which then becomes a search for causes and effects. Cooperation of this sort is to be sought everywhere; the authors to be studied must be selected with this end in view, and interpreted accordingly.

Herbart, J. (1904). *Outlines of Educational Doctrine* (C. De Garmo, Trans.). New York: The Macmillan Company, pp. 134–138. Reprinted with permission of the Macmillan Company.

Herbart in the Classroom

Herbart not only identified the school as the place to arouse the six interests introduced earlier but also provided numerous suggestions as to how this goal was to be accomplished. In terms of the overall curriculum, philosophers and scholars had focused on either a historical/classical education or a scientific education. Herbart's paramount concern was to arouse both the strength and variety of student interests, so it is not surprising that he believed both should be incorporated in the curriculum—they were equally necessary for human advancement.

Ideas would provide the core of the curriculum, and Herbart believed it was the teacher's responsibility to determine what ideas would be incorporated in the overall curriculum and how they would be organized and presented. He began with words, though words do not communicate the same thing to all students because of differences in reading comprehension, vocabulary, and so on. Herbart further believed teachers can provide more accuracy by using "things" as opposed to words. Although this approach might be better, it does not guarantee that the same "ideas" will be conceptualized or called to mind by any two students. The work of Friedrich Froebal, which laid the foundation for kindergartens, suggested that "showing" is better than "telling," which would be difficult to argue if "telling" was the be all, end all of a pedagogical approach. However, for Herbart words merely provided a foundation for a more common conceptualization through the development of pictures, which led to models, which led to objects. He believed this process enabled teachers to modify and thereby enable more accurate apperception masses and further believed that the best-educated human being was the person who had the biggest and best-arranged apperception masses with the life he or she was likely to lead (Stoops, 1971). To accomplish this goal, Herbart offered the following three components of pedagogy (Dunkel, 1969, pp. 66–68):

1. Government: Controlling students is a precondition to moral development.
2. Discipline: Influence of the teacher's will upon the student's will.
3. Instruction: What objects should be exhibited and in what order?

In addition to the components of pedagogy, Herbart also provided us with guidelines in the form of specific steps that would facilitate the acquisition of ideas and the development of apperception masses. Those five steps are (Stoops, 1971, p. 267):

1. Preparation: the development of student interest
2. Presentation: exposition of a new idea
3. Association: showing the new idea's relationship to ideas already acquired
4. Generalization: the forming of a general idea or a concept
5. Application: the use of acquired ideas in solving problems

Working backward, to lead a good life one must be able to problem solve (5). Successful problem solving often depends on the accuracy of one's apperception masses, which is affected by steps 4, 3, and 2; the bedrock of this effort is found in the promotion of student interest (step 1). With this in mind, read the following scenario in terms of the techniques being employed to promote student interest.

Scenario 7.1

Ms. Harriet Priest, a first-grade remedial reading teacher at McCann Elementary School, sat on the inside of an L-shaped table, around which sat four children. Behind her, on the board, she had suspended a sentence strip organizer on which there were three categories: CVC, CVCe, and CVVC.

Ms. Priest began her lesson by saying, "Today we are going to go over a thinking skill called *categorizing*. First of all, how many of you go to the grocery store with your mother?"

"I do," Brandon said.

"Does she buy everything on one row in the grocery store or does she have to go down different rows?"

"Different rows," the students responded together.

"Good. How many people eat cereal in your family, Joey?"

"Four, all of them."

"Does everyone like the same kind cereal, Joey?"

"Ah, nope."

"What kind do you like?"

"Pops."

"Sugar pops?" Ms. Priest inquired.

"Corn pops," Joey replied.

"How about your sister and your dad. What do they like?"

"Pops."

"And your mom?"

"Raisin Bran."

"So, Joey, three of the four of you like corn pops and one likes raisin bran. Good. That makes a group of cereals, but you eat other things during the week. Cereal is just one category of things you buy to eat. Another might be vegetables. What is an example of a vegetable?"

"Carrots," Prentice said.

"How about you, Angel?"

"Celery."

"Great. Fruit is another category. How about the name of a fruit, Brandon?"

"Grapes," Brandon said.

"Good. Now, do you think the cereal, vegetables, and fruits will all be in the same aisle?"

"Nooo," the children responded together.

"Right," Ms. Priest said enthusiastically. "Now today, rather that going to the store to take food out of the aisles, we are going to do a categorizing activity with words and we are going to put the words in different columns in our organizer. Now, let's look at category 1. What does *CVC* stand for? (Pause.) Joey?"

"One vowel and two consonants," Joey said.

"Right, consonant, vowel, consonant. Prentice, what does category 2 stand for?"

"Two consonants and a vowel."

"And what is this on the end?" (No response.) Ms. Priest continued, "a silent . . . ?"

"*E*," Prentice said.

"How about category 3, Angel?"

"Two consonants and two vowels. Consonant, vowel, vowel, consonant."

"Good. Now let's look over here on the board next to our organizer, where I have written the words of some songs we have learned this year that go with the categories. Let's do the first one together." Ms. Priest and the four children then repeated the following:

"Two consonant soldiers and a vowel in-between.

Ms. vowel is very shy and she cannot say her name.

She says her short vowel sound."

"Which category over here does that song go with?" Ms. Priest asked the children.

"One," Brandon said.

"Category 1. That is correct. Consonant, vowel, consonant. So that makes the vowel . . . ?"

"Short," Joey said.

"Good. Okay now let's look at our next song." Ms. Priest continued to work the children through the next two songs and allowed them to apply the lyrics to the appropriate category.

She then placed a number of cards with words on them face down in front of the children.

"Now let's play a game. We'll start with Joey. I want you to choose one of the cards on the desk, place it under one of the categories in our organizer, and be prepared to be questioned," Ms. Priest said with a smile. Joey turned over the word *'hate'* and placed it under the CVCe.

"Who would like to be the questioner? (Prentice raised his hand.) Okay, Prentice, seeing as you are sitting next to Joey, you can ask the questions I have written down for you."

"What category did you choose?" Prentice began.

"I chose category 2," Joey replied.

"Why did you choose that category?" Prentice inquired.

"I chose that category because it had two vowels."

"What vowel sound was in your word?" Prentice continued.

"The vowel sound I heard was *A*."

"Which song helped you choose that category?"

"When silent *e* appears."

"Good job! All right!" Ms. Priest said. "I'll play it on our electric keyboard, and let's see if we can do 'When Silent *e* Appears.'"

After finishing the song, Ms. Priest worked all the children through many words with the same question-and-answer and song procedure. She also introduced a new category called "special vowel sounds," for those words that did not fit into the first three columns. She concluded by telling them they could make categories by finding out things that fit together. The students then removed all the words from the organizer, mixed them up, and began the grouping process again at their desks. Ms. Priest moved about the room and provided individual assistance.

Ms. Priest's use of Herbart's preparation—which is the first of his steps in the teaching and learning process—is reflected in the variety of ways she is developing the students' interest in the lesson. Her immediate goal is to place examples of words in the proper category, and she begins by using their personal experiences with groceries to initiate the idea of categorization. She then employs song and verse in an enjoyable way, which enhances their attention to the task at hand, then uses keyboard music to further establish the rules underlying the categorization of the word examples. Having presented the new idea, Ms. Priest moves toward Herbart's third step, association, by providing an opportunity for the students to generate their own categories. Additionally, if you review the scenario, you will find that Ms. Priest has employed all three of Herbart's components of pedagogy by initially controlling and centering the experience, directing and focusing the activities, and sequencing the procedures and materials used in the language arts lesson.

Exercise 7.2

Examine the following statements to determine if they are consistent (c) or inconsistent (i) with Herbart's philosophy. Then compare your responses to the feedback at the end of the chapter.

_____ 1. Ideas are obtained exclusively through the use of the senses.
_____ 2. Whether or not we recall an idea depends upon how often we have recalled that specific idea in the past.
_____ 3. Ideas can be exactly shared by human beings.
_____ 4. Apperception masses result from the interaction of ideas in the mind.
_____ 5. Peoples' interests are directly related to the development of their ideas.

Exercise 7.3

Briefly discuss three of Herbart's pedagogical contributions and include a statement as to why you might employ them. Then check your response against the one at the end of the chapter.

Exercise 7.4

With regard to the Washington/Arthur example on page 192, read the following scenario, identify the primary teaching technique being employed, and briefly discuss how that technique reflects the application of Herbart in the classroom. Then compare your thoughts to the feedback at the end of the chapter.

Ms. Bridgit Bodefeld, an eighth-grade German teacher at Eggers Elementary/Middle School, began her class by saying good morning to the students.

"Guten Morgen, Studenten."

"Guten Morgen, Frau Bodefeld," the students replied.

"Please open your agenda books. What is the first thing we are going to write? Ben?"

"The word *review,*" Ben said.

"Fine, Ben, and under that write 'new expressions' and also write 'selected states—coat of arms.' Now, everyone quiet please, pay attention and sit back and let's do our review. You've done very well with the expressions we have learned so far this year. So respond to me in German. What would you say if I said to you, 'Guten Morgen,' Cheryl?"

"Guten Morgen, Frau Bodefeld."

"Good," Ms. Bodefeld said. "What if I were to say to you 'wie heisst du, Daniel?"

"Ich heisse Daniel," Daniel replied.

"Sehr gut. Very good, Daniel," Ms. Bodefeld said and continued by asking a number of the students to tell her their names in German. Then she asked, "Frank, how about this one. Wo warst du geboren?"

"Ich war in Chicago geboren," Frank said.

"Good, Frank, you were born in Chicago. Gloria, wo warst du geboren?"

"Ich war in Hammond geboren," Gloria responded.

"Und wie alt bist du?" Ms. Bodefeld inquired.

""Ich bein vierzehn Jahre alt," Gloria said.

""You're 14 years old. Well done, Gloria. So class, sprechen sie Deutsch?

"Ja," the class responded in unison.

"And if you didn't speak German, you would say . . . ?"

"Nein."

"And if you spoke a little German you would say . . . ?"

"Ich spreche wenig Deutsch."

"And," Ms. Bodefeld continued, "if you spoke no German you would say . . . ?"

"Ich spreche kein Deutsch," the class said together.

"Sehr gut, Klasse. Excellent! Now let's look at the expressions I have written on the board in English. I will read one and then you give it to me in German. Okay, Hector, how about 'what's the matter'?"

"Was ist los?" Hector said.

"Good . . . and Joan, try 'I am sleepy.'"

"Ich bin müde," Joan responded.

"Kenybisha, how about 'I am angry'?"

"Ich bin böse."

"Well done, Kenybisha. Maria, go with, 'I am sad.'"

With permission. Eggers Elementary/Middle School, Hammond, Indiana. Mr. Walter J. Watkins, Principal.

"Ich bin traurig."

"And what if you were happy?"

"Ich bin froh!" Maria added.

"Und ich bin auch froh!" Ms. Bodefeld said, "because you all did so well with the review. Now let's go over here and look at this expression, which applies to what we are going to do just a little bit later and also deals with what we have been working on with our maps. Please stay with me. You are doing a great job and I like your pronunciation and you are learning from listening to each other."

Ms. Bodefeld then read the following question that she had written on the board. "Wieviele Staaten sind in Deutchland?"

"Sechszehn," the students replied together.

"Very good. There are 16 states in Germany. Let's practice asking the question." The students repeated the statement a number of times.

"Now," Ms. Bodefeld continued, "I want to pass your folders out and at this time I want you to put your reviews in them, and then let's start off with a new sheet of paper. Look up this way and put your pens down. As we said earlier, there are 16 states in Germany and we have had discussions on what goes on, what the major industries are and so forth. And I told you that for each state there is a coat of arms. When you travel in a given state, you will see it all over the place—on phone booths, buildings, on T-shirts and the like. They are quite beautiful and I am going to show all of them to you in groups of four on the overhead."

Ms. Bodefeld then displayed the coat of arms representing each of the German states and engaged the students in a brief discussion regarding the unique characteristics of each shield. She then said, "This might be a good time for you to look in your folder. You will see the location of all the coats of arms as shown in their states on the map."

Ms. Bodefeld then explained to the students that the final step of their project would be for each of them to select a coat of arms and develop an original artistic presentation of that particular shield. For the remainder of the period, she moved about the class to help the students make their final selections and begin the activity.

HERBERT SPENCER, 1820–1903

Spencer was clearly influenced by the significant social and economic upheavals that took place in his lifetime as well as by the continued focus on the sciences in intellectual thought. Much of his work was devoted to his belief in individual freedom and the right to develop naturally through the employment of sensory data or empirical knowledge, which provided the foundation for the establishment of general principles or laws. Influenced by the *Origin of the Species*, Spencer saw this process as evolutionary in nature but went beyond the work of Darwin by suggesting that all human activity was the result of an evolutionary process. In fact, when Spencer coined the phrase "survival of the fittest"

*Learning the meaning of things
is better than teaching the
meaning of things.*

Herbert Spencer

prior to the publication of Darwin's revolutionary thoughts, his focus was societal as opposed to biological. This focus provided a central theme of his work, which became known as Social Darwinism or evolutionism.

Life and Times

Spencer was born in Derby, England, on April 27, 1820. Because his father was a schoolteacher, he primarily spent his first 13 years in what today is referred to as home schooling. Deviating from the accepted curriculum of the times, William George Spencer stayed away from classical studies and let his son freely pursue ordinary mathematics and other subjects of his choice. Because at an early age he was drawn to science, Spencer came to know something of physics, chemistry, biology, geography, and anthropology. Due to the nature of these subjects, he was impressed at an early age with the mental discipline approach and the desirability of intellectually furthering himself. When Spencer was a teenager, his uncle moved in with the family. He encouraged the young man to take an interest in mathematics and mechanical things, which, Spencer said later, led to a deficiency in subjects like history and literature.

When he finished his studies, he sought employment of a varied and exciting nature and settled on working on the London and Bristol railroad. His father wanted him to be a teacher, but the thought of teaching bored Spencer. A nasty strike ended his brief tenure in the railroad business. Needing to make a living and being well versed in the sciences, Spencer became an engineer and plied that trade for 12 years, from 1837 to 1849. During this time, he showed the influence of the Victorian, middle-class frame of mind and was, among other things, socially inhibited and uncomfortable around women. He never married. Although he was thought of as being all head and no heart, he was certainly affected by the industrialization and urbanization of England's peaceful neighborhoods. He increasingly entered into the political and social discussions of the day and generally did so in a critical and argumentative way. Due to his growing interests and concerns and his articulateness, Spencer entered the world of journalism, where he not only toiled as a writer but eventually became editor of the prestigious *Economist.* After five years, he devoted himself to a full-time writing career; he wrote voluminously for the remainder of his life. Many of his thoughts in the areas of political deregulation and social evolution—for example, natural development and natural rights—were considered radical. But eventually the rapidly changing times absorbed such thinking, and he faded from the playing fields of controversy and the philosophical center stage of 19th-century England.

Philosophical Contributions

Throughout the 19th century, the sciences grew in importance to the increasingly expanding intellectual communities of the world. Additionally, the need to educate the ordinary person was becoming recognized, particularly in the nations moving toward or adopting democratic governments. Spencer was clearly influenced by these movements and used scientific concepts to anchor his philosophical ideas. More specifically, "Spencer proposed that philosophy was not a critique of reason or a methodology for science but simply the coping-stone of science, the most general knowledge to be had of nature" (Peel, 1971, p. 6). Although he admitted that nothing could be conceived to be objectively real, he insisted that

> phenomena should not suggest elusiveness since they all lent themselves to investigation and the formulation of scientific generalizations by exhibiting characteristics and establishing a persistent and recurrent nature and, therefore, were real for man. Spencer further argued that this process was directed by evolutionary principles and that advance in intelligence was not only gradual (a characteristic of evolution) but was also very slow (Kennedy, 1978, pp. 37–38).

Because of his scientific background, we would expect Spencer to have emphasized empiricism as the primary source of knowledge, and he certainly acknowledged the importance of experience in the acquisition and development of ideas. However, with regard to the subjectivity of human interactions with the world of reality, he believed that we can never know "exactly" what a thing or object really is. Reasoning from sensory data for the purpose of meeting and solving environmental and social problems can take us just so far because there were apparently things that could not be reduced to observables. Nevertheless, the manifestation of reality through patterns and relationships does allow for the acquisition of genuine knowledge. The development of such knowledge, Spencer pointed out, was a process of moving from simplicity to complexity and therefore was evolutionary in nature. Spencer used this argument in developing his universal philosophical theory of how knowledge is derived by combining Darwin's scientific data theories with empiricism and inductive reasoning.

Spencer's theories are often referred to as reflecting Social Darwinism, for his primary concern was that of applying the principles of evolution, the accumulation of scientific data, and the utilization of inductive reasoning to problems affecting human life. He identified these problems as involving (Kazamias, 1966, p. 126)

- Activities which directly minister to self preservation
- Activities, which by securing the necessities of life, indirectly minister to self preservation
- Activities which have for their end the rearing and discipline of offspring
- Activities which involve the maintenance of proper social and political relations
- Activities which are miscellaneous and make up the leisure part of life and gratification of feelings

Spencer believed that his philosophical theory could be used to address these activities and provide solutions for social problems by unifying and organizing knowledge. He was one of the first to recognize the critical role of an educated populace in fostering a more harmonious world community.

The close observer soon discovers that the teacher's task is not to implant facts but to place the subject to be learned in front of the learner and, through sympathy, emotion, imagination, and patience, to awaken in the learner the restless drive for answers and insights which enlarge the personal life and give it meaning.

Nathan Pusey

Exercise 7.5

Reread the passage from Nathan Pusey and write a brief statement on how this quotation reflects an aspect of Spencer's philosophy. Then compare your response to the feedback at the end of the chapter.

From *What Knowledge Is of Most Worth?*, Herbert Spencer

The question which we contend is of such transcendent moment, is, not whether such or such knowledge is of worth, but what is its relative worth? When they have named certain advantages which a given course of study has secured them, persons, are apt to assume that they have justified themselves: quite forgetting that the adequateness of the advantages is the point to be judged. There is, perhaps, not a subject to which men devote attention that has not "some" value. A year diligently spent in getting up heraldry, would very possibly give a little further insight into ancient manners and morals. Any one who could learn the distances between all the towns in England, might, in the course of his life, find one or two of the thousand facts he had acquired of some slight service when arranging a journey. But in these cases, every one would admit that there was no proportion between the required labour and the probable benefit. And if here the test of relative value is appealed to and held conclusive, then should it be appealed to and held conclusive throughout.

To this end, a measure of value is the first requisite. And happily, respecting the true measure of value, as expressed in general terms, there can be no dispute. Every one in contending for the worth of any particular order of information, does so by showing its bearing upon some part of life. In reply to the question—"Of what use is it?" the mathematician, linguist, naturalist, or philosopher, explains the way in which his learning beneficially influences action—saves from evil or secures good—conduces to happiness. When the teacher of writing has pointed out how great an aid writing is to success in business—that is, to the obtainment of sustenance—that is, to satisfactory living; he is held to have proved his case. And when the collector of dead facts (say a numismatist) fails to make clear any appreciable effects which these facts can produce on human welfare, he is obliged to admit that they are comparatively valueless. All then, either directly or by implication, appeal to this as the ultimate test.

How to live?—that is the essential question for us. Not how to live in the mere material sense only, but in the widest sense. The general problem which comprehends every special problem is—the right ruling of conduct in all directions under all circumstances. In what way to treat the body; in what way to treat the mind; in what way to manage our affairs; in what way to bring up a family; in what way to behave as a citizen; in what way to utilize those sources of happiness which nature supplies—how to use all our faculties to the greatest

> advantage of ourselves and others—how to live completely? And this being the great thing needful for us to learn, is, by consequence, the great thing which education has to teach. To prepare us for complete living is the function which education has to discharge; and the only rational mode of judging of an educational course is, to judge in what degree it discharges such function.
>
> Spencer, H. (1860). *Education: Intellectual, Moral, and Physical.* Akron, Ohio: D. Appleton and Company, pp. 8–12.

Spencer in the Classroom

Unlike many European philosophers, Spencer clearly applied his philosophical thoughts to education and classroom teaching. His four pedagogical essays, which appeared in British journals between 1854 and 1859, provide us with his ideas, which covered topics ranging from educational goals and aims to methodology, practice, and procedures. Beginning with goals, Spencer believed that education should be a preparation for complete living and that achieving this goal depended on a curriculum that focused on the worth and relative use of knowledge to the student or other individual. As mentioned earlier, Spencer's educational experience had not been classically oriented, and he continued to criticize the common classical education of his time because he believed it conformed to public opinion, which suggested a subjective selection of curricular material to be studied. For Spencer, science was the essence of the modern curriculum (Kazamias, 1966). He supported this position through the following line of reasoning (Kazamias, 1966, pp. 194–195):

1. A curriculum founded upon science requires the examination of knowledge as opposed to the subjectivity of the classical or literary curriculum.
2. The science curriculum requires the development of processes which allow the student to know and determine what knowledge is useful and include such things as classification systems and the development of hierarchies. In the classical curriculum, knowledge is dependent upon student memory.
3. The science curriculum cultivates the organized development of judgment as opposed to the classical approach, which is more focused upon the mental discipline concept.

In addressing the actual implementation of science in the classroom, Spencer believed the laboratory method was the most valuable, and much of the contemporary focus on laboratory experiences is a direct result of his pioneering efforts in this area. It also follows that laboratory lessons are student centered, so that he was opposed to the common authoritarian learning environment of 19th-century England, which he considered submissive, artificial, dogmatic, and restraining with specific regard to intellectual development

(Kazamias, 1966). He also believed that experimentation required self-discipline and control and that a dictatorial classroom would, to some degree, negate the development of these characteristics in students. Furthermore, if the classroom environment was to promote self-development, it should be interesting and, to some degree, fun or pleasurable.

Finally, Spencer believed the science curriculum, with its emphasis on scientific laboratory experiences, was the most effective way to have students focus on objects as opposed to ideas. He strongly held that "true science is that which generates profound respect for and an implicit faith in those uniformities of action which all things disclose and gives us the true conception of ourselves and our relation to the mysteries of existence" (Spencer, 1963, p. 93). Keep this in mind as you read the following lesson showing Spencer's work in the classroom.

Scenario 7.2

Mrs. Lee McKelvey, a second-grade teacher at Loretto Elementary School, began her lesson by telling the students they were going to learn about the parts that help a plant live. She first directed them to look at the large potted tree she had brought into her room. Then she said, "Plants have roots that grow under the ground, and the roots help hold plants in the soil. Now, can you see the roots on a plant . . . Morgan?"

"Uh huh."

"Okay . . . sometimes . . . but when can you see roots on a plant, Morgan?"

"When they're growing," Morgan responded.

"Okay," Mrs. McKelvey said. "Sometimes when the plant gets very big you can see the roots coming up out of the ground, but who can tell me what you think would cause the roots to show that are usually out of the ground? Logan?"

"When the tree gets very big."

"Okay, sometimes when the tree gets very big. Matthew, what else?"

"When the roots get very big?"

"Yes . . . when the roots get big. Now, what could happen to the land to make the roots show sometimes . . . Kelsey?"

"It could dry up," Kelsey replied.

"Okay . . . but what happens when it rains? Doesn't it rain sometimes and the dirt goes to the side?" Mrs. McKelvey asked.

"Yes," Kelsey said.

"Right, and doesn't the ground and the dirt wearing away uncover some of the roots of a plant? How many of you have seen a tree that was growing and then the roots became uncovered by the rain coming down very very hard or a wind was blowing and you could actually see the roots from under the ground?" (Students nod with understanding.)

"Great," Mrs. McKelvey said. "Now, do you know what the roots have to have in order to live . . . David?"

"Um . . . water?"

"Okay, good job, but where do they get the water from, TJ?"

"From the rain and when you water them," TJ answered.

"Okay, when you water them with a hose, but how do the roots actually get the water that they need in order to live, Josh?"

"The soil."

"Right," Mrs. McKelvey said. The soil or the ground. Okay, the roots take in the water from soil, but does the water go directly to the roots?"

"I don't know," Josh responded.

"Okay, when it rains or when you water the plant, Josh, where does the water go?"

"On the ground."

"On the ground or the dirt. Right. Okay, so we know that roots help keep trees and other plants stay alive. Now," Mrs. McKelvey continued, "here is a picture of a tree and I want you, Jesse, to come up and point to where the roots would be on this tree."

Jesse approached the picture and said, "right down there."

"Okay. Good job, Jesse. The roots are under the grass. You can hardly seen them because most of them are hidden deep down under the grass, and that is where they get their water. Now, Jesse, can you see where some of the roots are above the ground, just a little bit, in our real tree?"

"Well, just a little," Jesse said.

"Yes, because this is a very, very big tree," Mrs. McKelvey added. "Now everybody look at our tree and find the trunk and then someone tell us what it does. What is its main job, Ashley?"

"It holds the tree up," Ashley said.

"Right, and what comes out of the trunk part of the tree, Karen?"

"The branches."

"Right, the trunk holds the heavy branches on the tree. Now, look at our tree and see if you think all the branches are heavy. Logan?"

"No, I think some of them you can break off," Logan said.

"Yes," Mrs. McKelvey said. "Some branches are very heavy, but then some are light and very thin. Megan, can you climb on the heavy branches of a tree?"

"Yes, sometimes."

"Can you climb on the lighter branches, too?"

"No, because you could fall and hurt yourself," Megan replied.

"True. You can fall out of a tree and hurt yourself. They are too thin and wouldn't be able to hold your weight. Now, how about the stems of a tree or plant? What do they do? Michael?"

"They let the leaves grow on them."

"Right, and what else, Stephen?"

"They help the tree," Stephen answered.

"That's true, Stephen, but specifically, how do they help the tree? What is their one big job?" Mrs. McKelvey asked.

"It helps it grow bigger by getting the water."

"Exactly right, Stephen," Mrs. McKelvey said with a smile. "The stem part of the plant carries the water from the roots to the other parts of the plant. If the water just stayed in the roots, the tree couldn't grow. Now let's look at the leaves on our tree. What are they closest to that is not part of the tree . . . Jessica?"

"The air," Jessica said.

"Yes, the air, and what else could you say they are closest to that the tree needs?"

"The sun."

"Right, the sun or the sunlight, and what do the leaves use the sunlight for, Scott?"

"To get stuff that helps make food for the plant."

"That's right, Scott. Now we know from our laboratory experiment last month that plants also produce seeds. When nature plants them, seeds grow and become plants and trees and many of them grow to be quite large. Does anyone remember what the biggest living thing on earth is that we read about in a story? Brandon?"

"The sequoia tree."

"Yes, the sequoia tree. Does it have roots, Brandon?"

"Yes."

"Does it have a trunk, Jesse?"

"Yes."

"Does a sequoia tree have branches, Meredith?"

"Yes."

"Does a sequoia tree have leaves on it, too?"

"Yes," Meredith added.

"You're right, Meredith, and these big trees grow to be more than 250 feet and are found in California. Now just like our tree here, what do they need to grow?" Mrs. McKelvey asked.

"Soil," Jessica said.

"Good. What else? Anyone?" Mrs. McKelvey inquired.

"Sunlight and air and water," Morgan added.

"Great job, everybody. Now, for our last laboratory experiment we planted some seeds and they are really doing very nicely. Today, we are going out to the fence corner and we are going to plant our tree, and for the rest of the year we are going to make sure the soil is rich and the tree gets plenty of sunshine and water. During that time, we are going to make observations and chart the growth of our tree, and I hope it will be fun when you all come back years from now to see the tree we planted."

Mrs. McKelvey then divided the class into teams and assigned each one a responsibility. They then proceeded to go outdoors and plant their tree.

In this classroom lesson, we see a number of Spencer's ideas being applied. First, Mrs. McKelvey is teaching a lesson that involves objects as opposed to ideas—that is, she is teaching the physical components of a tree as part of a unit on plants. Earlier, a lesson had been devoted to the concrete nature of seeds, which the students had planted and had been nurturing. That experience, along with the conclusion of the lesson on the planting of the tree, resonate with Spencer's strong belief in the use of laboratory experiences. It is important to note that such experiences do not necessarily have to be limited to such things as test tubes, flasks, and burners. Mrs. McKelvey utilized the schoolyard as her living laboratory. Needless to say, the preceding lesson was a science lesson, and Spencer championed the sciences as the focus for the curriculum. Finally, the behavior of the children, particularly in the schoolyard, reflected Spencer's position that educational experiences should be interesting and fun. Not only did the children enjoy the planting of the seeds and tree, but their interest was sustained by nurturing and observing the progress of their work.

Exercise 7.6

Examine the following statements to determine if they are consistent (c) or inconsistent (i) with Spencer's philosophy. Then check your answers against the feedback at the end of the book.

_____ 1. The school curriculum should focus on ideas as opposed to physical or concrete objects.
_____ 2. All knowledge is observable, and the nature of an object can be exactly determined.
_____ 3. The theory of evolution is only applicable to the biological sciences.
_____ 4. Philosophy can be used to solve human and societal problems.
_____ 5. The test of knowledge is found in its relative value to human society.

Exercise 7.7

Briefly discuss two ways Spencer's work influences the science curriculum in today's classrooms. Then compare your work to the feedback at the end of the chapter.

SUMMARY

The 19th century was, in part, characterized by the Industrial Revolution, the rise of democratic nations, and the growing belief that through science, human beings could change the world. What followed was the increasingly important role of the individual and a growing emphasis on education in order to produce individuals who could be change agents. Therefore, the thoughts of philosophers and other members of the intellectual community were more directed toward formal education than had been the case in the past. Herbart is often seen as the founder of pedagogy, in that his focus was as much on the art of teaching as on the knowledge to be taught. His primary concern was that ideas in the body of classical knowledge be taught in such a way as to promote the self-realization of the student through the stimulation of a number of interests. Pedagogically, this task was accomplished by the teachers controlling the learning environment, imposing their will on the students, and providing

orderly instruction through the preparation, presentation, association, generalization, and application of ideas. Herbart believed such an approach would give
the individual the tools with which to engage in a good life.

Spencer also dealt with education but differed from Herbart in emphasizing
a practical, scientifically oriented curriculum as opposed to a curriculum centered around classical knowledge. Spencer also believed the focus in the classroom should be on the concrete, material world in the form of objects, not
ideas (which Herbart emphasized).

This emphasis on the material world was due in part to Spencer's theory of
evolution, for which he was labeled a Social Darwinist—although a more accurate interpretation would be that Darwin was a "biological Spencerian" (Turner,
1985, p. 11). Because Spencer was more concerned with the solution of societal
problems, he stressed the practical nature of education. However, like Herbart,
he was concerned with methodology, and "the laboratory method of instruction, now common for scientific subjects in good schools, is an application of
his doctrines of concrete illustration, training in the accurate use of the senses,
and subordination of book work" (Spencer, 1966, p. xiii). Although Spencer believed such methodologies could give people problem-solving tools, his belief
in the inevitability of social evolution produced in his work a certain fatalism.
This fatalism was to provide a springboard for American pragmatism, which
stressed the possibility and desirability of social manipulation.

Questions for Discussion

1. What role do ideas play in the development of Herbart's apperception masses?
2. What role do Herbart's apperception masses play in the refinement of ideas?
3. How do Herbart's six kinds of interests affect the development of concepts?
4. In the reading from Herbart on page 193, how does he suggest teachers can maintain student interest?
5. What does Spencer mean when he suggests that, as in the theory of biolog-ical evolution, social development moves from the simple to the complex?
6. Why is Spencer opposed to a classical educational curriculum?
7. Of Spencer's five activities presented on page 203, which do you think needs to be most emphasized in the elementary classroom? The secondary class-room? Why?
8. Reread the passage from Spencer on page 204. What do you think is meant by *relative worth*?

Suggested Field Laboratory Activities

1. Using curriculum guides and lesson plan books, identify lessons that present classical knowledge and further identify the specific concepts or facts being taught.
2. Using curriculum guides and lesson plan books, identify lessons that focus on objects and further identify the specific objects being taught.

3. Obtain sample lesson plans and see if you can locate examples of material being presented in sequential fashion.
4. Using available lesson plans, locate examples of "presentation" and "associate" as defined in the chapter.
5. Given the opportunity, plan and implement a short lesson that focuses on a particular "idea."
6. Given the opportunity, plan and implement a short lesson that focuses on a particular "object."
7. With a small group of students, plan and implement a lesson that incorporates Herbart's use of association.
8. With a small group of students, plan and implement a hands-on laboratory experience that is science- and object-oriented and that hopefully is fun!

Exercise Feedback

Exercise 7.1

When reading this passage, you might have focused on the expression suggesting that education should not be a "tour through a jail." This certainly would be in line with Herbart's belief that an educational environment should foster in the student a "buoyancy of spirit." He would accomplish this end through the use of an exciting curriculum that would not only arouse interest but would facilitate self-realization. Among other things, he also proposed a very organized approach to classroom teaching, which hopefully would guarantee such outcomes.

Exercise 7.2

1. (i)   Inconsistent. Initially, ideas are gathered empirically, but they are then internalized, mixed, and potentially altered in the mind.
2. (c)   Consistent. The more we use information, the more readily we recall it.
3. (i)   Inconsistent. Since no two minds are the same, which is also the case regarding human experience, ideas cannot be exactly shared.
4. (c)   Consistent. And such interactions can strengthen, retard, or produce new apperception masses.
5. (c)   Consistent. Herbart's list of "interests" can be found on page 192.

Exercise 7.3

The pedagogical contributions of Herbart that you might have chosen to discuss could be any of the following:

- Focusing on ideas
- Providing an interest-oriented experience
- Delimiting of "forced" attention
- Delimiting of homework

■ Providing recreational activities
■ Establishing a cooperative learning environment
■ Organizing instruction, Herbart's five steps which are found on page 195.

Your reasons for employing these measures will vary, but hopefully you recognize the potentially positive impact of Herbart's pedagogy.

Exercise 7.4

The Washington/Arthur example is meant to emphasize Herbart's point of view that the more often we use information, the more readily available it becomes to us—that is, we are efficiently able to recall the information. This suggests the utility of the common classroom practice of repetition, or practice, or drill—a methodology employed in Ms. Bodefeld's German class during her question-and-answer session. Additionally, by allowing the students to create their own "shields," she is providing an experience that has the potential of promoting the students' interest in the language as well as the country.

Exercise 7.5

Pusey's words lend themselves to the philosophy of Spencer by suggesting that an authoritarian learning environment is not in the best interests of the students. His words suggest the teacher should be a facilitator, which is similar to the view of Spencer. Pusey also refers to the need to awaken a (student) drive for answers and insights, and Spencer's emphasis on the implementation of laboratory experiences in the classroom is consistent with this goal.

Exercise 7.6

1. (i)   Inconsistent. Spencer believed that the curriculum should be object as opposed to idea oriented. Herbart took the opposite postion.
2. (i)   Inconsistent. Although Spencer focused on the need for observable knowledge, he admitted some things could not be observed and therefore were unknowable.
3. (i)   Inconsistent. Spencer believed evolution could be applied to all aspects of human life and endeavor.
4. (c)   Consistent. This statement serves as the centerpiece of Spencer's philosophy.
5. (c)   Consistent. Also a major tenet of Spencer's work.

Exercise 7.7

First and foremost, Spencer championed the implementation of laboratory experiences in the classroom, and much of today's focus on laboratory methods is a result of his pioneering effort. Additionally, Spencer focused on teaching science in a practical, interest-oriented fashion. He felt that much of what is done should be student focused, with the teacher facilitating the classroom environment.

CHAPTER 8

KNOWLEDGE, THEORY, AND ACTION: JAMES AND DEWEY

After completing Chapter 8, you should be able to accomplish the following objectives:

1. You will increase your understanding of the philosophy of pragmatism, and so when given a number of statements you will be able to identify them as being consistent or inconsistent with the philosophy of William James.

2. You will increase your knowledge of pragmatism, so that in your own words, you will be able to briefly discuss William James's view of the nature of truth and the way this view affects classroom teaching.

3. You will become aware of how the philosophy of pragmatism affects classroom practice, and so when given a number of statements you will be able to identify them as being consistent or inconsistent with the positions of John Dewey.

4. You will become familiar with Dewey's contributions to classroom teaching so that, in your own words, you will briefly discuss what is meant by the following statement: "Education is not a preparation for life; education is life."

With a growing focus on pedagogy, as presented in Chapter 7, and a trend toward universal elementary education, educators and others moved into the 20th century vigorously debating not only what should be taught but what methodologies would be most appropriate in educating the masses. In the United States, educators had been significantly influenced by all the philosophers presented in the previous chapters. The majority of school systems around the year 1900 reflected the philosophical theories of idealism and realism and took a conservative position in emphasizing the need to transmit existing knowledge in teacher-centered learning environments.

The two philosophers you will study in this chapter, William James and John Dewey, departed from the traditional approach by championing pragmatism as the philosophical foundation for education. To a degree, such an educational philosophy called for practical and verifiable experiences—something others had argued for. Bacon believed inductive reasoning could be used to solve problems and generally advance society, and Locke believed that knowledge was verified or obtained through a perceptual interaction with the world. For James and Dewey, the use of empirical observation was merely the first step in increasing the accuracy of knowledge.

A personal example may be helpful here. I was recently on a plane flight that took off from St. Louis, Missouri, at 5:22 P.M. The sun had gone down and the horizon was marked by the horizontal red glow or line often characteristic of a sunset. As the aircraft rose sharply to its cruising altitude of 33,000 feet at a speed in excess of 500 miles per hour, the sun "rose" and within ten minutes was completely visible in the western sky. Needless to say, as the plane leveled, the sun rapidly "set." However, if my total knowledge of this experience had been limited to the facts that the round orb was the sun and the plane was flying west, I would have concluded that the sun rises, however briefly, in the west.

James would reject this conclusion, not in terms of the actual occurrence, but on the basis that truth is that which has been tried by experience and experiment. Dewey would reject this conclusion by expressing his belief in reflective thinking, which requires an "active, persistent, and careful consideration of any belief or supposed form of knowledge in the light of the grounds that support it and the further conclusions to which it tends" (Dewey, 1910, p. 6). For both of them, the implementation of these and other pragmatic principles in an activity-oriented classroom built on real-life experiences would be the most effective way for students to inquire into a wide range of concerns, acquire knowledge, and come up with solutions to social problems.

WILLIAM JAMES, 1842–1910

In some respects, James was no different from the Western philosophers who had come before him in that he had been influenced by the theories of great minds and by the time and place in which he lived. Specifically, Bacon's inductive reasoning, Locke's empiricism, Kant's practical reason, and Spencer's focus on science played a role in the development of James's pragmatism. What sets James apart from many of his philosophical forerunners was his focus on the practical utility of philosophy and his attempt to move philosophy from the abstract playing fields of intellectuals to the concrete streets and lives of ordinary people. Therefore, when reading James, we find the central theme of his pragmatic approach to be that of a useful application to daily life. Although much of his thought found its roots in European philosophy, his voice clearly reflected the life and times of 19th-century America:

> His appeal to the common man, his forceful call for action and results and his desire to explore and conquer the social and cultural frontiers of this relatively new nation led some to declare that William James was the first great American philosopher. (Davidson, 1952, p. 224).

People can alter their lives by altering their attitudes.

William James

Life and Times

James was of Irish descent and was born in New York City on December 10, 1842. He was one of five children born to Mary Robertson Walsh James and Henry James. Henry James's father had settled in Albany and amassed a fortune in excess of $1 million. Because of his wealth, Henry James had been able to study literature and philosophy at Princeton and get involved in a wide range of cultural activities. Apparently, he was extremely pleasant as well as learned, and his congenial personality as well as his penchant for challenging conventional thought and championing unpopular ideas and movements seem to have influenced William.

Due to the wealth and cultural prominence of his family, William James was educated in the finest institutions of his time, including private schools in France, England, and Switzerland. During that time in Europe, the sciences had come to the fore and James's focus became that of biology. Much of his early life was spent traveling back and forth between the United States and the Continent, where he also became interested in painting. Unlike Rousseau's untalented attempt at music, James was a fairly accomplished artist. But realizing the limits of those endeavors, he returned to the world of science, entered Harvard, and received a medical degree in 1870. Unlike his famous literary brother Henry, who remained abroad and actually became a British citizen, William accepted a position at Harvard in 1871 and was rapidly promoted. Having established himself in his career, James married at age 36 and, unlike many philosophers before him, had a secure family life. He died in 1910, while still employed at Harvard.

Although he had a medical degree, James was uninterested in the actual practice of medicine. He devoted his early career to the teaching of anatomy, physiology, and especially experimental psychology, which resulted in the publication of his *Principles of Psychology* in 1890. During his 20 or so years at Harvard, he became increasingly interested in philosophy through discussions with friends, students, and peers, who included George Santayana and Josiah Royce. James was particularly influenced by the writings of Charles Peirce, who argued that to find the meaning of an idea, we must examine the consequences to which it leads in action.

In his mid-fifties, he began to pursue his interest in a more concrete and practical philosophy, which resulted in the publication of his *Essays on Radical Empiricism* in 1912. His philosophical orientation was captured in a note found on his desk after he died. The note said: "There are no fortunes to be told and there is no advice to be given. Farewell" (Durant, 1953, p. 389).

Philosophical Contributions

James addressed many philosophical issues, but for us his most significant contribution involved the continuation of Bacon and Locke's focus on things or objects. James took Bacon's inductive reasoning a step further by emphasizing the critical function of hypothesizing. He went beyond Locke's work by introducing additional factors influencing empiricism as a source of knowledge. He undertook both these efforts by contributing to pragmatism that arose in 19th-century America. This philosophical school is not only a school of thought but is a method of getting results. When it gets results, something is said to be true or good; when it does not get results, something is said to be false or bad. Thus,

> that something (call it an idea) can be useful or useless and the only criterion is success in practical action. Pragmatism is therefore an action oriented philosophy that asserts only our minds really exist, that the natural and social world exists only in our sensations and ideas, will and emotions (Well, 1971, p. 15).

Although this statement could be interpreted as reflecting the traditional empiricism of Aristotle and Locke, James stressed the subjective nature of a given experience. He "believed knowledge depends on being known; it changes, and therefore is subjective" (Ford, 1982, p. 63). According to James, "experience past and present is found in the self and consists of a stream of thoughts" (Ford, 1982, p. 14). The components of this stream are found in his five characteristics of the thought process, which are as follows (Scheffler, 1974, p. 130):

1. Every thought tends to be part of a personal consciousness. Thoughts are not isolated or clustered into a single whole.
2. Within each personal consciousness, thought is always changing. Humans contribute their own will . . . no two thoughts are exactly the same.

3. Within each personal consciousness, thought is sensibly continuous. Thought moves across time gaps.
4. [Thought] always appears to deal with objects independent of itself. It is cognitve or possesses the function of knowing.
5. [Thought] is interested in some parts of these objects to the exclusion of others and welcomes or rejects . . . chooses from among them, in a word . . . all the while. This emphasis is present in every perception we have.

As you know, metaphysics is concerned with the search for reality and, for James, the search involved the preceding characteristics and the subjective nature of humankind. Note that "the inability of human experience to be objective (i.e., neutrally disinterested) does not preclude our knowing the real, for man and his activities are part and parcel of reality" (Dooley, 1974, p. 173).

Peirce, with whom James interacted for more than 40 years, laid the foundation for pragmatism by focusing on an analysis of logic and its application to the sciences. But James

> went beyond Peirce's work by showing how the meaning of any idea can be found ultimately in nothing save in the succession of experiential consequences that it leads through and to; that truth and error, if they are within the realm of the mind at all, are identical with those consequences, (Davidson, 1952, pp. 246–247).

Using these theories as a base, in a speech at the University of California in 1898, James then put forth his "method" of pragmatism.

James's primary concern was that of making philosophy a practical matter that required a method of systematically thinking things out in a clear fashion. Previously the philosophies of idealism and realism had presented truth as eternal and concrete, but James's pragmatism suggested that truth was relative, was in a constant state of flux, and was directly related to human judgment and societal need. James believed in a world full of change and chance that was perpetuated by spontaneous acts and human freedoms. This being the case, a method was needed that would focus on examining the results and consequences of putting thought into action because truth could only be determined in terms of whether or not something "worked." Specifically, James believed all that the pragmatic method implies is that truths should have practical consequences (James, 1978, p. 204).

James's pragmatic method was nothing more than a technique for locating answers that included three steps (Bird, 1986, p. 17):

1. Clarifying our concepts
   a. How do things work?
   b. How do we "put" concepts [thoughts] to work?
   c. What is [the concept] known as?
2. Differentiate or identify hypotheses
3. Reject as spurious hypotheses which have no practical consequences

The result of answering questions was that of establishing true ideas, and the preceding steps allowed for the assimilating, validating, corroborating, and verifying of concepts, ideas, or thoughts. For James, "truth 'happens' to an idea. It 'becomes' true, is 'made' true by events. It's verity 'is' an event, a process" (Ford, 1982, p. 64).

What James's method does is that of presenting a practical, concrete problem-solving effort, and his use of a hypothesis was central to this process. James viewed a hypothesis as anything that may be proposed as our belief and further believed it could be either alive or dead. To him, "a live hypothesis is one that appeals as a real possibility, whereas a dead hypothesis refuses to scintillate with any credibility at all" (James, 1992, p. 458). Put another way, we tend to believe in things we perceive as having a use and disbelieve in things for which we have no use. James's pragmatic method begins with the perception of a need or a problem, but its power is found in the process of validating the practical utility of the solution—a process that can and should be used in the classroom to enable our students to seek and acquire knowledge.

The creative experience is always seeking to be fed; it derives nourishment from the everyday experience.

Paula Sheehy

Exercise 8.1

After rereading the quotation by Paula Sheehy, write a brief statement on how you think James might interpret her use of the term *nourishment*. Then compare your response to the feedback at the end of the chapter.

From *What Pragmatism Means*, William James

Some years ago, being with a camping party in the mountains, I returned from a solitary ramble to find every one engaged in a ferocious metaphysical dispute. The corpus of the dispute was a squirrel . . . a live squirrel supposed to be clinging to one side of a tree-trunk; while over against the tree's opposite side a human being was imagined to stand. This human witness tries to get sight of the squirrel by moving rapidly around the tree, but no matter how fast he goes, the squirrel moves as fast in the opposite direction, and always keeps the tree between himself and the man, so that never a glimpse of him is caught. The resultant metaphysical problem now is this: Does the man go round the squirrel or not? He goes round the tree, sure enough, and the squirrel is on the tree; but does he go round the squirrel? In the unlimited leisure of the wilderness, discussion had been worn threadbare. Everyone had taken sides, and was obstinate; and the numbers on both sides were even. Each side, when I appeared therefore appealed to me to make it a majority. Mindful of the scholastic adage that whenever you meet a contradiction you must make a distinction, I immediately sought and found one, as follows:

"Which party is right," I said, "depends on what you *practically mean* by 'going round' the squirrel. If you mean passing from the north of him to the east, then to the south, then to the west, and then to the north of him again, obviously the man does go round him, for he occupies these successive positions. But if on the contrary you mean being first in front of him, then on the right of him, then behind him, then on his left, and finally in front again, it is quite as obvious that the man fails to go round him, for by the compensating movements the squirrel makes, he keeps his belly turned towards the man all the time, and his back turned away. Make the distinction, and there is no occasion for any farther dispute. You are both right and both wrong according as you conceive the verb 'to go round' in one practical fashion or the other."

Although one or two of the hotter disputants called my speech a shuffling evasion, saying they wanted no quibbling or scholastic hairsplitting, but meant just plain honest English 'round,' the majority seemed to think that the distinction had assuaged the dispute.

I tell this trivial anecdote because it is a peculiarly simple example of what I wish now to speak of as the pragmatic method. The pragmatic method is primarily a method of settling metaphysical disputes that otherwise might be interminable. Is the world one or many?—fated or free?—material or spiritual?—here are the notions either of which may or may not hold good of the world; and disputes over such notions are unending. The pragmatic method in such cases is to try to interpret each notion by tracing its respective practical consequences. What difference would it practically make to any one if this notion rather than that notion were true? If no practical difference whatever can be traced, then the alternatives mean practically the same thing, and all dispute is idle. Whenever a dispute is serious, we ought to be able to show some practical difference that must follow from one side or the other's being right.

A glance at the history of the idea will show you still better what pragmatism means. The term is derived from a Greek word meaning action, from which our words "practice" and "practical" come. The principle of pragmatism, introduced by Mr. Charles Peirce, states that

(continued)

in order to attain perfect clearness in our thoughts of an object, we need only to consider what conceivable effects of a practical kind the object may involve—what sensations we are to expect from it, and what reactions we must prepare. Our conception of these efforts, whether immediate or remote, is then for us the whole of our conception of the object, so far as that conception has positive significance at all.

McDermott, J. (Ed.). (1977). *The Writings of William James.* Chicago: University of Chicago Press, pp. 376–378. Reprinted with permission of the University of Chicago Press.

James in the Classroom

Although the most direct application of James's work to classroom teaching is found in his pragmatic method, his views regarding the aims and curriculum of educational institutions are also of value. James thought "the aim of (American) education is the same in other countries, and that is to organize capacities for conduct" (Myers, 1986, p. 731). This, of course, varies from nation to nation, depending on local needs and aspirations: "Education in Germany in the nineteenth century meant advancing scientific knowledge and serving the State, while the school system in Great Britain was focused on inculcating the personality and image of the English gentleman" (Myers, 1986, p. 731). Unlike the nationalistic systems of many European countries, the U.S. system made education a state's right, which obviously produced a decentralized approach. Nevertheless, many "conduct" commonalities can be found, such as being an educated participant in a democracy and being able to engage in problem solving.

James further believed the function of the curriculum was that of facilitating the acquisition and refinement of ideas that had a practical value. The more we can store and access a multitude of ideas, the more capable we are of meeting and overcoming the demands of individual and society living. James also believed ideas or knowledge are most effectively acquired in the classroom when students are given a chance to generate hypotheses and employ the steps of his pragmatic method to practical as opposed to abstract experiences. He thought it was incumbent on the school curriculum to provide such experiences in the classroom. These experiences should be designed to spark the curiosity and investigative interests of students. James's reference to confirming ideas or thoughts has particular value in the classroom, because it is important for teachers to provide learning situations and materials that allow students to come closer to truth by personally and methodically investigating a given concept. Now let's take a look at James in the classroom.

Scenario 8.1

Mr. Greg Garman, a sixth-grade science teacher at A. A. Slade Elementary School, continued his lesson on erosion by telling his class they were going to work on their experiment, which would simulate the building of the Grand Canyon. The day before, his students had used their stream tables and maps to observe and chart the effects of water on a flat surface.

"Is there one thing you can think of that can make the erosion in our water trays take place faster than it did yesterday? In other words, something we can do that will cause even more erosion?" Mr. Garman asked.

"We could put a bigger hole in our water cup," Tara said.

"That would definitely work because it would do what, Tara?"

"Make our water source larger."

"Great, Tara," Mr. Garman said. "What is something else we could use to make erosion take place faster or more dramatically? (Pause.) Brady?"

"Use more water," Brady replied.

"Use more water. Okay. Would that make erosion take place faster or more dramatically or just produce erosion over a longer period of time, Brady?"

"It would take more years maybe but more erosion would still take place," Brady said.

"You're right. That would be one way to cause more erosion to take place. Good. I'll put 'more water over time' on the board along with the size of the water source. Anything else we can do? Any other ideas? Kashmira?"

"We could spread out the sand and make it thinner in our trays," Kashmira said.

"You're on the right track, Kashmira. You're on to something. Stretch what you are saying a little further. There is something we can do other than adding more water or adding it at a faster rate. (No response, and Mr. Garman pulls down a large map of the United States.)

"Okay," he continued, "here is the Grand Canyon in Northern Arizona and the Colorado River runs through it south to where?"

"The Gulf of California," Sidney said.

"Good. Now what is the approximate elevation at the Grand Canyon? Take a guess?"

"I'm not sure, but the Gulf of California is at sea level, so there must be a pretty big slope from the Grand Canyon," Sidney answered.

"Right," Mr. Garman said. "So the river does not flow on a flat or level plane like ours did in yesterday's stream table experiment. Now, scientists don't know exactly how the Grand Canyon was formed, but one of the possible reasons is that because of the slope the river is dropping rapidly, which will cause a lot of erosion. They're not sure. We want to see today if that will happen. So, how can we set up our water trays in order to have some slope?"

"We could put something under it," Amber said.

With permission. A. A. Slade Elementary School, Laramie, Wyoming. Mr. Dick Greenlee, Principal.

"What could we put under it?"

"A piece of wood," Amber replied.

"Right. If we set our water tray on a piece of wood, we are going to have a slope, but I don't know if that will cause more erosion. I don't know if it will cause erosion to occur more dramatically. You need to find that out and you need to make the decision, so let's get going."

Mr. Garman then provided instructions on how to do the experiment. He made sure that the three or four students at each lab station properly assembled their equipment. Each green plastic stream tray, approximately 2 feet by 1 foot, was placed at the end of a desk, with the opposite end of the tray being elevated by a 1–inch piece of wood. Earth material—a combination of diatomaceous earth and fine-grained sand—was packed, leveled, and carefully measured at 20 centimeters. A 16-ounce plastic cup with a small hole in the bottom was balanced on a ruler placed across the elevated end of the tray.

"Okay," Mr. Garman said. "Is everybody about ready? Check to make sure and be very careful about your earth material being flat. We don't want any bumps. Now, unlike yesterday we are going to add one more step because today we are going to time. Everybody will pour water into their plastic cup at the exact same time, and I will watch the second hand on the clock and call off times."

"What I want you to do today," Mr. Garman continued, "is to look for things that happen. When does a water stream first start to flow? When do we start having canyons form? When do we start to have a channel? When do we notice a slump, and when does a delta start to form? And by 'when,' do I mean 30 seconds after the water has started to flow? A minute and 10 seconds? You will need to record that on the elapsed-time section of your handout, and I want you to look specifically for slump, stream, canyon, and delta as important events."

Mr. Garman had written the following information on the board as a reinforcer of previously learned terms or knowledge:

Slump: The downward movement (collapse) of a mass of earth material
Stream: A flow of water in a channel
Canyon: A V-shaped valley eroded by a river or a stream
Delta: A fan-shaped (triangular) deposit of earth material at the mouth of a stream

"As you know," Mr. Garman said, "the experiment has been designed so that 1 minute equals approximately 1 million years. Now . . . what are we trying to figure out? What are we looking for? (Pause.) Zach?"

"The different times that things happen," Zach said.

"Good, because that will give us the big picture as to whether or not erosion is going to happen more quickly or more dramatically in the sloped tray, or was erosion more dramatic in the flat tray . . . or is it going to make no difference at all? We want to figure these things out today."

"You'll be able to compare what you recorded on your map yesterday with what you will record now. Okay. Everybody with me? Get ready to pour your water into the cup. I'll call off the times and you write down your observations in the 'Important Events' space. Okay. You may begin."

The students at the lab stations began the experiment and observed the events as Mr. Garman called off the elapsed time every five seconds. The experiment lasted for approximately five minutes.

"Now class," Mr. Garman began, "I want you to think about how slope has affected what happened with slump, stream formation, and canyon formation, and what happened with the formation of your delta. Compared to yesterday's flat experiment, what kind of things went on with these areas? Take a few minutes in your groups and consult with each other."

On the completion of their group discussions, the students shared their observations with Mr. Garman and the whole class. Mr. Garman then asked, "What might be one major conclusion you could state based on all the observations? Candace?"

"Since the tray was at a tilt, the water flowed faster and had more energy to take the sand further and make faster changes."

"Good observation, Candace. Anything else?"

"The water cut into the earth deeper," Raynaldo added.

"And if it cut into the earth deeper, what did it form?"

"A canyon," Raynaldo said.

"Very good. A really deep canyon. Now, is this canyon deeper than the canyon you saw yesterday?"

"Yes, because the water was moving faster," Raynaldo said.

"Great . . . and did the deltas form like yesterday's? (Pause.) I see lots of heads shaking no. Okay then. Do you think water speed is affected by slope? (Affirmative nods.) Do you think erosion, then, is affected by the speed at which water travels? (More affirmative nods.) If you were going to write a statement about erosion and water speed, what would that be? Talk that over in your group, and in a few seconds I will ask one group to answer that. (Pause.) Jackie's group. What did you guys decide about erosion and water speed?"

"The more the slope, the more the erosion," Jackie said.

"Fine," Mr. Garman replied, "but why?"

"As the slope increases the speed of the water increases."

"So?" Mr. Garman urged.

"The faster the water travels, the more erosion will take place," Jackie concluded.

"Great job, everybody! In the time remaining, finish up your map of today's work on your stream table handout. While you are doing that, I will come around to each lab station so you can share with me the events that took place in your trays."

The most obvious aspect of James's work that Mr. Garman is employing involves the students' generating cause-and-effect statements, which are representative of framing a hypothesis. The students were able to do so by observing and recording the events of the stream table experiment. Additionally, Mr. Garman is using the first step of the pragmatic method by posing a problem—in this case, having the students discuss ways the water might flow more rapidly. The students were then allowed to put their suggestions into play, monitor the action, and develop their concluding statements. Finally, the practical implications of increasing the students' knowledge of erosion are obvious in an environmentally and ecologically conscious world.

Exercise 8.2

Examine the following statements to determine if they are consistent (c) or inconsistent (i) with James's pragmatic philosophy. Then check your answers against those at the end of the chapter.

_____ 1. Knowledge is relative as opposed to absolute.

_____ 2. Pragmatism utilizes components of both inductive reasoning and empiricism.

_____ 3. Pragmatists are more concerned with what we know as opposed to the process of acquiring knowledge and truth.

_____ 4. Ideas are useful only if they are practical.

_____ 5. Human perception does not play a role in pragmatic thinking.

Exercise 8.3

The development of a hypothesis is one of the critical steps in James's pragmatic method. Briefly discuss how the nature of a hypothesis is consistent with James's view of the nature of knowledge. Then compare your response to the feedback at the end of the chapter.

JOHN DEWEY, 1859–1952

Like James, Dewey was significantly influenced by philosophers who preceded him. A difference is found, however, in the way these influences affected the two American philosophers. Whereas James built on the work of Bacon, Locke, and others, Dewey chose to depart from the foundational work of such philosophers as Aristotle and Kant.

Metaphysically, Aristotle believed some truths about the world were intuitively or demonstrably certain. Kant believed certain postulates about the world were founded on morality, which was a priori. Both reflected a belief in the certainty or absolute nature of knowledge. Since Dewey "did not subscribe to the theory of an unchangeable nature and an omnipotent environment, his focus was upon a methodology which began with identifying difficulties or problems and ended with synthesizing and co-ordinating knowledge and desire, resulting in the controlling and remaking of the external world" (Durant, 1953, p. 393).

The influence of Aristotle and Kant on Dewey is most easily understood when considering the function of reason. Aristotle championed *theoretical* reason, for he believed the most important human activity was that of the "intellectual excellence of knowing." Kant championed *practical* reason, for he believed the most important human activity was that of the "moral excellence of doing." Dewey denies the existence of this dualism and therefore rejects any separation or distinction between theoretical and practical reasoning or philosophy, something with which Aristotle and Kant were very comfortable. Dewey champions the belief that Aristotle's "knowing" and Kant's "doing" are both

*Education is literally and all
the time its own reward.*

John Dewey

employed in the effort he referred to as "making." Because Dewey theorized that "reality is a liquid process which is constantly changing and in which there is no absolute spirit, his making or supreme imperative was that man must ever be alert to his changing environment and active in solving the problems it unceasingly presents" (Butler, 1968, p. 39).

Life and Times

Dewey was born on October 20, 1859, on a farm in Burlington, Vermont. He was the third of four sons born to Lucina Rich Dewey and Archibald Dewey, who operated a small village grocery store. Although Dewey spent most of his formative years in New England, his family lived in northern Virginia in the early 1860s to be near Archibald, who fought in the Civil War. The young Dewey later wrote that the violence of this divisive conflict marked him in terms of its futility and its horrendous social and human consequences.

On returning to Vermont—where his now middle-aged parents opened a cigar and tobacco store—Dewey was enrolled in the public school system and was impressed at an early age by the importance of such an education in a democratic society. Moreover, there can be little doubt that growing up in a small New England town, with its town meetings and other cooperative institutions, would have influenced him not only in terms of the positive nature of the societal interactions but also in the sense of making him aware of the problems of a growing industrial town and nation. New thinking in the areas of science (including evolution), economics, and politics as well as changes in social institutions marked the dynamic times and influenced the curriculum of America's institutions of higher learning. These institutions included the University of Vermont, from which Dewey graduated Phi Beta Kappa in 1879.

Dewey's professional career in education began with two years of high school teaching in Pennsylvania, after which he returned to the University of Vermont for a year of study in philosophy. He then transferred to Johns Hopkins, wrote a dissertation on Kant, and earned his Ph.D. in 1884. Dewey entered the world of higher education as an instructor at the University of Michigan. Having fulfilled the contemporary criterion of "career first," Dewey then married Alice Chipman, with whom he had 6 children and, it is said, shared 40 years of happiness.

With the exception of the academic year 1888–89, spent at the University of Minnesota, Dewey remained at Michigan until 1894, when he accepted the position of head of psychology, philosophy, and education at the University of Chicago. During these years he came to feel that an emphasis should be placed on the cultural environment as having pervasive influence in forming the ideas, beliefs, and intellectual attitudes of individuals (White, 1943). It was also at this time that Dewey became prominent in the area of education, with his view that a school should be a microcosm of the community or the society—that is, the real world. He therefore attempted to shift the focus in schools from what knowledge should be known to the methodology of learning, including practices, trial and error, and most important, reflective thinking and his experimental method.

In 1904, Dewey accepted a position as chair of the philosophy department at Columbia University, where he continued to focus on the need for inquiry as opposed to the pursuit of truth until his retirement in 1930. For the remaining 22 years of his life, Dewey continued to publish his work; he continued to be intellectually active until his death at age 93 in 1952. Throughout his long public career, popular writings, and many volumes of scholarly work, Dewey "persistently sought to identify challenges to democracy and to articulate intelligent responses to these changing challenges" (Stuhr, 1993, p. 40).

Philosophical Contributions

By the time Dewey arrived at the doorway of his professional life, the foundation of the philosophy of pragmatism had been laid by Peirce, whose work emphasized the sciences, and by James, who focused on the psychological and religious applications of the new American philosophy. As early as age 19, Dewey had expressed his view that "if you lose faith in yourself, you lose faith in humankind" (White, 1943, p. 58). He therefore tried to apply the principles of pragmatism to the achievement of the individual as well as the societal "good life," which he defined as a "harmonious whole consisting of good experiences and values . . . experiences that are achieved through intellectual action, that are approved after reflection in light of the full knowledge of their conditions and consequences, and that are enjoyed as being so achieved and so approved" (Frankena, 1965, p. 161). Dewey further believed that the purpose of philosophy was that of addressing and solving the problems and conflicts of human life. This purpose, coupled with his belief in the relative and changing nature of knowledge as well as society, marked a significant departure from the Greek philosophy that had dominated Western society for centuries. Though "Greek philosophers removed the imaginative forms, i.e., mythology, they put in place a 'Supreme Reality,' a higher realm of fixed reality with change being a movement toward inherent ends, a fulfillment in perfect objects" (Westbrook, 1991, p. 349).

Although Dewey rejected the theory of absolute nature as expressed in the philosophies of idealism and realism, he recognized the traditional need to communicate existing and time-honored abilities, traits, and knowledge, which were required if individuals were to interact in a dynamic and fluid social environment. Thus, "he believed society must be concerned with transmitting habits of doing, thinking, and feeling from the older to the younger" (Dewey, 1966, p. 3). As noted in the preface to this book, you cannot employ knowledge unless you possess knowledge. In other words, the transmission of knowledge is not an end in itself but is a critical foundation for further inquiry and eventual action—what Dewey referred to as "making." Here is the core of Dewey's pragmatism: "his belief that ideas are the instruments for social action in a continually developing world" (Hickman, 1990, p. 195). He called this belief *instrumentalism.*

For Dewey, instrumentalism involved the application of pragmatism in solving human problems. In the event a given idea did help solve problems, it approximated truth. This conception of truth was frequently attacked as being too narrow, and Dewey felt strongly that no misconception of his instrumental logic had been more persistent than that of supposedly making knowledge a means to a practical end, or to the satisfaction of practical needs—*practical* being taken to signify something useful and of a material or everyday nature. Dewey relentlessly affirmed that instrumentalism meant only the rule of referring all thinking, all reflective considerations, to consequences for final meaning and test. Nothing is said about the nature of the consequences; they may be aesthetic, or moral, or political, or religious in character. All that the theory requires is that "whatever theoretical conclusions we might reach, we must also take account of their practical consequences" (Hendley, 1986, p. 42).

Because of the practical and concrete nature of instrumentalism, Dewey believed that philosophy must be empirically based and empirically tested. He saw this as an ongoing process, and in the event a traditional idea did not "hold up" when subjected to experimental inquiry, it would obviously lose its practical value and no longer be tenable. The process Dewey proposed that would accomplish this end was *reflective thinking,* which he defined as an "active, persistent and careful consideration of any belief or supposed form of knowledge in the light of the grounds that support it and further conclusions to which it tends" (Dewey, 1910, p. 6). Fundamental to the concept of reflective thinking is the development or disposition to reflect; to inquire and deliberate prior to action; to perceive a problem or a felt need. Once undertaken, the following steps in Dewey's reflective thinking process are employed (Jacobsen, Eggen, and Kauchak, 1993, p. 215):

1. The perceived problem is defined and clarified.
2. A tentative hypothesis is developed.
3. The consequences of the tentative hypothesis are considered.
4. The hypothesis is tested by acting on it to determine whether or not it "holds up" or is validated by further Experience.

The end result of this process was not only that of confirming a thought or hypothesis but also that of assuming its practical and social utilization. For Dewey, reflective thinking is not a quest for truth as though the truth were a static and eternal quality in things. Thinking rather is the act of trying to achieve an adjustment between people and their environment through a "straightforward, flexible, intellectual interest or an open-minded will to learn, an integrity of purpose and an acceptance of responsibility for the conse-quences of one's activity including thought or intellectual thoroughness" (Dewey, 1966, p. 179).

Look forward. Turn what has been done into a better path. If you're a leader, think about the impact of your decisions on seven generations into the future.

Chief Wilma Mankiller

Exercise 8.4

Revisit the words of Wilma Mankiller and briefly discuss one aspect of Dewey's philosophy that is expressed in the quotation. Then check your work against the response at the end of the chapter.

From *The Quest for Certainty*, John Dewey

The business of thought is not to conform to or reproduce the charac-ters already possessed by objects but to judge them as potentialities of what they become through an indicated operation. This principle holds from the simplest case to the most elaborate. To judge that this object is sweet, that is, to refer the idea or meaning "sweet" to it without actually experiencing sweetness, is to predict that when it is tasted—that is, subjected to a specified operation—a certain consequence will ensue. Similarly, to think of the world in terms of mathematical formulae of space, time and motion is not to have a picture of the independent and fixed essence of the universe. It is to describe experienceable objects as material upon which certain operations are performed.

The bearing of this conclusion upon the relation of knowledge and action speaks for itself. Knowledge which is merely a reduplication in ideas of what exists already in the world may afford us the satisfaction of a photograph, but that is all. To form ideas whose worth is to be judged by what exists independently of them is not a function that (even if the test could be applied, which seems impossible) goes on within nature or makes any difference there. Ideas that are plans of operations to be performed are integral factors in actions which change the face of the world. Idealistic philosophies have not been wrong in attaching vast importance and power to ideas. But in isolating their function and their test from action, they failed to grasp the point and place where ideas have a constructive office. A genuine idealism and one compatible with science will emerge as soon as philosophy accepts the teaching of science that ideas are statements not of what is or has been but of acts to be performed. For then mankind will learn that, intellectually (that is, save for the esthetic enjoyment they afford, which is of course a true value), ideas are worthless except as they pass into actions which rearrange and reconstruct in some way, be it little or large, the world in which we live. To magnify thought and ideas for their own sake apart from what they do (except, once more, esthetically) is to refuse to learn the lesson of the most authentic kind of knowledge—the experimental—and it is to reject the idealism which involves responsibility. To praise thinking above action because there is so much ill-considered action in the world is to help maintain the kind of world in which action occurs for narrow and transient purposes. To seek after ideas and to cling to them as means of conducting operations, as factors in practical arts, is to participate in creating a world in which the springs of thinking will be clear and ever-flowing. We recur to our general issue. When we take the instance of scientific experience in its own field, we find that experience when it is experimental does not signify the absence of large and far-reaching ideas and purposes. It is dependent upon them at every point. But it generates them within its own procedures and tests them by its own operations. In so far, we have the earnest of a possibility of human experience, in all its phases, in which ideas and meanings will be prized and will be continuously generated and used. But they will be integral with the course of experience itself, not imported from the external source of a reality beyond.

Dewey in the Classroom

Unlike many of his philosophical predecessors, including Aristotle and Kant, Dewey was committed to a completely democratic society and was further committed to the critical role of the school in providing students with the processes and dispositions needed to sustain a democratic way of life. Prior to Dewey, the aim of most educational institutions was that of facilitating a student's acquisition of knowledge. But with the appearance of his theories and reflective method, educators became increasingly concerned with increasing students' ability to process information and with enhancing their problem-solving skills and intellectual acumen. Nevertheless, the implementation of Dewey's process-oriented education was slow, because the schools were overwhelmingly staffed with traditionalist educators who fostered such dispositions as authoritarianism and revelation—which promoted the "storage" of classical knowledge as opposed to the development of critical thinking skills.

The relative nature of Dewey's philosophical theories when applied to classroom teaching is clearly shown in his belief that education should not have any preconceived, fixed, or determined ends. His so-called progressive classroom is characterized by a learning environment that is a practical, simplified version of society. Within this environment, Dewey emphasized a student-centered, activity-oriented curriculum with the focal point being the promotion of a cognitive methodology—that is, his reflective thinking. He further believed it was the teacher's responsibility to provide problems or situations that would not only be interesting and challenging but would be worthwhile in promoting social growth.

Although the application of the reflective method to a wide range of problems is central to the implementation of Dewey's pragmatism, teachers who bring him into their classrooms are equally concerned with facilitating an experience that is relevant, practical, and in the present, as opposed to being theoretical and having a potential for future application. As has often been stated, for Dewey, education *is* life, not a preparation *for* life. It is a dynamic, ongoing, and never-ending experience in which the most effective way to learn is found in the active doing of something. The following lesson provides an example of Dewey's "learning by doing."

Scenario 8.2

Ms. Elvia Rodriguez, a second-grade teacher at Centennial Elementary School, wrote the five parts of a friendly letter on the board. She then asked the children to take out a piece of paper and fold it in half. She then said, "Now children, open it up. Right where you see the crease, look to the right-hand side and think about what belongs there."

"The heading goes there," said Lisa.

With permission. Centennial Elementary School, Denver, Colorado. Mr. Gerald R. Gilmore, Principal.

"That's right," Ms. Rodriguez responded. "Now write the date and start at the crease toward the top and go across to the right. (Pause.) Now, here's the big question. What kind of punctuation mark are we going to have after the 23rd of November, Charles?"

"A comma."

"A comma. That's right. That is the punctuation mark used after the date on all the letters you will write. Now, skip a line and go to the left-hand side of the crease just to the edge of your paper. What are we going to do here? (Pause.) Look at the list on the board."

"The greeting," said Selena.

"Yes, you're right. Now look at your pen pal letter that you received from my sister's class (Ms. Sylvia Adams, Conlee Elementary School, Las Cruces, New Mexico) and look at the way he or she wrote a greeting to you. What is the word most of the children started with before your name?"

"*Dear*," some of the students replied.

"Yes, that is a very common greeting. Did anyone have anything else? (No response.) Okay, then, let's all start our letter with *dear*, and then you fill in the first name of your pen pal. And don't forget, what kind of a letter does *dear* begin with?"

"A capital letter," said a number of students.

"My pen pal's name, *Jammie*, also begins with a capital letter," added Juli.

"You've got it, Juli," Ms. Rodriguez said. "Now, here comes another question. Right after the name—that is, the person you are writing to—what kind of punctuation mark do we use?"

"An exclamation mark."

"Kerry said an exclamation mark. Does anyone disagree? (Pause.) Sylvana, you disagree . . . so what is it?"

"A comma."

"A comma is correct. Why do you use a comma, Sylvana?"

"Because you wouldn't say it real excited and it's a friendly letter."

"Two very good reasons, Sylvana. Now, let's move on to the body of the letter. Who remembers what we do that is very special when we start the body of our friendly letter? Jenny remembers. What is it, Jenny?"

"I am going to say 'Are you doing okay?'"

"Great," Ms. Rodriguez said. "You could say that and it would be very nice."

"I would also start with a capital letter," Jenny added.

"That would be correct."

"Sam joined in by saying, 'I would ask how are you?' Ms. Rodriguez praised Sam and used what he said by writing his greeting on the board two ways and asking the students to try to determine what was different about them. George raised his hand and Ms. Rodriguez said, "Go for it, George."

"It's number 2 because you have to go in a little, right past the 'Dear pen pal.'"

"That's wonderful, George. You are a second grader and you are learning so much. Now this is a new word. We say 'moving in a little' . . . or *indenting*."

Ms. Rodriguez continued to work through and demonstrate the remaining components of a friendly letter. She then asked the students to begin writing their letters to their pen pal in order to mail them on Friday afternoon. The children began the assignment while Ms. Rodriguez provided individual assistance.

Ms. Rodriguez's lesson was the culmination of a short unit on writing a friendly letter. When she began by writing the five parts of the letter on the board, she was providing information the children had already learned through a student-centered, teacher-facilitated experience and was then engaging them in putting the information into practice. Dewey's belief in "learning by doing" and his philosophical position that education is not a preparation for life but is life itself are evident in this lesson, in that the students are not learning the structure of a friendly letter for future use; they are putting this information into practice by writing friendly letters to real people. In this instance, Ms. Rodriguez had arranged for each of her students to have a pen pal in her sister's elementary school in New Mexico. Furthermore, the experience was not designed to be a one-time-only assignment; the students continued to correspond throughout the term. What they learned about writing a friendly letter became useful and relevant and was incorporated into their repertoire of practical skills, reflecting Dewey's desire to bring the real world into the classroom.

Exercise 8.5

Examine the following statements to determine if they are consistent (c) or inconsistent (i) with Dewey's pragmatic philosophy. Then compare your answers with those at the end of the chapter.

_____ 1. In a progressive classroom, there is little need to present classical knowledge to the students.

_____ 2. Classroom experiences should enable the students to promote social action.

_____ 3. The primary method used in progressive classrooms is reflective thinking directed toward the solving of problems.

_____ 4. Truth is manifested in the consequences of individual and social actions.

_____ 5. Classroom experiences should provide a base of information for future use.

Exercise 8.6

One of the cornerstones of Dewey's philosophy, with specific regard to schools, is that education is not a preparation for life; education is life. Briefly discuss in your own words the relevance of this belief to classroom teaching. Then check your response against the feedback at the end of the chapter.

SUMMARY

Pragmatism is a philosophy characterized by an emphasis on the relative nature of knowledge and the changing nature of society. It seems obvious and predictable that such a philosophy would have its roots in a fledgling American

nation-state whose Constitution reflected the dynamic political and cultural upheavals of the times.

Along with Peirce, James and Dewey gave birth to what many believed to be
a radical new philosophy. It is often said that Peirce provided the initial concepts, James popularized the beliefs and methods, and Dewey was the high
priest calling for its practical application in a democratic society. Although
James and Dewey share a common spirit with regard to pragmatism, their
thinking reveals significant differences. The first difference is found in the fact
that, unlike Dewey and the pragmatists who followed, James was not opposed to
traditional religious beliefs. He actually applied and used the inductive method
to explain moral and religious questions and beliefs that had value if they provided "suitable consequences" (Ozmon and Craver, 1995, p. 140). For James,
science says "things are"; morality says "some things are better than other
things"; and religion says "the best things are the more eternal things." In
keeping with pragmatism, the "best things" would be those that withstood the
consequences of time and action and so approximated truth.

Dewey "credited *Psychology* by James with much of his development, particularly in the application of James's inductive reasoning to all facets of human life,
which helped his slow drift from Hegel and brought his philosophy into the
mainstream of psychology with its emphasis on behavior rather than consciousness" (Smith and Smith, 1994, pp. 292–293). However, a second significant difference between the two philosophers was that Dewey was much more focused
on ethics and social thought, whereas the pragmatic focus for James was psychology and religion. His concern for the individual's ability to problem solve
and serve as an active participant in the effort to improve society clearly had an
impact on the methodology of 20th-century U.S. education. One scholar offers
the following assessment: "No major U.S. philosopher has been more diligently
committed to the ideal that philosophical inquiry, like any other form of inquiry, takes place as part of, and is directed toward, specific times and places"
(Hickman, 1990, p. 3).

Questions for Discussion

1. According to James, how do we go about increasing the accuracy of knowledge?
2. What is the role of experience and experiment in establishing truth?
3. Regarding the passage from James's "What Pragmatism Means," how do we
   know if something *works* or if it is *right*?
4. As expressed in the philosophy of pragmatism, what is the connection between usefulness and truth?
5. With regard to James's employment of the pragmatic method, what is the
   purpose of "hypothesizing"?
6. How did the work of Aristotle and Kant contribute to Dewey's philosophy?
7. What is Dewey's theory of *instrumentalism*?

8. What are the key features of the method of learning Dewey referred to as *reflective thinking*?
9. In the passage from *The Quest for Certainty*, Dewey expresses his concern about the common educational practice of *reduplication*. What does this term mean and how would Dewey replace it in the classroom?

Suggested Field Laboratory Activities

1. Using lesson plan books and curriculum guides, look for examples of units and/or lessons designed to engage students in real-life experiences.
2. Using lesson plan books and curriculum guides, look for examples of units and/or lessons designed to allow students to usefully apply what they have learned.
3. Discuss with your fellow students and site directors why the implementation of pragmatic principles and Dewey's progressive ideas are controversial and are often viewed in a skeptical way by the educational community.
4. Given the opportunity, prepare and implement a lesson that enables the students to generate a hypothesis and employ James's pragmatic method.
5. Working with either a small or large group of students, develop and teach a lesson that allows the students to engage in Dewey's reflective thinking.
6. Given the opportunity, design and teach a lesson that gives students an experience of "learning by doing." You might also administer a short questionnaire to collect information on how students felt about the learning experiences.

Exercise Feedback

Exercise 8.1

When interpreting Paula Sheehy's use of the word *nourishment,* James might suggest a connection between what we do and what we experience. For him, there was a clear connection between the life activities in which we engage and the way those interactions nourish or promote human growth.

Exercise 8.2

1. (c)   Consistent. The belief in relativism as opposed to absolutism is a critical difference between James's pragmatism on the one hand and the philosophies of idealism and realism on the other.
2. (c)   Consistent.
3. (i)   Inconsistent. Pragmatists focus more on the "how" as opposed to the "what."

4. (c) Consistent. The proof of the pudding is found in whether ideas or knowledge can be applied to real situations, whether they work, and whether they withstand the test of time.

5. (i) Inconsistent. Knowledge is explained in terms of human experience that is varied, is subjective, and is within the consciousness of the individual.

Exercise 8.3

James viewed the nature of knowledge as being relative, thus rejecting the idea of absolute truth. Put another way, we cannot think of knowledge at the 100 percent level. Hypotheses too do not operate at the 100 percent level. When we validate a hypothesis, we are not saying it is absolutely true; we are saying it is generally so or statistically accurate. When thinking of a hypothesis as a cause-and-effect statement, its validation suggests that the predicted outcome is most likely to occur.

Exercise 8.4

Wilma Mankiller's concern about the need to consider contemporary decisions and actions in light of their impact on future generations reflects Dewey's concern with the usefulness of such actions being measured by their ability to withstand the test of time. It is assumed that if they can continue to provide society with viable approaches and solutions, they will have successfully served future generations.

Exercise 8.5

1. (i) Inconsistent. Dewey believed classical knowledge was important to the development of a base of information that could be used to promote problem solving. His concern was that, all too often, classical knowledge served as the end-all, be-all of the curriculum.

2. (c) Consistent.

3. (c) Consistent.

4. (c) Consistent. This statement also points out the relative nature of truth, for it is strengthened, altered, or abandoned if it cannot withstand the consequences of the test of time.

5. (c) Consistent.

By declaring that "education is life," Dewey is saying that education is "now." It is not something one engages in theoretically and passively for a period of time before actually putting information and knowledge to use. The cornerstone of Dewey's philosophy involves the need for human beings to successfully problem solve; all of us are confronted on a daily basis with problems, whether we are 8 or 80 years old. Because of this, Dewey believed the classroom should bring the "real" world into the school and provide students with opportunities to engage in problem-solving activities that are not only practical but also relevant. In this way, teachers facilitate the "living of life" as opposed to the "getting ready" for life.

CHAPTER 9

SUBJECTIVITY AND TRUTH: KIERKEGAARD AND SARTRE

After completing Chapter 9, you should be able to accomplish the following objectives:

1. You will gain an understanding of the philosophical contributions of Søren Kierkegaard by identifying statements as being consistent or inconsistent with his philosophy.

2. You will expand your knowledge of dialectics by writing a short paragraph that compares Kierkegaard's employment of the dialectic to that of Hegel's.

3. You will increase your knowledge of existentialism by labeling a series of statements as being consistent or inconsistent with the philosophy of Jean-Paul Sartre.

4. You will expand your conceptualization of existentialism by writing a short paragraph explaining Sartre's assertion that existence precedes essence.

In Chapter 8, you learned about the theories and applications of James's and Dewey's pragmatism. Part of the significance of their contributions is found in their departure from earlier philosophies that emphasized absolute knowledge and the predetermined nature of human beings. For these U. S. philosophers, human beings were individually characterized by the philosophical belief in "free choice" and the ability to engage in problem-solving activities that had the potential to produce desirable change in the world.

In this chapter, you will be introduced to the existentialist philosophies of Søren Kierkegaard and Jean-Paul Sartre, whose work also focused on individuals. However, a significant difference between the American pragmatists and the European existentialists is found in the former's focus on the *intellectual* nature of individual free choice, as opposed to the latter's focus on the *subjective* nature of individual free choice. For Kierkegaard, each person possesses an essential self that should be actualized. Despair and guilt create an awareness of qualitative differences in various modes of existence, and some are more authentic than others. Arriving at an authentic existence is not based on or a matter of intellect; it is a matter of faith and a process of choice. Furthermore,

Kierkegaard believed there was no such thing as objective certainty, because eternal truth was directly related to the individual and was therefore totally subjective: "Truth is reserved for the individual human being. To exist implies being a certain kind of individual, an individual who strives, who considers alternatives, who chooses, who decides, and who, above all, commits himself" (Stumpf, 1966, p. 462).

Sartre also addressed the concept of existence, which up to his time, was thought to be preceded by the concept of essence—that is, the predetermined nature or character of human beings. Sartre's basic principle of existentialism was that existence preceded essence. By this he meant that human beings first exist and do so with no predetermined traits or knowledge and with no objective system of values. They have no essence, which is attained throughout life through free choice and subjective interactions in the social and physical world. For Sartre, essence is found in the course of living and cannot be developed until one has lived. As in Herbart's theory of ideas, no two lives can be the same, and therefore each individual must make sense out of life's experiences and determine its value on a subjective basis. Sartre's beliefs, along with those of Kierkegaard, contributed to what became the 20th-century focus on the individual as opposed to the society or state.

SØREN KIERKEGAARD, 1813–1855

Kierkegaard is often referred to as the "melancholy Dane," since he lived a solitary life of self-imposed loneliness in a world he considered adrift. His "gloom" was caused by his belief that people in Western society were preoccupied with the objective world and that this was an exercise in futility because reality could not be grasped by reason. Reality could not be taught or communicated rationally and academically; it had to be grasped personally, passionately, and anti-intellectually (Clark, 1957). Kierkegaard, therefore, was concerned not only about the existence of human beings but about their individual quality of life. He believed that quality of life depended on truth, which was obtained through personal freedom and subjective interactions, not through human reason. This view was diametrically opposed to Hegel's, since Hegel used the dialectic as an intellectual process for fostering human progress. As you are about to see, Kierkegaard also employed the dialectic, but his "gloom" was once again manifested because he thought the use of the dialectic would lead not to a world of progress but to a world of tragedy. Though his foundational work in the area of existentialism reflected a preoccupation with moving from what is to what ought to be, for Kierkegaard, unlike most of the idealists, realists, and pragmatists you have studied, the role of human beings was not that of improving or saving the world but to let it be known it was perishing. This belief was most clearly expressed when he wrote the following (Kierkegaard, 1986, p. 591):

> It happened that a fire broke out in the theatre. The clown came out to inform the public. They thought it was a joke and they applauded. He repeated

Truth is objective uncertainty passionately held fast.

Søren Kierkegaard

his warnings, they shouted him down. So I think the world will come to an end amid general applause from all the wits, who believe that it is a joke.

Life and Times

Kierkegaard was born in Copenhagen on May 5, 1813. As a boy he was aloof and considered strange and certainly precocious. His appearance was "odd." He was small and had so obvious a stoop that he seemed to be a hunchback (Dru, 1959, p. 8). Though "Kierkegaard was anything but a melancholy child, in his early years, everything in his home life centered around his father, whose faith in God was deeply vulnerable and undermined by silent despair" (Dru, 1959, p. 11)—a despair that was clearly reflected in Kierkegaard's writings throughout his life. His mother played a subordinate role in the family. After the death of his first wife, Kierkegaard's father had married his housekeeper, whom he continued to treat as a servant. Her cheerfulness was not enough to shield Kierkegaard from his father's pessimism.

Much of Kierkegaard's life was uneventful. He was educated at the University of Copenhagen, where he briefly considered studying law but then turned to philosophy. His higher education culminated in a master's degree, for which he wrote a thesis titled *The Concept of Irony, with Constant References to Socrates.*

Kierkegaard's pessimism was quickly established in this work. He argued that Socrates lived ironically, taught ironically, and went to his death ironically, offering an example of his own definition of irony: infinite negativity. It is not surprising that on his graduation he adopted a reclusive lifestyle and removed himself from the real world. This may have had something to do with his suspicion that he could never marry or share his life with another human being and with his decision to dissolve his engagement to a woman he truly loved. Kierkegaard sustained himself through his inheritance and his writings but never held a job and, like Kant, lived his entire life in one city. Though he never attended social gatherings and therefore was not seen publicly, he became well known in Copenhagen through his writings, published under his own name as well as a variety of pseudonyms. Although his work varied poetically, philosophically, and religiously, the thread running throughout was that of the world's suffering as well as his own. Kierkegaard died in 1855 at the young age of 42 and was generally considered to be a broken man throughout his life. But "even in the smallest matters, he preserved a gentleness and even humour, a sense of proportion and a clarity of thought, and above all, a calm and peaceful faith" (Dru, 1959, p. 32).

Philosophical Contributions

Kierkegaard is considered to have laid the foundation for the philosophy of existentialism by expressing his beliefs regarding the nature of human existence. But existentialism has many forms, and the philosophers who have viewed themselves as existentialists may have had more differences than similarities. Kierkegaard begins with the subjective and

> absolute certainty of an individual's existence and the belief that such an existence is private and incommunicable and is characterized by an awareness of (1) being non–self derived, (2) being free to make choices, (3) being with and experiencing time as an eternal present to which past and future refer, and (4) being in a state of anxiety or dread. (Auden, 1971, p. 7).

Such views clearly broke with the commonly accepted metaphysics of according eternal truth to an Absolute. By providing a subjective foundation for aesthetic, ethical, and religious existence, Kierkegaard attempted to offset the idea of predetermination with this example (Stumpf, 1966, p. 462):

> There are two kinds of men in a wagon, one who holds the reins in his hands but is asleep and the other who is fully awake. In the first case, the horse goes along the familiar road without any direction from the sleeping man, whereas in the other case, the man is truly a driver. Surely, in one sense, it can be said that both men exist, but the term *existence* does not properly belong to inert or inactive things. Existence must refer to a quality in the individual, namely, his conscious participation in an act.

This passage presented Kierkegaard's belief that nothing is certain; there is only uncertainty and individuals must look inwardly and subjectively employ imagination, feeling, passion, suffering, and guilt in order to ascertain for themselves what is true. He called this *objective uncertainty,* which was based on his belief that eternal truth is related to the individual. He further believed that truth was not something that could be "taught" directly to human beings because to do so would require bringing knowledge from the outside by someone who knew that which he could not absolutely know; only God can absolutely know! Therefore, human beings had to lead themselves to the truth, or subjectively become, through the exercise of freedom and choice. In order to know, individuals must look inward and be concerned not only with what is true but with how their words relate to their own existence. This involves what Kierkegaard referred to as the *passion of the infinite,* whereas objectivity is focused on thought content and is not infinite. This is the justification he employs to determine that subjectivity constitutes truth. He "also has trouble with speculative philosophy because the end result of speculation would be that of refining knowledge, which in the long run would prevent further speculation" (Bretall, 1946, p. 204).

Hegel sought to refine knowledge through his use of the dialectic, which required an intellectual awareness and a rational process of thought that would culminate in fostering human progress and was therefore positive in nature. Kierkegaard's use of the dialectic was significantly different, for he was more concerned with being than thinking. He further viewed the end result as being that of a constant state of dissatisfaction—something that was inherently tragic. For him, dialectical thinking is not the objective thought process it is for Hegel, because its purpose is not that of objectively validating truth. His is a search through a continuous dialogue with self (not others, as in Socrates' case) aimed at conceptualizing his own existence and the degree to which he could acquire a personal knowledge of truth. When the question of truth is raised subjectively, reflection is directed subjectively to the nature of the individual's *relationship,* as opposed to the objective approach, in which reflection is directed to the *truth.*

Finally, Kierkegaard's use of the dialectic establishes the role of religion in his existentialist philosophy as presented in the following three stages of individual actualization (Stumpf, 1966, pp. 464–466):

1. Aesthetic stage: behaves according to impulses and emotions. Governed by senses but is aware that life ought to be more if he is to become an individual which produces an antithesis (no universal standards; only personal taste).
2. Ethical stage: recognizes rules of conduct and accepts them using reason. Takes a firm stand and, like Socrates, to know good is to do good. Tries to fill moral lows, cannot, falls short and feels guilty. Guilt is the real antithesis, which now presents an either/or. Either remain there and fulfill the moral law or respond to a new awareness.
3. Religious state: movement from (1) to (2) involves choice and reason. First, no objective or conceptual knowledge is available. The only way to cross the span between man and God is not through speculative reason but through faith. Therefore, truth is a subjective matter, a consequence of commitment. With faith, the individual realizes his true self.

As you have seen in Chapter 7, all dialectical thought begins when an antithesis contradicts something that has come before it, which in turn leads to an endless series of nullifications. For Kierkegaard, the aesthetic stage is canceled by the ethical stage, which in turn is canceled by the religious stage, and, if God created everything from nothing, the inevitable result of this process is a state of nothingness—hence, Kierkegaard's belief that all was doomed.

Although Kierkegaard was concerned with how far it is possible to acquire truth, he believed the freedom to seek the Absolute could only result in the dissatisfaction of settling for the finite as opposed to the infinite, for, as implied earlier, we cannot *know* the thoughts of God. Here again, his gloom arose in his concept of irony, which he viewed as infinitely and absolutely negative in that it may guide people but eventually results in disaster, as shown by the following anecdote: "In his youth, Dean Swift founded a lunatic asylum where he himself was placed in old age. It is told that while there he would often look at himself in a mirror and say: Poor old man" (Rohde, 1960, p. 27).

Kierkegaard's "gloomy view of irony was further expressed in his view that irony is an abnormal growth; like the abnormally enlarged liver of the Strassburg goose it ends by killing the individual" (Dru, 1959, p. 58). But there is another side to the picture: "As negative as this may sound, Kierkegaard saw the use of irony as beginning on a positive note with fantastic grandiose ideas not yet disturbed by an ingenuous world" (Hong and Hong, 1970, p. 251). Clearly, Kierkegaard viewed his life as one replete with irony and estrangement, and although he believed the world to be in a state of decline ready to applaud the clown's announcement, he stood opposed to it and tried throughout his life to get his fellow human beings to attend to his thoughts and beliefs.

Life is the only real counselor; wisdom unfiltered through personal experience does not become a part of the moral tissue.

Edith Wharton

Exercise 9.1

Reread the quotation from Edith Wharton and write a brief statement on one aspect of Kierkegaard's philosophy that might be reflected in her words. Then compare your work to the feedback at the end of the chapter.

From *Philosophical Fragments*, Søren Kierkegaard

If the Teacher serves as an occasion by means of which the learner is reminded, he cannot help the learner to recall that he really knows the truth; for the learner is in a state of Error. What the teacher can give him occasion to remember is, that he is in Error. But in this consciousness the learner is excluded from the Truth even more decisively than before, when he lived in ignorance of his Error. In this manner the Teacher thrusts the learner away from him, precisely by serving as a reminder; only that the learner, in thus being thrust back upon himself, does not discover that he knew the Truth already, but discovers his Error; with respect to which act of consciousness the Socratic principle holds, that the Teacher is merely an occasion, whoever he may be, even if he is a God. For my own Error is something I can discover only by myself, since it is only when I have discovered it that it is discovered, even if the whole world knew of it before. (Under the presupposition we have adopted concerning the moment, this remains the only analogy to the Socratic order of things.)

. . . . Now if the learner is to acquire the Truth, the teacher must bring it to him; and not only so, but he must also give him the condition necessary for understanding it. For if the learner were in his own person the condition for understanding the Truth, he need only recall it. The condition of understanding the Truth is like the capacity to inquire for it: the condition contains the conditioned, and the question implies the answer. (Unless this is so, the moment must be understood in the Socratic sense.)

But one who gives the learner not only the Truth, but also the condition for understanding it, is more than teacher. All instruction depends upon the presence, in the last analysis, of the requisite condition; if this is lacking, no teacher can do anything. For otherwise he would find it necessary not only to transform the learner, but to recreate him before beginning to teach him. But this is something that no human being can do; if it is to be done, it must be done by God himself.

Philosophical Fragments. Copyright 1985 by Howard V. Hong, Published by Princeton University Press. Reprinted with permission of Princeton University Press.

Kierkegaard in the Classroom

Although the previous excerpt discusses a teacher-learner relationship, Kierkegaard's writing more often than not addressed a more global relationship as opposed to that of institutional classroom environments. His work questioned how teachers in all walks of life, who cannot be absolutely and objectively certain, can "teach" truth. For this reason, his value to us in the classroom is found in his belief in the subjectivity of knowledge. Generally, the classroom applications you have studied in this book are designed to objectively acquire knowledge and could therefore be referred to as *objective* methods. When applying the philosophy of Kierkegaard to classroom teaching, we have what must be termed a *subjective* method. This label can, initially, produce some discomfort, for the word *subjective* is often taken to mean biased, falsified by prejudice, or even something akin to wishful thinking. However, "especially when we talk about the subjective method, it ought to mean nothing more nor less than a particular approach, of equal validity to the objective methods, to be used where objectivity is insufficient—that is where personal participation is required for the gaining of any knowledge at all" (Roubiczek, 1964, p. 99).

In the classroom, the use of the subjective method is most applicable to the affective domain of the taxonomy of educational objectives. Unlike the cognitive domain, which focuses on the intellectual processing of information in such areas as comprehension, application, analysis, and evaluation, the affective domain involves the expression of opinions and attitudes and the positive interaction of the students in a valuing environment. Whereas the cognitive domain is mostly concerned with convergence culminating in the acquisition of objective knowledge, the affective domain meets the essence of Kierkegaard's concept of subjectivity in that it is criterionless. This further involves his views on choice, for if criteria determines what is chosen, the individual does not make the choice; outside forces do.

Although we are most likely to employ Kierkegaard when implementing lessons involving the affective domain, there is one exception in the cognitive domain, and it is found at the level called *synthesis,* which requires the creating of a new "whole" based on a criterion. If the individual student is allowed to develop the criterion as opposed to the teacher supplying it, one component of Kierkegaard's subjective method is satisfied. As for the other component, although synthesis is an intellectual process, by definition it requires the creation of something new and unique unto the student. For example, if I build a boat, having drawn it and purchased the materials, I surely am applying objective knowledge, but the finished product, the boat itself, is my unique, subjective creation and it does not matter that the whole world has been building boats for 5000 years and more.

The difficulty that presents itself when utilizing the subjective method is that teachers must be very careful to avoid making judgments about student creations, expressions, and so on. In a competency-based classroom, the only legitimate "evaluation" is to determine whether or not the student accomplished the task. In other words, did the student "build the boat" or did the student "express" an attitude on a given subject? You will occasionally find this is not an easy task. All of us have our own value structures, and it can be difficult when you provide an open-ended, divergent experience that allows the students to freely and subjectively process information and they do so in a direction with which you are not in agreement. It is important, therefore, that you seriously plan and structure such activities and that you be *prepared* to take what comes. Now let's take a look at subjectivity in the classroom.

Scenario 9.1

Mrs. Susie Ackis, a second-grade teacher at Mandarin Oaks Elementary School, began her class by asking her students to think about a song that they really liked a lot. She also instructed them not to tell her but to just get it in their minds.

After providing a few moments for undertaking the task, Mrs. Ackis then asked, "How would that music make you feel if you could hear it right now?"

"Excited," Georgianne said.

"That's fine. How about another one, Gene?"

"Happy," Gene replied with a smile.

"Happy, okay," Mrs. Ackis said. "Martha, do you have something?"

"Well, I feel sad sometimes because I don't get to hear it very much."

"Because it isn't played very often. Yes. But how do you feel when you hear it, Martha?"

"Joyful."

"That's a good describing word, Martha, and it is a good feeling also. You all did a fine job telling us about the words. Now think about the music. Why is the song you thought of so important to you? Why do you like it so much . . . Charlie?"

"Because it's cool."

"How is it cool?" Mrs. Ackis asked. "What do you mean by cool?"

"Well, the words are cool because they are talking about being down on a lake and they ski and stuff."

"Okay, so you like the subject of it. What it is about?"

"Yeah," Charlie replied.

"That's fine. How about you, Arabella?"

"I like it because it is fast."

"When you say fast, Arabella, what do you mean?" Mrs. Ackis asked.

"I like it quick but I can still hear it all."

"So you can understand it?"

"Yes."

"Okay. Anything else?"

"I like the tune," William said.

"What is it that you like about your tune?" Mrs. Ackis inquired.

"I like the volume and I like it because it is country and you can understand it, not like rock and roll, which is them talking real fast and they go dotta, dotta, dotta." (Other students giggle.)

"That's his opinion and he is entitled to his opinion," Mrs. Ackis said to a suddenly quiet class.

"I agree with Charlie," Missy said, "because I don't understand how you can even sing fast words in rock and roll."

"Yeah, but some of it isn't always fast," Laura observed.

"And what do you call that?" Mrs. Ackis asked.

With permission. Mandarin Oaks Elementary School, Mandarin, Florida. Mrs. Jo Doty, Principal.

"Soft rock," Laura replied.

"Okay, so you like to learn the words and you like to be able to listen to the tune. What is it that appeals to you so much about a certain tune? For instance, Arabella said she likes a fast beat, while somebody else might like a slow beat. What is it that it makes you feel when you hear that slow beat or when you hear that fast one?"

"It makes you feel nice because you heard your favorite song," Nadeen said.

"That's true," Mrs. Ackis said.

"I like the more medium beat," Carly added.

"You like the more medium beat, Carly. Why is that?"

"Well, it kind of wakes me up a little bit."

"Okay, it kind of makes you feel a little more energetic, it gives you a little more energy. Fine."

"Sometimes you just think you are going to die," Maria said adding a somewhat somber note to the conversation.

"Why is that?" Mrs. Ackis asked.

"Because sometimes the words are just so sad."

"Do you have something to add, Russell?"

"Well, words can put you in a good mood, too."

"Okay. Great job everybody. Now I am going to play some music for you and it is not rock and roll and it's not country either. It's music that is called classical, which means that it is a musical style that began a long time ago. It was written by composers who became famous and whose music many people still love to listen to today. The first piece we are going to listen to this morning was written by Strauss. Has anyone ever heard of him?"

"Oh! I can play something on my piano that was written by him," Maureen said.

"Can you really. That's great!"

"My mom has a CD," Roy said.

"I think I heard some in a movie," Betty added.

"Fine. Now I want you to just sit quietly. In fact, I think it might be a good idea if you close your eyes and really concentrate on how the music sounds and think about how it is making you feel. Okay. I'm going to start it." Mrs. Ackis then played a brief section of Strauss's "Blue Danube." After about four or five minutes, she stopped the recording and asked the students how the music made them feel.

"I think I heard it in *Fantasia*," Bernadine said.

"Okay, Bernadine, but how did the music make you feel when you were listening to it today, not when you were watching the movie?"

"I felt like I was dancing at a ball."

"I felt joyful," Bailey added.

"I felt happy and thought I was leading the music," Pete said.

"So you were conducting the orchestra?" Mrs. Ackis asked.

"Yes, and everybody else was dancing."

"I felt good because I saw myself writing the notes."

"Oh, so you were creating the music, Donna?"

"Yeah, and I got it to rock a little when it got real loud."

"I'm glad you brought that up, Donna, because the music changed. How was it at the beginning?"

"It was low and then it was high."

"When you say low and high, what do you mean, Donna?"

"Some of the notes were kind of deep and then some were kind of screechy."

"Okay, everybody. Now I have another piece of music. This was written by Beethoven, and again, I want you to close your eyes and sit very still and really think about the music as you listen to it and feel the music coming in through your ears and down through your body. Again, think about how it makes you feel and imagine where you might be when the music was being played." Mrs. Ackis then played a selection from Beethoven's "Moonlight Sonata," after which she again asked the students to share their reactions to the music.

In concluding the discussion, Mrs. Ackis introduced her students to a follow-up activity by saying, "What I am going to have you do next is to take the piece of paper I am going to give you, and I am going to play a little more music for you. As I am playing it I would like you to use your crayons and just draw the way the music is making you feel. There is no right or wrong way. Okay. Just draw what the music makes you feel." Mrs. Ackis then began playing a portion of Beethoven's "Rondo in C" and spent the remainder of the time allocated for the lesson moving around the room and observing the students' progress.

Obviously, the entire tone of this lesson is subjective. Ms. Ackis, through the use of personal experience and the playing of classical music, is providing the students with a creative, divergent opportunity to express how music makes them feel, what the music might mean, and how they think about the selections. She also provided them with different avenues of expression, the primary one being that of verbalization and the follow-up exercise being artistic. It should be noted that Mrs. Ackis avoided any value judgments and maintained a classroom environment of respect and one free of any possibility of embarrassment, humiliation, or contradiction. Establishing such an atmosphere is absolutely critical to the successful implementation of subjectivity in the classroom.

Exercise 9.2

Examine the following statements to determine if they are consistent (c) or inconsistent (i) with Kierkegaard's philosophy. Then compare your answers with those found at the end of the chapter.

_____ 1. A priori knowledge is a critical component of the philosophy of existentialism.

_____ 2. Individuals employ subjectivity to arrive at the truth.

_____ 3. The purpose of philosophy is speculative with specific regard to the nature of reality.

_____ 4. The primary role of the classroom teacher is that of disseminating knowledge.

_____ 5. Existentialism in the classroom is most frequently employed in activities that utilize the intellectual processes of the cognitive domain.

Exercise 9.3

Kierkegaard, like Hegel, critically employed the dialectic in his existentialist philosophy. Write a paragraph that briefly discusses two significant differences between Kierkegaard's and Hegel's use of the dialectic. Then compare your response to the one at the end of the chapter.

JEAN-PAUL SARTRE, 1905–1980

Throughout Kierkegaard's professional life, philosophical critics and commentators expressed the view that his foundational work in what he called existentialism would be little noted in the future. This "evaluation" was due in part to the times in which he lived, a time dominated by centralized nations and economies, the need for the common person to serve industry or the state, and a continued focus on the private education of the upper classes. Such conditions did not have the same importance in Sartre's lifetime. His years spanned two world wars, successful challenges to the captains of industry, a movement toward universal public education, the social upheaval of the 1960s, and a march toward the recognition and worth of the individual. Because of these and other societal changes, Kierkegaard transcended his lifetime by having his philosophical contributions absorbed and expanded in the work of Sartre and other 20th-century existentialists. As mentioned earlier, there are significant differences between many of the philosophers we have covered; Kierkegaard and Sartre are no exception. Possibly the biggest difference between them was the former's steadfast commitment to the concept of religion or human faith and the latter's belief that there is no God as well as no determinism or guidelines guaranteed to us in this world. Sartre presented his philosophical theories in a variety of genres, ranging from novels and plays to formal essays. He was important to the existentialist movement because, among other things, he was able to communicate the tenets of this rather "heavy" philosophy to the common person through his open and irresistible writing style.

Life and Times

If Kierkegaard's life was uneventful and reclusive, Sartre's went to the other extreme. He was born in Paris on June 21, 1905, and after the death of his father one year later, he lived and was raised by his mother and grandparents. He was educated at the École Normale Supérieure in Paris, and it was recognized early on that he was extremely adept in the literary arts. However, his rebellious nature manifested itself early when he failed his national exams in philosophy in 1928 due to his extensive "original" responses to the questions. The following year, understanding what needed to be done, he approached the examination in a scholarly and traditional fashion and "set the curve."

After earning his credentials, Sartre taught philosophy in various institutions and then continued his studies between 1933 and 1935 as a research student at the Institute Français in Berlin and the University of Freiburg. By about 1936,

*Man is only the sum of his
actions and purposes.*

Jean-Paul Sartre

Sartre had established himself as a writer by publishing novels, essays, and sto-ries. His work quickly provided him with sufficient fame and fortune to allow him to exclusively devote himself to writing. However, with the outbreak of World War II in 1939, he found himself in the service, and within a year was in-terned as a German prisoner of war. He was released after the armistice and re-turned to teaching philosophy in Paris until 1944. But again his resistance to authority surfaced with his active participation in the French resistance movement. He also continued to write during these years and produced *Being and Nothingness,* often considered his most significant work.

After the war, Sartre co-founded a political and literary review, *Les Temps Modernes,* which basically was a vehicle for his existentialist point of view. His politics were considered leftist but not communist, although there were times, such as the Cold War, when he sided with the Soviet Union. He also produced written works that attempted to establish certain compatibilities between exis-tentialism and Marxism but that, on the other hand, denounced the Soviet in-vasion of Hungary and its treatment of Russian literary giants. Another example of his political flexibility was found in his support both for the existence of Israel and for the need to establish a Palestinian State.

The power and influence of his work was clearly recognized when France ac-corded him the Legion d' Honneur. Another major honor was the Nobel Prize for Literature, which he was awarded in 1964 but which he turned down because he claimed he did not want to become an institution. This declining of honors was characteristic of what was considered at that time an unorthodox lifestyle. Sartre never married but chose instead to engage in a long-running, unencumbered affair with the writer Simone de Beauvoir, in her own right one of the principal figures in the postwar existentialist movement.

Despite the fact that "many believed her to be an existentialist philosopher, de Beauvoir considered herself to be a literary writer who had philosophical differences with Sartre primarily in the areas of voluntarism vs. social conditioning and embodiment, individualism vs. reciprocity, and ontology vs. ethics" (Simons, 1992, p. 27). However, there certainly was agreement on the basic existentialist tenet of existence preceding essence, de Beauvoir's conceptualization of which allowed her to express her belief that one is not born a woman; rather, one becomes, and is forced to become, a woman. One scholar notes that "these and other theories of women's oppression established her as the sole female voice to be heard among the first generation of existentialists and phenomenologists of twentieth century France" (Pilardi, 1989, p. 18). De Beauvoir's

> admitted project in life was to make herself into an independent, intellectual woman and as such she became an icon of the twentieth century feminist movement. Her interpretation of "independent" was material and intellectual; what it very often was not was emotionally independent of Sartre. Frequently separated from him as she was, she nevertheless remained deeply involved in his life. (Evans, 1996, p. 3).

Sartre's relationship with de Beauvoir did not last through his later years, which certainly could not be characterized as "golden." He chose to live in cheap hotels, had few material possessions, and gave away his fortune to a variety of charitable causes and political movements. By the 1970s, Sartre was all but blind and unable to read or write. As a result, he was heavily in debt when he died in Paris on April 15, 1980. His burial was revealing:

> Even in death, his character was exemplified by his request that he be buried quietly without any processions, ostentatious gestures or acts. Nevertheless, it is estimated that in excess of fifty thousand Parisians mourned his passing, attesting to his work, which anticipated, projected, and solicited the social upheavals of the post World War II world. (Wood, 1990, p. xviii)

Philosophical Contributions

From their very beginnings, both Kierkegaard and Sartre exhibited, in varying degrees, the existentialist view of a pessimistic, lonely individual traveling through a hostile world that characterized the human condition. However, Sartre's existentialist theories differed from those of Kierkegaard in terms of both tone and content. With specific regard to the first, Kierkegaard believed human beings were on a one-way road to oblivion and that all he could do philosophically was to sound the alarm, focus the issues, and stand back and witness the inevitable march to the end. Sartre's tone is equally pessimistic, in that he views the world as composed of ignorant and imperfect individuals living in an uncertain universe in which nothing is rational or right. He agrees that we do not live in a good society but, unlike Kierkegaard, he takes the role of an activist and believes that society can be better and that human beings should attempt to remedy serious injustice. In this respect, "Sartre is foremost among existentialists in the importance which he gave to the problem of communication, as expressed in his belief that what men think, and communicating it, is vital not only to the conduct of their personal lives but also to the righting of social evils" (Greene, 1960, p. vi).

With regard to content, the significant difference between the two was that Kierkegaard was a Christian existentialist and Sartre was an atheistic existentialist. You have already become familiar with the role religion and faith played in Kierkegaard's work. From Sartre's perspective, in order for his belief that life cannot be anything until it is lived to be valid, it is necessary to deny the existence of God. For example, in a earlier chapter, I used a reference to a sculptor producing a bust of an ancient philosopher. For Sartre, in that example, essence would have preceded existence of the bust because the sculptor conceptualized it prior to its material or physical production. Following this line of thought, God creates human beings just as the sculptor creates the head of a person; hence, in the case of human beings, essence precedes existence. But if one adheres to an atheistic point of view, as did Sartre, there can be no master plan, no grand design or conceptualization that allows existence to precede essence and further allows human beings to become or make of themselves what they will. Such an absence of predetermination not only allows such development to take place but also requires individuals to make decisions and choices that influence their essence. Moreover, "when doing so, the individual sets a course of action which has the potential of prescribing attitudes and activities for men and help to determine how they live" (Greene, 1960, pp. 8–9).

For many existentialists, including Sartre, the theories of this philosophy centered more on an intellectual mood or atmosphere than on a coherent creed or body of doctrine: more a method or approach than a school of thought. One of the mechanisms of this approach was that of using reflection in examining the knowledge of the physical world, for like Descartes and other idealist philosophers before him, Sartre did not look to empiricism, materialism, and the sciences. It was his existentialist belief that subjective human experience provided the fountain of truth and that such experiences involved reflection, freedom of choice, decision making, and accepting responsibility for the outcomes or results of our choices. This process or approach by nature produces what Sartre refers to as "anguish," for we must make choices throughout our lives and frequently we have no idea whether they are right or wrong: "All leaders know this anguish. That doesn't keep them from acting: on the contrary, it is the very condition of their action. For it implies that they envisage a number of possibilities, and when they choose one, they realize that it has value only because it is chosen" (Sartre, 1947, p. 25).

During the 20 or so years that followed World War II, Sartre and other European existentialists helped bring to the forefront a focus on the individual through their philosophical writings. However, Sartre lived long enough to realize that the paramount concern of the world was that of social change, as opposed to the self-realization of human beings. Some would attribute this to such things as Western materialism, the growth of the applied sciences, and the rise of global economics. Nevertheless, Sartre believed that the hope of a better world was, in the final analysis, still in the hands of the individual, and his work was devoted to providing a structure that would initiate this effort.

You miss 100% of the shots you never take.

Wayne Gretsky

Exercise 9.4

Return to the quotation from Wayne Gretsky and write a statement suggesting how his words might encompass an aspect of Sartre's philosophy. Then check the feedback at the end of the chapter.

From *Existentialism*, Jean-Paul Sartre

What is meant by the term *existentialism?* Most people who use the word would be rather embarrassed if they had to explain it, since, now that the word is all the rage, even the work of a musician or painter is being called existentialist. . . . It seems that for want of an advance-guard doctrine analogous to surrealism, the kind of people who are eager for scandal and flurry turn to this philosophy, which in other respects does not at all serve their purpose in this sphere.

Actually, it is the least scandalous, the most austere of doctrines. It is intended strictly for specialists and philosophers. Yet it can be defined easily. What complicates matters is that there are two kinds of existentialists; first those who are Christian, among whom I would include Jaspers and Gabriel Marcel, both Catholic; and on the other hand the atheistic existentialists, among whom I class Heidegger, and then the French existentialists and myself. What they have in common is that they think that existence precedes essence, or, if you prefer, that subjectivity must be the starting point.

Just what does that mean? Let us consider some object that is manufactured, for example, a book or a paper-cutter: here is an object which has been made by an artisan whose inspiration came from a concept. He referred to the concept of what a paper-cutter is and likewise to a known method of production, which is part of the concept, something which is, by and large, a routine. Thus, the paper-cutter is at once an object produced in a certain way and, on the other hand, one having a specific use; and one cannot postulate a man who produces a paper-cutter but does not know what it is used for. Therefore, let us say that, for the paper-cutter, essence—that is, the ensemble of both the production routines and the properties which enable it to be both produced and defined—precedes existence. Thus, the presence of the paper-cutter or book in front of me is determined. Therefore, we have here a technical view of the world whereby it can be said that production precedes existence.

When we conceive God as the Creator, He is generally thought of as a superior sort of artisan. Whatever doctrine we may be considering, whether one like that of Descartes or Leibnitz, we always grant that will more or less follows understanding, or, at the very least, accompanies it, and that when God creates He knows exactly what He is creating. Thus, the concept of man in the mind of God is comparable to the concept of the paper-cutter in the mind of the manufacturer, and, following certain techniques and a conception, God produces man, just as the artisan, following a definition and a technique, makes a paper-cutter. Thus, the individual man is the realization of a certain concept in the divine intelligence.

Atheistic existentialism, which I represent, states that if God does not exist, there is at least one being in whom existence precedes essence, a being who exists before he can be defined by any concept, and that this being is man or, as Heidegger says, human reality. What is meant here by saying that existence precedes essence? It means that, first of all, man exists, turns up, appears on the scene, and, only afterwards, defines himself. If man, as the existentialist conceives him, is indefinable, it is because at first he is nothing. Only afterward will he be something, and he himself will have made what he will be. Thus, there is no human nature since their is no God to conceive it. Not only is man what he conceives himself to be, but he is also only what he wills himself to be after this thrust toward existence. Man is nothing else but what he makes of himself.

Man is nothing else but what he makes of himself. Such is the first principle of existentialism, whose first move is to make every man aware of what he is and to make the full responsibility of his existence rest on him. And when we say that man is responsible for himself, we do not only mean that he is responsible for his own individuality, but that he is responsible for all men.

Sartre in the Classroom

Two recurrent themes found in the educational reform literature are those of promoting student critical thinking skills and advancing the concept of student empowerment. The overwhelming focus of philosophical classroom applications has been that of presenting methodologies that attempt to secure knowledge through the use of reason and problem solving. Thus, it only seems fitting that we conclude our bridge-building with Sartre's existentialist belief in free choice, which (when implemented in classrooms) supports positive teacher-pupil partnerships and enhances student empowerment.

As you read earlier, Sartre's concept of freedom is twofold, in that the freedom to choose can either advance freedom or negate it. In terms of classroom applications, this suggests that providing experiences that empower students by allowing them to engage in free choice is something that should be well planned and not entirely devoid of constraints or limitations. As the saying "success breeds success" implies, it is important that, if at all possible, students' choices result in positive achievements or outcomes, which in turn reinforce the usefulness of such experiences in the minds of the teachers as well as of the students.

Providing students with the freedom to engage in choice always carries with it the potential to backfire, and, due to the potentially controversial nature of existentialism in the classroom, teachers need to avoid negative experiences at all costs. Therefore, it is suggested that activities that include aspects of student freedom of choice be introduced into the learning environment at the onset of the academic term in a limited and structured way. Hopefully, as students become comfortable with the responsibilities that accompany the concept of free choice, the number of such activities can be increased and the number of constraints can be reduced. With that in mind, let's take a look at how one teacher utilizes the concept of freedom of choice in the classroom.

Scenario 9.2

Ms. Vicki DeAnda, a sixth-grade teacher at Blanton Elementary School, began her class by informing the students that they were going to finalize their organization and plan for their fifth social studies project of the year. As an overview, she briefly presented highlights of the first four projects, which included an Egyptian museum in the school's hallways, a Grecian play, a Roman festival, and a Chinese New Year celebration. In addition, Ms. DeAnda reminded her students of the parameters within which they must operate, which included the selection of any chapter or chapters in their social studies text and the presentation of the minimal knowledge base offered by the book. She then asked the students to move into the groups in which they had been brainstorming the task at hand and to review the information they intended to share.

With permission. Blanton Elementary School, Arlington, Texas. Mr. John Demore, Principal.

"Okay," Ms. DeAnda began. "How about the focus group? What do you have for us . . . Jan?"

"We want to recommend to the class that we tie in the three chapters on Africa with our interest in Black History Month," said Jan, who had been chosen by the group to be the spokesperson.

"What do you think, group? It's your decision?" Ms. DeAnda replied.

"I like it," responded Mo, who was sitting comfortably on the floor with her group."

"Me too," added Ralph, who was sitting on a table with his group in a back corner of the classroom.

"Okay. Anyone else have something to say? (Pause.) Any disagreements? (No response.)"

"Fine," Ms. DeAnda said. "We are agreed. As with our other projects, we now need to develop a primary objective. How about it, group?"

"It seems to me that we want to learn about the past and present African civilizations," Anita said.

"Yeah, and just like our other projects, we want to teach what we learn to the other kids in the schools," Laura added.

"I think they've got it," Saul concluded. (Class verbally agrees with Saul.)

"Great," Ms. DeAnda said, "so we are going to learn and teach about the past and present African civilizations. But we need to be more specific with our objective, so let's brainstorm some topics we might include in our studies."

"Colonization," Doreen said.

"How about wildlife!" Marita chimed in.

"Can we do a specific country, like Kenya?" Rhonda inquired.

"Sure, if that is what you all want to do," Ms. DeAnda responded.

"I've always wanted to learn more about the rain forests," Annalisa said.

"Right . . . and I've always been interested in deserts," Bill added.

"The savannahs are pretty unique," Abby said, "and I think we should study them too."

"All really solid selections," Ms. DeAnda said. "You'll have a chance to focus on them and expand the list if you like when we get back into groups, but for the moment, let's turn our attention to maybe some major threads that we could run throughout the past and present. Ideas please?"

"We could use religion," Mimi said.

"I think industry or the economy or stuff like that could work," Aretha added.

"Good ones," Ms. DeAnda said. "We can further explore this list too in our groups. (Pause.) How about a time line?"

"Four weeks," Brady said.

"I'm for five," Brent said.

"How about like our last project," Zora interjected. "Let's stay loose and say five to six weeks." (Appears to be verbal consensus on this last comment.)

"Okay, unless there is a problem, we will go with the five to six weeks," Ms. DeAnda said. "Now," she continued, "how are we going to achieve our objective? How are we going to both learn and teach this unit?"

"Written reports," Mark said.

"I'd like to illustrate things like we have done before," Bob added.

"Gee, with all the wildlife, let's do some sculpting and some modeling," Mickey said enthusiastically.

"Can we do another video documentary?" Doreen inquired.

"Wow," Ms. DeAnda said with a laugh. "You're really turning up the burner now. Tell you what. Let's break up into our groups and make a master list of our activities. For the moment, why don't you prioritize your top three or four. Then we will come back as a large group and finalize our activities, which of course will also provide us with our assessments. Problems? (None.) Okay everybody . . . let's get to it," Ms. DeAnda said as she moved toward the group to begin facilitating the work at hand.

In this unit of instruction, Ms. DeAnda has brought Sartre into her classroom by empowering her students and giving them the freedom to choose and design the scope and content of the educational experience. It should be noted, however, that if this experience were to be totally existentialist, the students would have exercised their freedom by "choosing" to come to school, selecting an academic discipline to study, determining who would be their teachers, if any, and so on. It therefore becomes obvious that existentialism in schools is limited due to the mission and other practical considerations that face a system committed to universal education. One could argue that Ms. DeAnda compromised the existentialist flavor of the unit by imposing on the students the requirements of selecting a chapter from the assigned textbook and ensuring a minimum coverage of the material selected, and one would be accurate in doing so. However, the important point to be made is that Ms. DeAnda was developing a partnership with her students by including them in the decision-making process and allowing them the freedom to choose for themselves the content, form, and assessment of the learning experience.

Exercise 9.5

Examine the following statements to determine if they are consistent (c) or inconsistent (i) with Sartre's philosophy. Then check your responses against those at the end of the chapter.

_____ 1. Existentialism begins with a rejection of the belief in the Absolute or God.

_____ 2. Individuals can right societal wrongs or evils.

_____ 3. Existentialism does not adhere to any aspect of predeterminism.

_____ 4. Truth is established through subjective human experience.

_____ 5. Freedom of choice results in positive outcomes.

Exercise 9.6

Write a short paragraph explaining what Sartre meant when he said that "existence precedes essence." Then check your response against the feedback at the end of the chapter.

SUMMARY

It is said that Kierkegaard was the first existentialist and that Sartre was the greatest latter-day existentialist. For both philosophers, the primary goal of existentialism was that of supplying the individual with a guide to life by making philosophy the servant of the full scope of individual demands on life. Philosophy for the true existentialist is not a discipline among other disciplines, but a vocation (Greene, 1960). Although existentialists do agree on basic tenets, they also have significant and fundamental differences. Had he been alive, Kierkegaard would have taken issue with Sartre's position that we can only understand human nature in purely finite terms; Kierkegaard believed that human beings represented a synthesis of the finite and the infinite. The deeper view was purely religious: Kierkegaard was a Christian existentialist, whereas Sartre was an atheistic existentialist.

Both philosophers viewed freedom of choice as a fundamental characteristic of human beings. Kierkegaard expressed this position by writing the following (Stumpf, 1966, p. 462): "Do not wish to be a philosopher in contrast to being a man . . . do not think as a thinker . . . think as a living real being . . . think in existence . . . meaning, recognize that one is faced with personal choices."

Sartre also championed the concept of freedom of choice, but unlike Kierkegaard, he believed that individual choice could in fact impact on an undesirable world. He was therefore an activist, as shown by his wide-ranging political views. Kierkegaard, on the other hand, believed all he could do was call attention to the inevitable doom that lies ahead. Though

> Sartre did not approach Kierkegaard's level of "gloom," he did suppose that his view of utter freedom was a difficult one to live with, and that men always do have a propensity to try to cast the burden off, to live as though they were settled objects, to look for excuses for their conduct in a world they had in fact made and were responsible for. (Danto, 1975, p. 80)

To conclude

> the core of Sartre's existentialism was found in his views on the subjective nature of knowledge defining subjectivity as an immediate, untheorized self awareness; the spontaneous reflexivity of consciousness when it is directed toward something other than itself. Sartre, like Descartes and Kant before him, attempted to grapple with the problems or dualisms inherent in any theory of subjectivity: freedom/determinism, praxis/structure, and self/other. These dualisms, along with Sartre's existentialist views, are expressed in a variety of literary forms, and the sheer range and volume of his work is astonishing as was the degree to which he was vilified. However, he also aroused intense enthusiasm and loyalty, and no other writer or philosopher has ever dominated French thought as completely and massively as he did between the end of World War II and the early 60's. (Wood, 1990, p. 2)

Questions for Discussion

1. How does existentialism differ from pragmatism with regard to the specific concept of "free choice"?
2. How does Kierkegaard's theory of existentialism differ from Sartre's?
3. Metaphysically speaking, how does Kierkegaard conceptualize the nature of reality?
4. What does Kierkegaard mean when he says that, "existence is self-derived"?
5. In the passage from Kierkegaard's *Philosophical Fragments,* what is the "requisite condition"?
6. How does Sartre define *essence* and how does it evolve or come to be?
7. What is the role of *uncertainty* in Sartre's existentialist philosophy?
8. Why did Sartre consider his view of existentialism to be action oriented?
9. What role does communication play in Sartre's existentialist philosophy?
10. Why does Sartre reject the labeling of artistic and musical works of art as existentialist?
11. What does Sartre mean in the passage from *Existentialism* where he says, "Man is nothing else but what he makes of himself"?

Suggested Field Laboratory Experiences

1. Review prepared lesson plans and curriculum guides and determine whether any of them provide students with subjective learning experiences. If so, determine how the lessons are being planned to facilitate their successful implementation in terms of desired outcomes and the maintenance of a positive, healthy, and respectful learning environment.
2. Using a copy of Bloom and Krathwahl's *Taxonomy of Educational Objectives,* review selected lessons and curriculum guides in an area in which you hope to teach and identify any levels of the affective domain that are being utilized in those plans or guides.
3. Identify a cognitive unit of instruction in a teacher's curriculum guide and determine one way you might incorporate a "subjective" lesson.
4. Organize and present a lesson that allows the students to engage in a subjectively oriented activity. Pay careful attention to how you intend to measure and assess student involvement or achievement.
5. Review lessons in a number of curriculum guides or teacher-prepared units and try to identify experiences that have any components that allow for student choice. If you locate such experiences, determine the flexibility of the experience—what are the constraints within which the students must operate?
6. Given the opportunity, observe a number of teacher presentations in terms of whether they are action oriented, thereby providing students with an opportunity to physically change something.
7. Given the opportunity, have a teacher assist you in planning and implementing an appropriate topic that will provide an opportunity for students

to exercise free choice within an established set of classroom and content constraints. Be sure you have carefully considered the measurement and evaluation components of your plan.

Exercise Feedback

Exercise 9.1

Edith Wharton's reference to personal experience embodies Kierkegaard's belief in the subjective nature of truth. Personal experiences *are* subjective and serve as the flesh and bone of a human being's essence. Kierkegaard would also be comfortable with Wharton's reference to "moral tissue," in that he viewed himself to be a religious man and believed that morality and religion were intertwined.

Exercise 9.2

1. (i)   Inconsistent. A priori knowledge can be viewed as a form of predetermination, which is rejected in existentialist philosophy.
2. (c)   Consistent.
3. (i)   Inconsistent. Kierkegaard rejected speculative philosophy, believing its purpose was that of moving human beings in the direction of absolute knowledge.
4. (i)   Inconsistent. This would suggest an absolute or certain truth regarding knowledge, and Kierkegaard rejected the concept of "certainty."
5. (i)   Inconsistent. The most common existentialist activities in classrooms involve the affective domain, which focuses on opinions, attitudes, and values.

Exercise 9.3

The two most significant differences between Hegel's dialectic and Kierkegaard's dialectic involve the driving mechanisms and the end result. Regarding mechanisms, Hegel employed intellect and what he believed to be logic to "move [human beings] down the road," whereas Kierkegaard focused on the tool of subjectivity. In terms of the end result, "down the road" for Hegel meant positive progress toward the acquisition of absolute knowledge, whereas this passage for Kierkegaard was negative and would result in the end of humankind.

Exercise 9.4

The quotation from Wayne Gretsky could existentially suggest that human beings not only have the freedom to exercise choice but the requirement to do so. Sartre might say, along with Gretsky, you have to do more than be on the ice, grinding, checking, and passing. You cannot score unless you shoot. In a sense, this suggests Sartre's belief in activism: if you don't make choices, you cannot advance yourself or the society in which you live.

Exercise 9.5

1. (c)   Consistent. The existence of God presumes a master plan, which implies people have an essence prior to their physical birth.

2. (c)   Consistent.

3. (c)   Consistent. Predetermination would not allow essence to precede existence.

4. (c)   Consistent.

5. (i)   Inconsistent. Not necessarily. Freedom of choice can result in anguish and sorrow, for there is no guarantee that a choice is a right one or a good one.

Exercise 9.6

Most philosophers believe that people begin life with some aspect of predeterminism. This being the case, some or all of their essence (their character, thoughts, values, knowledge, or even destiny) are in place prior to their physical existence. By adopting an atheistic position, Sartre negated the concept of predeterminism, which allowed human beings to come into existence and begin their life and spend all their days subjectively experiencing the world and constantly developing their essence.

GLOSSARY OF PHILOSOPHICAL TERMS

Absolute   The perfect. The all-inclusive. Often referred to as God.

Abstraction   The process through which we formulate ideas; it generally focuses on common characteristics.

Aesthetics   The component of philosophy that addresses the contemplation of what is beautiful, ugly, and so on. Commonly centered around the arts.

Altruism   The belief that one should act in terms of the benefit for all.

Analogy   An expression based on similarities.

Analysis   The process of determining the essence of an object or thought by examining its parts.

Apology   A defense by the use of intellectual argument.

A posteriori   That which can only be discovered and verified by experience. A factual statement; an empirical statement.

A priori   That which appears to be so clear and rational that no sense experience is needed to establish it. Truth independent of experience. That which precedes experience.

Attribute   A necessary characteristic or property; something fundamental to the essence of an object.

Axiology   The branch of philosophy that involves the study of value. Subcomponents include ethics and aesthetics.

Axiom   A statement assumed to be true as the basis of a proof.

Behaviorism   A method in psychology that limits empirical investigation of the mind to the study of human behavior.

Cartesianism   The philosophy of René Descartes.

Categorical imperative   As put forth by Immanuel Kant, the unconditional moral law for all rational beings.

Category   A fundamental class; a basic conception; one of the primary ideas to which all other ideas can be reduced.

Class   A group or category of things that share common characteristics or properties.

Cosmology   The component of metaphysics that inquires into the structure of the universe.

Deduction   Reasoning that involves the logical movement from laws and rules to specifics and examples.

Determinism   The philosophical position that all events have a cause and an effect and that the event is a function of the cause.

Dialectic   A rational method of constructing ideas by resolving apparent contradictions.

Dilemma   An argument with two alternatives or choices, neither of which will produce a totally satisfactory result.

Direct knowledge   Awareness of consciousness such as feelings, thoughts, and emotions.

Dualism   Any metaphysical theory that reduces the kinds of existing things to two basic substances.

Egoism   The theory that one ought to act so as to secure the greatest possible good for oneself.

Empirical statement   A statement that can be verified through experience.

Empiricism   The theory that the source of knowledge is that of experience and no knowledge is innate or a priori.

Epistemology   The branch of philosophy that tries to clarify ideas about knowledge and the methods for securing knowledge.

Essence   The distinctive nature of something.

Eternity   A condition that goes beyond time or includes all time.

Ethics   The part of axiology that deals with morality or questions of value.

Existentialism   A philosophy founded on the belief that existence precedes essence and that character is determined by how one lives or exists.

Fallacy   A mistake or error in reasoning.

First principle   A truth that serves as a foundation for other ideas.

Free will   The will or power to decide.

Humanism   A view that considers human beings rather than the supernatural as the central focus.

Idea   Either a universal thing in terms of an idea or an object known directly through experience.

Idealism   A philosophy that believes reality is composed of ideas in the mind.

Induction   Inferring the general from the specific.

Intuition   Knowing or being aware without the use of deductive or inductive reasoning.

Logic   That which involves rational arguments.

Logos   Divine reason; the words of God.

Materialism   The philosophical view that matter alone is real.

Metaphysics   Greek for "after the physics." Speculative inquiries regarding the nature of human beings and the nature of the universe.

Mysticism   A belief that the knowledge of reality involves the immediate awareness of God's nature and presence.

Naturalism   The theory that reality is understandable without reference to the supernatural.

Nominalism   The position that terms do not designate universal properties.

Ontology   The study of the nature of existence and the attempt to discover the fundamental categories of all being.

Percept   A specific element in a given perceptual experience.

Perennialism   An educational ideology founded primarily on the philosophy of realism, which mainly sees the role of schools as that of transmitting the existing culture or body of traditional knowledge.

Phenomenon   An appearance of a thing as opposed to the thing itself.

Philosophy   Greek for "love of wisdom." An intellectual pursuit attempting to resolve issues regarding matters of reality and experience. Includes the major fields of metaphysics, epistemology, and axiology.

Pluralism   A theory that there are many ultimate substances in the world.

Postmodernism   A philosophical movement that rejects theories of universals and asserts that reality or truth is found in specific cultures and the locales of the present.

Pragmatism   A philosophy that holds that the sense effects of an object are the whole of the object and that an idea is true if it works satisfactorily.

Predestination   The belief that all events are determined by the action of God's will.

Premise   A proposition, often considered true, on which the conclusion of an argument is based.

Progressivism   The educational ideology founded primarily on the philosophy of pragmatism, which mostly sees the role of the school as that of evaluating the existing culture and promoting critical thinking skills.

Rationalism   The source of knowledge that states that what we know is achieved through the use of reason without reference to experience.

Realism   The philosophical school that maintains that physical objects reflect reality and are independent of thought or perception.

Reconstructionism   An educational ideology founded on the philosophies of pragmatism and existentialism. It primarily views the role of schools as that of transforming the existing culture through the immediate application of critical thinking skills.

Secondary qualities   Characteristics of physical objects that do not belong to the objects themselves except as powers to cause sensations.

Skepticism   The position that knowledge is probable as opposed to certain.

Substance   That which has properties; the enduring system of properties considered as a system in abstraction from the properties.

Tabula rasa theory   Locke's belief that the mind is a blank tablet at birth without innate ideas.

Teleology   Any theory of ends or purposes. Or the study of events as signs of purpose.

Theology   The philosophical study of God using the sources of revelation or empiricism.

Validity   The property of an argument in which the premises imply the conclusion.

PHILOSOPHERS' TIME LINE

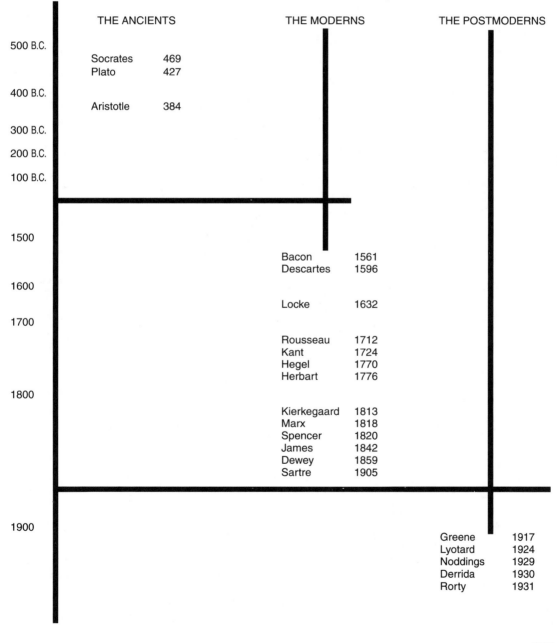

	THE ANCIENTS		THE MODERNS		THE POSTMODERNS	
500 B.C.	Socrates	469				
	Plato	427				
400 B.C.	Aristotle	384				
300 B.C.						
200 B.C.						
100 B.C.						
1500			Bacon	1561		
			Descartes	1596		
1600			Locke	1632		
1700			Rousseau	1712		
			Kant	1724		
			Hegel	1770		
			Herbart	1776		
1800			Kierkegaard	1813		
			Marx	1818		
			Spencer	1820		
			James	1842		
			Dewey	1859		
			Sartre	1905		
1900					Greene	1917
					Lyotard	1924
					Noddings	1929
					Derrida	1930
					Rorty	1931

265

REFERENCES

Aaron, R. (1971). *Knowing and the Function of Reason.* Oxford, England: Oxford University Press.

Acton, H. (1967). "G. W. F. Hegel." In *The Encyclopedia of Philosophy,* vol. 3. (P. Edwards, ed.). New York: Macmillan.

Adams, J. (1899). *Herbartian Psychology Applied to Education.* Boston: Heath.

Adler, M. (1978). *Aristotle for Everybody.* New York: Macmillan.

Adler, M. (1985). *Ten Philosophical Mistakes.* New York: Macmillan.

Adler, M. (1988). *Reforming Education.* New York: Macmillan.

Adler, M. (1993). *The Four Dimensions of Philosophy: Metaphysical, Moral, Objective, Categorical.* New York: Macmillan.

Adorno, T. (1993). *Hegel: Three Studies.* Cambridge, Mass.: MIT Press.

Allen, J. (1989). "An Introduction to Patriarchal Existentialism." In *The Thinking Muse: Feminism and Modern French Philosophy* (J. Allen and I. Young, eds.). Bloomington: Indiana University Press.

Allen, J., and Young, I. (eds.). (1989). *The Thinking Muse: Feminism and Modern French Philosophy.* Bloomington: Indiana University Press.

Anderson, F. (ed.). (1960). *The New Organon and Related Writings.* New York: Liberal Arts Press.

Appelbaum, R. (1988). *Karl Marx.* Newbury Park, Calif.: Sage.

Armstrong, D., Henson, K., and Savage, T. (1993). *Education: An Introduction,* 4th ed. New York: Macmillan.

Aronson, R. (1980). *Jean-Paul Sartre: Philosophy in the World.* London: NLB.

Auden, W. (1971). *The Living Thoughts of Kierkegaard.* Bloomington: Indiana University Press.

Ayers, M. (1991). *Locke,* vol. 1: *Epistemology.* London: Routledge.

Barnes, J. (1991) *Founder of Thought: Aristotle.* New York: Oxford University Press.

Barrow, R. (1976). *Plato and Education.* London: Routledge and Kegan Paul.

Benjamin, A. (1993). *The Plural Event: Descartes, Hegel, Heidegger.* London: Routledge.

Bernstein, J. (1980). *Shaftsbury, Rousseau, and Kant.* Cranbury, N.J.: Associated University Presses.

Bird, G. (1986). *William James.* London: Routledge and Kegan Paul.

Bloom, A. (1979). *Emile or on Education.* New York: Basic Books.

Bloom, B., Englehart, M., Furst, E., Hill, W., and Krathwohl, D. (1956). *Taxonomy of Educational Objectives, Handbook I: Cognitive Domain.* New York: David McKay.

Bluck, R. (ed.) (1964). *Plato's Meno*. London: Cambridge University Press.

Bontempo, C. and Odell, S. (eds.). (1975). *The Owl of Minerva: Philosophers on Philosophy*. New York: McGraw-Hill.

Bottomore, T. (ed. and trans.). (1963). *Karl Marx: Early Writings*. New York: McGraw-Hill.

Boyd, W. (ed. and trans.). (1956). *The Emile of Jean-Jacques Rousseau: Selections*. New York: Teachers College Press.

Boydston, J. (ed.). (1984). *John Dewey: The Later Works, 1925–1953*. Carbondale: Southern Illinois University Press.

Brameld, T. (1950). *Education for the Emerging Age*. New York: Harper & Row.

Brameld, T. (1955). *Philosophies of Education in Cultural Perspective*. New York: Holt, Rinehart and Winston.

Brazill, W. (1970). *The Young Hegelians*. New Haven, Conn.: Yale University Press.

Bretall, R. (ed.). (1946). *A Kierkegaard Anthology*. New York: Modern Press.

Briggs, J. (1989). *Francis Bacon and the Rhetoric of Nature*. Cambridge, Mass.: Harvard University Press.

Bronstein, D., Krikorian, Y., & Wiener, P. (eds.). (1955). *Basic Problems of Philosophy*. Englewood Cliffs, N.J.: Prentice Hall.

Brumbaugh, R. (1989). *Platonic Studies of Greek Philosophy: Forms, Arts, Gadgets, and Hemlock*. Albany: State University of New York Press.

Bryant, W. (1896). *Hegel's Educational Ideas*. New York: Werner School Book Company.

Butler, C. (1977). *G.W.F. Hegel*. Boston: Twayne.

Butler, J. (1968). *Four Philosophies and Their Practice in Education and Religion*. New York: Harper & Row.

Caponigri, A. (1971). *A History of Western Philosophy*. Notre Dame, Ind.: University of Notre Dame Press.

Cassirer, E. (1963). *Rousseau, Kant, Goethe* (J. Gutmann, trans.). New York: Harper & Row.

Charlesworth, M. (1975). *The Existentialists and Jean-Paul Sartre*. New York: St. Martin's Press.

Clark, G. (1957). *Thales to Dewey: A History of Philosophy*. Boston: Houghton Mifflin.

Clegg, H. (1977). *The Structure of Plato's Philosophy*. Cranbury, N.J.: Associated University Presses.

Colletti, L. (1973). *Marxism and Hegel*. London: Atlantic Highlands Humanities Press.

Cotkin, G. (1990). *William James: Public Philosopher*. Baltimore, Md.: Johns Hopkins University Press.

Cottingham, J. (1988). *The Rationalists*. Oxford, England: Oxford University Press.

Counts, G. (1952). *Education and American Civilization*. Westport, Conn.: Greenwood Press.

Counts, G. (1962). *Education and the Foundations of Human Freedom*. Pittsburgh: University of Pittsburgh Press.

Cranston, M. (1991). *The Noble Savage: Jean-Jacques Rousseau.* Chicago: University of Chicago Press.

Cullen, B. (ed.). (1988). *Hegel Today.* Aldershot, England: Avebury.

Danto, A. (1975). *Jean-Paul Sartre.* New York: Viking Press.

Davidson, R. (1952). *Philosophies Men Live by.* New York: Dryden Press.

Davidson, T. (1971). *Rousseau.* New York: AMS Press.

Dennis, L. and Eaton, W. (eds.). (1980). *George S. Counts: Educator for a New Age.* Carbondale: Southern Illinois University Press.

Descartes, R. (1960). *Meditations and First Philosophy* (L. Lafleur, trans.). Indianapolis, Ind.: Bobbs-Merrill. (Original work published 1641)

Descartes, R. (1986). *Meditations on Philosophy* (J. Cottingham, trans.). Cambridge, England: Cambridge University Press.

Descartes, R. (1988). *Descartes: Selected Philosophical Writings* (J. Cottingham, R. Stoothoff, and D. Murdoch, trans.). Cambridge, England: Cambridge University Press. (Original work published 1684)

Descartes, R. (1990). *Meditations on First Philosophy* (G. Heffernan, trans.). South Bend, Ind.: University of Notre Dame Press.

Desmond, W. (ed.). (1989). *Hegel and His Critics: Philosophy in the Aftermath of Hegel.* Albany: State University of New York Press.

Dewey, J. (1910). *How We Think.* Boston: Heath.

Dewey. J. (1921). *Reconstruction of Philosophy.* London: University of London Press.

Dewey, J. (1929). *The Quest for Certainty: A Study of the Relation of Knowledge and Action.* New York: Minton, Balch and Company.

Dewey, J. (1938). *Experience and Education.* New York: Macmillan.

Dewey, J. (1960). *Theory of the Moral Life.* New York: Holt, Rinehart and Winston.

Dewey, J. (1966). *Democracy and Education.* New York: Free Press.

Dooley, P. (1974). *Pragmatism as Humanism: The Philosophy of William James.* Chicago: Nelson-Hall.

Dru, A. (trans.). (1959). *The Journals of Kierkegaard.* New York: Harper & Brothers.

Dunkel, H. (1969). *Herbart and Education.* New York: Randon House.

Dunkel, H. (1970). *Herbart and Herbartianism: An Educational Ghost Story.* Chicago: University of Chicago Press.

Durant, W. (1953). *The Story of Philosophy.* New York: Simon and Schuster.

Edwards, P. (ed.). (1967). *The Encyclopedia of Philosophy.* New York: Macmillan.

Evans, M. (1996). *Women of Ideas: Simone de Beauvoir.* London: Sage.

Farrell, F. (1994). *Subjectivity, Realism, and Postmodernism: The Recovery of the World.* Cambridge, England: Cambridge University Press.

Faulkner, R. (1993). *Francis Bacon and the Project of Progress.* Lanham, Md.: Rowman & Littlefield.

Feibleman, J. (1973). *Understanding Philosophy: A Popular History of Ideas.* New York: Horizon Press.

Fine, G. (1993). *On Ideas.* New York: Oxford University Press.

Flay, J. In L. Stepelevich, (ed.). (1993). *Selected Essays on G. W. F. Hegel.* Atlantic Highlands, N.J.: Humanities Press.

Ford, M. (1982). *William James's Philosophy: A New Perspective.* Amherst: University of Massachusetts Press.

France, P. (1987). *Rousseau: Confessions.* Cambridge, England: Cambridge University Press.

Frankena, W. (1965). *Three Historical Philosophies of Education.* Glenview, Ill.: Scott, Foresman.

Fraser, N. (1997). *Justice Interruptus.* New York: Routledge.

Fraser, N., and Bartky, S. (eds.). (1992). *Revaluing French Feminism: Critical Essays on Difference, Agency, and Culture.* Bloomington: Indiana University Press.

Freire, P. (1995). *Pedagogy of the Oppressed.* (M. Ramos, trans.). New York: Continuum.

Gaukroger, S. (1989). *Cartesian Logic.* Oxford, England: Clarendon Press.

Gay, P. (1966). *Age of Enlightenment.* New York: Silver Burdett.

Gemkow, H. (1975). *Karl Marx: A Biography.* New Delhi, India: People's Publishing House.

Goldman, A. (1986). *Epistemology and Cognition.* Cambridge, Mass.: Harvard University Press.

Goldman, A. (1988). *Empirical Knowledge.* Berkeley: University of California Press.

Greene, M. (1973). *Sartre.* New York: Franklin Watts.

Greene, M. (1988). *The Dialectic of Freedom.* New York: Teachers College Press.

Greene, N. (1960). *Jean-Paul Sartre: The Existentialist Ethic.* Ann Arbor: University of Michigan Press.

Griese, A. (1981). *Your Philosophy of Education? What Is It?* Santa Monica, Calif: Goodyear.

Grimsley, R. (1973a). *Kierkegaard: A Biographical Introduction.* New York: Charles Scribner's Sons.

Grimsley, R. (1973b). *The Philosophy of Rousseau.* London: Oxford University Press.

Grosholz, E. (1991). *Cartesian Method and the Problem of Reduction.* Oxford, England: Clarendon Press.

Gulley, N. (1968). *The Philosophy of Socrates.* London: Macmillan.

Gutek, G. (1988). *Philosophical and Ideological Perspectives on Education.* Boston: Allyn and Bacon.

Gutek, G. (1997). *Historical and Philosophical Foundations of Education.* Upper Saddle River, N. J.: Prentice Hall.

Guyer, P. (Ed.). (1992). *The Cambridge Companion to Kant.* New York: Cambridge University Press.

Hahn, R. (1988). *Kant's Newtonian Revolution in Philosophy.* Carbondale: Southern Illinois University Press.

Hamilton, E., and and Cairns, H. (eds.). (1961). *The Collected Dialogues of Plato Including the Letters.* Princeton, N.J.: Princeton University Press.

Hampshire, H. (1966). *Philosophy of Mind.* New York: Harper & Row.

Hartshorne, C. (1983). *Insights and Oversights of Great Thinkers: An Evaluation of Western Philosophy.* Albany: State University of New York Press.

Heffernan, L. (ed. and trans.). (1990). *Meditations on First Philosophy.* South Bend, Ind.: University of Notre Dame Press.

Heiss, R. (1975). *Hegel, Kierkegaard, Marx: Three Great Philosophers Whose Ideas Changed the Course of Civilization*. New York: Delacorte Press.

Hendley, B. (1986). *Dewey, Russel, Whitehead: Philosophers as Educators*. Carbondale: Southern Illinois University Press.

Herbart, J. (1904). *Outlines of Educational Doctrine*. (A. Lange, trans.). New York: Macmillan.

Hickman, L. (1990). *John Dewey's Pragmatic Technology*. Bloomington: Indiana University Press.

Hong, H., and Hong, E. (eds.). (1970). *Søren Kierkegaard's Journals and Papers*, vol 2. Bloomington: Indiana University Press.

Hong, H., and Hong, E. (eds. and trans.). (1985). *Philosophical Fragments: Johannes Climacus*. Princeton, N.J.: Princeton University Press.

Howells, C. (ed.). (1992). *The Cambridge Companion to Sartre*. New York: Cambridge University Press.

Hudelson, R. (1990). *Marxism and Philosophy in the Twentieth Century: A Defense of Vulgar Marxism*. New York: Praeger.

Hunkins, F. (1989). *Teaching Thinking Through Effective Questioning*. Boston: Christopher-Gordon.

Hutchings, R. M. (ed.). (1952). *Great Books of the Western World: Kant*. Chicago: Encyclopaedia Britannica.

Hutchins, R. M. (ed.). (1952a). *Great Books of the Western World: Aristotle*. Chicago: Encyclopaedia Britannica.

Hutchins, R. M. (ed.). (1952b). *Great Books of the Western World: Hegel*. Chicago: Encyclopaedia Britannica.

Hyppolite, J. (1969). *Studies on Marx and Hegel*. New York: Basic Books.

Illich, I. (1970). *Deschooling Society*. New York: Harper & Row.

Jacobsen, D., Eggen, P., and Kauchak, D. (1993). *Methods for Teaching: A Skills Approach*, 4th ed. New York: Macmillan.

James, W. (1907). *Pragmatism: A New Name for Some Old Ways of Thinking*. New York: Longmans, Green.

James, W. (1978). *The Meaning of Truth*. Cambridge, Mass.: Harvard University Press.

James, W. (1987). *Writings: 1902–1910*. New York: Library of America.

James, W. (1992). *Writings: 1878–1899*. New York: Library of America.

Jolley, N. (1990). *The Light of the Soul: Theories and Ideas of Leibniz, Malebranche, and Descartes*. Oxford: Clarendon Press.

Jowett, B. (trans.). (1973). *The Republic and Other Works by Plato*. New York: Doubleday.

Jowett, B., and Loomis, L. (eds. and trans.). (1942). *Plato*. Roslyn, N.Y.: Walter J. Black.

Kaminsky, J. (1967). "Herbert Spencer." In *The Encyclopedia of Philosophy* (P. Edwards, ed.). New York: Collier-Macmillan.

Kazamias, A. (ed.). (1966). *Herbert Spencer on Education*. New York: Teachers College Press.

Kennedy, J. (1978). *Herbert Spencer*. Boston: Twayne.

Kenny, A. (ed.). (1994). *The Oxford History of Western Philosophy*. Oxford, England: Oxford University Press.

Kierkegaard, S. (1941). *Repetition: An Essay in Experimental Psychology.* (W. Lowrie, trans.). New York: Harper & Row.

Kierkegaard, S. (1986). *Either/Or,* vol. 1.(G. Stengren, trans.). New York: Harper & Row.

Kitching, C. (1988). *Karl Marx and the Philosophy of Praxis.* London: Routledge.

Kneller, G. (ed.). (1971). *Foundations of Education.* New York: Wiley.

Kolenda, K. (1990). *Rorty's Humanistic Pragmatism: Philosophy Democratized.* Tampa: University of South Florida Press.

Korsch, K. (1970). *Marxism and Philosophy* (F. Halliday, trans.). New York: NLB.

Krathwohl, D., Bloom, B., and Masia, B. (1964). *Taxonomy of Educational Objectives—The Classification of Educational Goals, Handbook II. Affective Domain.* New York: David McKay.

Kraut, R. (ed.). (1992). *The Cambridge Companion to Plato.* Cambridge, England: Cambridge University Press.

Kyburg, H. (1983). *Epistemology and Inference.* Minneapolis: University of Minnesota Press.

LaCapra, D. (1978). *A Preface to Sartre.* Ithaca, N.Y.: Cornell University Press.

Lamb, D. (ed.). (1987). *Hegel and Modern Philosophy.* London: Croom Helm.

Lampert, L. (1993). *Nietzsche and Modern Times: A Study of Bacon, Descartes, and Freud.* New Haven, Conn: Yale University Press.

Lee, H.D.P (trans.). (1955). *Plato: The Republic.* Harmondsworth, Middlesex, England: Penguin Books.

Lehrer, K. (1990). *Theory of Knowledge.* Boulder, Colo.: Westview Press.

Lipman, M. (1988). *Philosophy Goes to School.* Philadelphia: Temple University Press.

Locke, J. (1959). *An Essay on Human Understanding* (A. C. Fraser, ed.). New York: Dover.

Locke, J. (1989). *Some Thoughts Concerning Education* (Jean Yolton and John Yolton, eds.). Oxford, England: Clarendon Press.

Lodge, R. (1970). *Plato's Theory of Education.* New York: Russell & Russell.

Loomis, L. (ed.). (1943). *Aristotle: On Man in the Universe.* Roslyn, N. Y.: Walter J. Black.

Lyotard, J. (1979). *The Postmodern Condition: A Report on Knowledge.* (G. Bennington and B. Massumi, trans.). Minneapolis: University of Minnesota Press.

Lyotard, J. (1986). *Phenomenology.* (B. Beakley, trans.). Albany: State University of New York Press.

Mackenzie, M. (1970). *Hegel's Educational Theory and Practice.* Westport, Conn: Greenwood Press.

MacVannel, J. (1905). *The Educational Theories of Herbart and Froebel.* New York: Teachers College, Columbia University.

Madison, G. (ed.). (1993). *Working Through Derrida.* Evanston, Ill.: Northwestern University Press.

Magill, F. (ed.). (1990). *Masterpieces of World Philosophy.* New York: Harper-Collins.

Mah, H. (1987). *The End of Philosophy, the Origin of Ideology: Karl Marx and the Crisis of the Young Hegelians.* Berkeley: University of California Press.

Malachowski, A. (ed.). (1990). *Reading Rorty: Critical Responses to Philosophy and the Mirror of Nature.* Cambridge, England: Blackwell.

Malcolm, N. (1963). *Knowledge and Certainty: Essays and Lectures.* Englewood Cliffs, N. J.: Prentice Hall.

Marcuse, H. (1972). *Studies in Critical Philosophy.* London: NLB.

Marler, C. (1975). *Philosophy and Schooling.* Boston: Allyn and Bacon.

Marx, K. (1964). *Economic and Philosophic Manuscripts of 1844.* New York: International Publishers.

McBride, W. (1977). *The Philosophy of Marx.* New York: St. Martin's Press.

McDermott, J. (ed.). (1977). *The Writings of William James.* Chicago: University of Chicago Press.

McGrew, T. (1995). *The Foundations of Knowledge.* Lanham, Md.: Littlefield Adams Books.

McInnes, N. (1972). "Karl Marx." In *The Encyclopedia of Philosophy* (P. Edwards, ed.). New York: Macmillan.

McKeon, R. (ed.). (1941). *The Basic Works of Aristotle.* New York: Random House.

Mill, J. (1924). *Autobiography of John Stuart Mill.* New York: Columbia University Press.

Modrak, D. (1987). *Aristotle: The Power of Perception.* Chicago: Unversity of Chicago Press.

Montagu, B. (ed.). (1831). *The Works of Francis Bacon,* vol. 14. London: William Pickering.

Montessori, M. (1965). *Spontaneous Activity in Education* (F. Simmonds, trans.). New York: Schocken Books.

Moser, P., and vander Nat, A. (eds.). (1995). *Human Knowledge: Classical and Contemporary Approaches,* 2nd. ed. New York: Oxford University Press.

Murillo, L. (1988). *A Critical Introduction to Don Quixote.* New York: Peter Lang.

Murray, P. (1988). *Marx's Theory of Scientific Knowledge.* Atlantic Highlands, N.J.: Humanities Press International.

Myers, G. (1986). *William James: His Life and Thought.* New Haven, Conn.: Yale University Press.

Nicholson, L. (ed.). (1990). *Feminism/Postmodernism.* New York: Routledge.

Noddings, N. (1984). *Caring: A Feminine Approach to Ethics and Moral Education.* Berkeley: University of California Press.

Noddings, N. (1992). *The Challenge to Care in Schools: An Alternative Approach to Education.* New York: Teachers College Press.

Noddings, N., and Shore, P. (1984). *Awakening the Inner Eye: Intuition in Education.* New York: Teachers College Press.

Norris. C. (1987). *Derrida.* Cambridge, Mass.: Harvard University Press.

Norris, C. (1993). *The Truth About Postmodernism.* Oxford, England: Blackwell.

O'Hear, A. (1985). *What Philosophy Is: An Introduction to Contemporary Philosophy.* Atlantic Highlands, N.J.: Humanities Press International.

O'Neill, O. (1989). *Constructions of Reason: Explorations of Kant's Practical Philosophy.* New York: Cambridge University Press.

Ornstein, A., and Levine, D. (1993). *Foundations of Education,* 5th ed. Boston: Houghton Mifflin.

Ozmon, H., and Craven, S. (1995). *Philosophical Foundations of Education,* 5th ed. Columbus, Ohio: Merrill.

Padover, S. (1978). *Karl Marx: An Intimate Biography.* New York: McGraw-Hill.

Papanoutsos, E. (1968). *The Foundations of Knowledge.* Albany: State University of New York Press.

Paringer, W. (1990). *John Dewey and the Paradox of Liberal Reform.* Albany: State University of New York Press.

Peel, J. (1971). *Herbert Spencer: The Evolution of a Sociologist.* New York: Basic Books.

Perez-Ramos, A. (1988). *Francis Bacon's Idea of Science.* Oxford, England: Clarendon Press.

Pilardi, J. (1989). "Female Eroticism in the Works of Simone de Beauvoir." In *The Thinking Muse.* (J. Allen and I. Young, eds.) Bloomington: Indiana University Press.

Pinkard, T. (1988). *Hegel's Dialectic: The Explanation of the Possibility.* Philadelphia: Temple University Press.

Pinkevich, A. (1929). *The New Education in the Soviet Republic.* New York: John Day.

Plato. (1955). *The Republic* (H.D.P. Lee, trans.). Harmondsworth, Middlesex, England: Penguin Books.

Pollock, J. (1986). *Contemporary Theories of Knowledge.* Totowa, N.J.: Rowman and Littlefield.

Popper, K. (1974). *The Philosophy of Karl Popper.* LaSalle, Ill.: Open Court.

Prichard, H. (1950). *Knowledge and Perception: Essays and Lectures.* Oxford, England: Oxford University Press.

Prokopczyk, C. (1980). *Truth and Reality in Marx and Hegel: A Reassessment.* Amherst: The University of Massachusetts Press.

Putnam, H. (1995). *Pragmatism: An Open Question.* Cambridge, Mass.: Blackwell.

Reavis, G. H. (1956). *The Animal School.* Chicago: Field Enterprises.

Rich, J. (1992). *Foundations of Education: Perspectives on American Education.* New York: Macmillan.

Richetti, J. (1983). *Philosophical Writing: Locke, Berkeley, Hume.* Cambridge, Mass: Harvard University Press.

Rohde, P. (ed.) (1960). *The Diary of Søren Kierkegaard.* (M. Anderson, trans.). New World: Philosophical Library.

Rorty, R. (1979). *Philosophy and the Mirror of Nature.* Princeton, N.J.: Princeton University Press.

Rorty, R. (1982). *Consequences of Pragmatism.* Minneapolis, Minn.: University of Minnesota Press.

Roubiczek, P. (1964). *Existentialism: For and Against.* Cambridge, England: Cambridge University Press.

Runes, D. (1963). *Pictorial History of Philosophy.* Paterson, N.J.: Littlefield, Adams.

Russell, B. (1948). *Human Knowledge: Its Scope and Limits.* New York: Simon and Schuster.

Sallis, J. (ed.). (1987). *Deconstruction and Philosophy: The Texts of Jacques Derrida.* Chicago: University of Chicago Press.

Santas, G. (1979). *Socrates.* London: Routledge and Kegan Paul.

Sartre, J. (1947). *Existentialism.* (B. Frechtman, trans.). Secaucus, N.J.: Carol Publishing Group.

Sarup, M. (1989). *An Introductory Guide to Post-Structuralism and Postmodernism.* Athens: The University of Georgia Press.

Sayer, D. (ed.). (1989). *Readings from Karl Marx.* London: Routledge.

Schaper, E. & Vossenkuhl, W. (eds.). (1989). *Reading Kant: New Perspectives on Transcendental Arguments and Critical Philosophy.* Oxford, England: Blackwell.

Scheffler, I. (1974). *Four Pragmatists: A Critical Introduction to Peirce, James, Mead, and Dewey.* New York: Humanities Press.

Schouls, P. (1989). *Descartes and the Enlightenment.* Montreal: McGill–Queen's University Press.

Schouls, P. (1992). *Reasoned Freedom: John Locke and the Enlightenment.* Ithaca, NY: Cornell University Press.

Scramuzza, V., and MacKendrick, P. (1958). *The Ancient World.* New York: Holt.

Seeskin, K. (1987). *Dialogue and Discovery: A Study in Socratic Method.* Albany: State University of New York Press.

Simons, M. (1992). "Two Interviews with Simone de Beauvoir." In *Revaluing French Feminism* (N. Fraser and S. Bartky, eds.) Bloomington: Indiana University Press.

Smith, L., and Smith, J. (1994). *Lives in Education: A Narrative of People and Ideas,* 2nd ed. New York: St. Martin's Press.

Sorell, T. (1987). *Descartes.* Oxford, England: Oxford University Press.

Spencer, H. (1904). *An Autobiography,* vol. 1. New York: D. Appleton and Co.

Spencer, H. (1963). *Education: Intellectual, Moral, and Physical.* Paterson, N.J.: Littlefield, Adams. (Originally published in 1860)

Spencer, H. (1966). *The Works of Herbert Spencer,* vol. 16. Osnabrück, Germany: Otto Zeller.

Stoops, J. (1971). *Philosophy and Education in Western Civilization: Summaries and Interpretations for Schoolmen and Churchmen.* Danville, Ill.: Interstate Printers and Publishers.

Struik, D. (ed.). (1964). *Economic and Philosophic Manuscripts of 1844.* New York: International Publishers.

Stuhr, J. (ed.). (1993). *Philosophy and the Reconstruction of Culture: Pragmatic Essays After Dewey.* Albany: State University of New York Press.

Stumpf, S. (1966). *Socrates to Sartre.* New York: McGraw-Hill.

Suckiel, E. (1982). *William James.* Notre Dame, Ind.: University of Notre Dame Press.

Suchting, W. (1986). *Marx and Philosophy: Three Studies.* New York: New York University Press.

Teloh, H. (1986). *Socratic Education in Plato's Early Dialogues.* Notre Dame, Ind.: University of Notre Dame Press.

Turner, J. (1985). *Herbert Spencer: A Renewed Appreciation.* Beverly Hills, Calif.: Sage.

Urmson, J. (ed.). (1960). *The Concise Encyclopedia of Western Philosophy and Philosophers.* New York: Hawthorn Books.

Vaught, C. (1989). "Hegel and the Problem of Difference: A Critique of Dialectical Reflection." In *Hegel and His Critics: Philosophy in the Aftermath of Hegel* (W. Desmond, ed.). Albany: State University of New York Press.

Viroli, M. (1988). *Jean-Jacques Rousseau and the "Well-Ordered Society"* (D. Hanson, trans.). Cambridge, England: Cambridge University Press.

Walker, A. (1989). Marx, *His Theory and Its Context,* 2nd ed. London: Rivers Oram Press.

Webb, L., Metha, A., and Jordan, K. (1992). *Foundations of American Education.* New York: Macmillan.

Well, H. (1971). *Pragmatism: Philosophy of Imperialism.* Freeport, N.Y.: Books for Libraries Press.

Westbrook, R. (1991). *John Dewey and American Democracy.* Ithaca, N.Y.: Cornell University Press.

White, M. (1943). *The Origins of Dewey's Instrumentalism.* New York: Columbia University Press.

Williams, B. (1978). Descartes: *The Project of Pure Inquiry.* Atlantic Highlands, N. J.: Humanities Press.

Witherell, C. and Noddings, N. (eds.). (1991). *Stories Lives Tell: Narrative and Dialogue in Education.* New York: Teachers College Press.

Wolff, R. (1989). *About Philosophy,* 4th ed. Englewood Cliffs, N.J.: Prentice Hall.

Wood, D., and Bernasconi, R. (eds.). (1988). *Derrida and Différance.* Evanston, Ill.: Northwestern University Press.

Wood, M. (ed.). (1985). *Hegel.* Oxford, England: Oxford University Press.

Wood, P. (1990). *Understanding Jean-Paul Sartre.* Columbia: University of South Carolina Press.

Wylleman, A. (ed.). (1989). *Hegel on the Ethical Life, Religion, and Philosophy.* Leuven, Belgium: Leuven University Press.

Young, I. (1990). *Throwing Like a Girl and Other Essays in Feminist Philosophy and Social Theory.* Bloomington: Indiana University Press.

INDEX